AUTOBIOGRAPHY

AUTOBIOGRAPHY

NEVILLE CARDUS

faber and faber

This edition first published in 2008
by Faber and Faber Ltd
3 Queen Square, London WC1N 3AU

A CIP record for this book is available from the British Library

ISBN 978-0-571-24433-1

CONTENTS

❖

ILLUSTRATIONS

*Grateful acknowledgment is made to Sir Thomas Beecham for per-
mission to reprint a letter originally published in the "Daily Telegraph,"
and to the "Manchester Guardian" for permission to reprint certain extracts.*

INTRODUCTION

A MAN PAST his middle years may resign himself to the thought that his life as a sower of seeds is more or less done with; he is now free to reap from memory, if he should feel that way inclined. I am aware that men of genius have been known to achieve fresh creative energy even in their seventies and their eighties; I speak here only of talented folk. I certainly speak for myself.

So, at the age of fifty-two, I sit myself down in a single top-room of a flat in Sydney, and begin my autobiography; the Australian summer blazes away outside my window, and blazes away the World War; and the immensity of both will no doubt remind me from time to time, and from page to page, of the need of proportion, most of all in a book intended to present merely a personal and temporal life, even if a life that has been full and rich in enjoyment, and sorely tried now and again, and curiously variegated.

In the olden style, I present herewith a Prospectus or Advertisement. Manchester was my place of birth, in a slum. Back-to-back tenements were not unknown in the neighbourhood, but there was a Free Library round the corner, and also there were fields or, let us say, an "open space" not yet built upon, and utilised in part for the disposal of rubbish; it was called, and called correctly, the "Corporation tip." In recent and more progressive years the authorities built an edifice called, with an equally nice sense of words, the "Destructor." During the summer cricket was played on these open spaces. Given a library and a cricket pitch, both free of charge, I was obviously blessed with good luck beyond the lot of most boys rich or poor. Here at any rate was the material I needed.

In the Manchester streets and on blasted heaths I began life, on slimy pavements in winter, in the summer when pavement and dust and grime threw back a heat as though from sunshine generated industrially. I attended what was known as a Board School, a place of darkness and inhumanity. I learned scarcely anything there, except to read and write. For four years only did I attend school, delicate years and

miserable. At the age of thirteen my formal education came
to an end. To this day I am incapable of coping with the
most elementary of school examination papers. Any child
knows more than I of mathematics (my studies in this direction
got as far as arithmetic). I am ignorant of chemistry. I cannot
grasp—not for long anyhow—what is a gerundial infinitive.
I confuse an isthmus with an archipelago, and cannot confidently spell either. Strictly speaking, I suppose I am formally
uneducated.

I earned my first money, my first wages, when I was ten
years old, as a pavement artist. I have sold, as well as written
for, newspapers. My parents conducted a home-laundry; or,
not to be tautological, they took in washing. I once delivered
the washing to the home and house of the Chairman of the
Hallé Concerts Society, delivered it in a perambulator at the
tradesmen's entrance. Years afterwards I dined with him one
night; I was now music critic of the *Manchester Guardian*,
and he wished to placate my pen on a point of musical policy.
As I smoked his cigars, and drank his Liebfraumilch, I could
not resist thinking to myself: "What a world! I have delivered
his washing. My grandmother ironed his dress shirts, and
ironed them well, bless her. And here I am and here is he—
and he is filling up my glass again, trying to make me see
reason."

Since the time when I was one of the submerged of Man-
chester, occasionally short of food, I have lunched in the
Savoy, and also in the house of Lady Cunard in Grosvenor
Square—once, as Oscar Wilde said of Frank Harris. Since those
proletarian years, I have dined at Lyons and in the Hotel
Vierjahreszeiten München. I saw my first play and my first
opera from the sixpenny gallery of the Manchester Theatre
Royal. I have met Richard Strauss and Bradman; George
Robey and James Barrie; Delius and Jack Hobbs; Schnabel
and Tom Webster; James Agate and Gustave Agate; Samuel
Alexander (the last of the classical metaphysicians) and Emmott
Robinson (also a philosopher of consequence); Sibelius and
Edward Elgar and Larwood; J. L. Garvin and Hammond of
Gloucestershire. I have been a professional cricketer, and I
have been secretary to C. P. Scott of the *Manchester Guardian*,
and secretary also to Cyril Alington when he was Headmaster

of Shrewsbury School. I have travelled to Australia to write about cricket, and I have travelled all over Europe to write about concerts and music.

The reader need not become uneasy; I do not intend to write of the boy that made good. This particular poor boy, as you will discover, lacked conscience somewhat. No self-help or duty or Ladders of Life for him. He declined, in a family which was always living close to the bone, to take on any job which threatened permanence *qua* real industry and was not related in any way to the enjoyment of life. Manchester was not all bricks and mortar and bread-and-dripping for this delicate boy who incredibly was myself. On one and the same day he saw Henry Irving and A. C. Maclaren and Hans Richter walking in the streets of the Manchester of forty years ago. Not, of course, together.

I spent sixteen years of my youth mainly in books and music and in the sixpenny galleries of theatres. The men on the cricket field were mixed up with the heroes of books and plays. When I went alone on Saturday evenings to the Free Library (and my early youth was spent much alone) I did not go in the spirit of a good boy stirred upward and on by visions of an improving kind. I revelled in it all: excitement and sensuous delight. I argued with Shaw and A. B. Walkley; I went up and down with Mr. Micawber; I heard the whinny of Grane, and I saw the flames consuming Valhalla. I was Kipps, Richard Feverel and David Copperfield—in a place whose odour and atmosphere of india-rubber mats and silence of a municipal reading-room come back to me as I write. I had no time, not even when I was emerging from my teens, for the routing pleasures of my first companions. The girl did not exist in the whole world who could win my heart and passions from Beatrix Esmond; besides, I was a shy youth, except in the world of imagination, where I could be as bold as brass. For "Book Learning" as such (to use the old term) I had no use; far different was absorption in the creations of rich minds; here was sport indeed. I could not even play cricket without aping the gods of Old Trafford and Lord's.

In my twenties, I had the good luck to come under the influence of the *Manchester Guardian*, in the period of Scott, Montague, Haslam Mills, Samuel Langford, Sidebotham and

Crozier. It was a strain, living up to these Olympians; now and again the atmosphere was not as humane as it might have been. But no finer school has ever been at hand for a young man with my notions and desires. Not that it really was at hand; for years it lay so remote from me that it might as well have been Balliol—and not merely a sort of extension of Balliol. "To bring to the day's diet of sights and sounds the wine of your own temperament"; this was C. E. Montague's credo. I have tried to give you an outline, a menu, of the diet of sights and sounds to be served in my book. I shall hope that the wine will be good enough; I was, at any rate, born in a vintage year.

Part One

STRUGGLE

TO
EDITH

"OUR HOUSE"—as all houses were in those days confidently known by their various denizens, everybody liable to be ejected any week for arrears of rent—stood at the end of a small row. It boasted bay-windows, and a narrow strip of earth, which occasionally put forth green growths, like Tannhäuser's staff. This was the garden; it was protected from the pavement by iron rails of penal aspect. Bay-windows and a garden were responsible for an unfounded rumour in the"Place" that the Carduses enjoyed social amenities of an abnormal order. The bay-windows gave us nothing more than a certain superiority of vantage-ground; from behind Klace curtains we could command every approach to the house, though it was difficult to peer through them and at the same time keep them quite still. The laundry or washing was taken in by my grandfather, who collected and delivered it by means of a cart and a cheerful pony, except in the case of a"rush" order, when usually the delivery was executed by me and the perambulator. My grandfather originally was a policeman, or to use his own fastidious language, a constable. He was wholly Victorian. A framed photograph of Mr. Gladstone hung over the mantelpiece in the living-room of Summer Place. The living-room was the one used every day and we called it the kitchen. The front room or parlour, which enjoyed the bay-windows, was occupied only on Sundays; in the brass fender was a collection of fire-irons, tongs and other accoutrements, none of which was put to any practical use, igneous or other. When a fire was lighted in the parlour in winter, a poker was brought from the kitchen.

My grandfather retired from the constabulary on a small pension, after receiving several blows on the head, administered in person by Mr. Charles Peace with a crowbar. My grandfather was proud of these bumps on his head, lasting evidence of an intimate association with a famous and, in his day, much respected criminal. A picture from my infancy is of my grandfather sitting by the kitchen fire, the lamplight touching the bumps to a shiny flesh-red clearness of outline which fascinatad me always and made me feel something of the pain sustained in the reception of them. On long winter evenings my grandfather would sit in his arm-chair reading in turn, as the fancy seized him, the Holy Bible, the *Manchester Guardian* or the *Sporting Chronicle Handicap Book*. At a given sign, a pint of beer would be handed to him in a jug, into which he would plunge a red-hot poker. He held strong views about Home Rule. While he pondered and occasionally spoke, my grandmother and her three daughters would be busy at two tables, getting on with the laundry, flicking water on the sheets, holding hot irons an inch from their cheeks, now and again spitting on them and making a fizzing sound. It was my habit and pleasure to sit under one of these tables drawn against the wall of the room and imagine that I was hidden, unobserved but an observer, solemnly in a tent. This is the first aesthetic emotion I can remember ever experiencing; I date it 1894.

My grandfather and grandmother, both God-fearing and hard-working, saw their daughters in the course of time go dancing down the primrose path. These girls were "post-war" long in advance of 1914 and long in advance of the Boer War. They grew tired of being poor but respectable. My mother began the movement of enlightenment when she begot me. She had a liberating influence on her sisters. My mother was indeed a pioneer for freedom in an epoch and a house which held loyally to the decrees of the century; respectability before all things. Blessed are the poor. The rich man drives round in his carriage. "I spurn your ill-gotten wealth," said the heroines of the melodramas which held up the mirror then; symbols and shining examples for the masses who crammed the pit and the gallery. And Sir Jasper was thwarted of his worst intentions. My mother and her sisters powdered their faces at a time in our island story when to powder a girl's face was scarlet sin—in a provincial city at any rate. The powder was contained on tissue paper in a little book; sometimes my mother would give me one; its slightly sickly-sweet flavour returns to me now. I loved to lie in bed and watch my mother as she prepared for the evening's adventuring. The structure of corsets of the period was peculiar; they were erected on a girder of steel, and the secret was to begin at the bottom, at the waist-line. One clip was fastened down there, then you worked upward. Often when connection had been made at the top, the lowest clip would burst asunder. My mother's reddening face and suppressed curses were my constant delight.

No word of reproach was ever uttered by my mother against my father when he vanished from her life. During my infancy I was led to believe that he had gone to the coast of West Africa on "Business." It was subsequently arranged for him to die there. The coast of West Africa, known as White Man's Grave, was a favourite place amongst the middle and lower orders of the 'nineties if a family secret needed to be hidden, or if the skeleton were too unwieldy to be kept safely in the family cupboard. I never believed the story about my father and West Africa, at least not after I had understood the first thing about it. I can account for my mother's reticence. But why didn't my Aunt Beatrice tell me? For Beatrice broke away entirely from the traces; in the course of time she brought into the life of Summer Place things as esoteric as evening gowns, hansom cabs to and from the theatre, the Turkish Consul of Manchester, and an action for Breach of Promise. The most she ever told me of my father is that he was tall, saturnine of countenance, and one of the first violins in an orchestra.

With the advent of shame into Summer Place, my grandmother declared that it would be the death of her; but it was really bronchitis that carried her off at the age of seventy-three. For several years—in fact as long as I knew her—she was afflicted by congestion, or, to use her own language, "phlegm." She would go black in the face with coughing, and my Aunt Beatrice would shout to her across the room: "For God's sake get a drink!" Beatrice was not being brutal; this was the way the working-classes talked to one another during the more searching crises of life. My grandmother put much faith in the healing properties of creosote; she also believed in red flannel. When she died, my grandfather put on black clothes, closed his *Sporting Chronicle Handicap Book* for ever, and would not take off his coat even at meal-times. He fell down the cellar steps with fatal results shortly before the relief of Ladysmith.

From my father, I suppose, I inherited my feeling for

music and an un-English æstheticism. From my mother I
inherited my less inhuman self and a very English love of the
brave humours of the street, expressed in her time and for all
time by Marie Lloyd, the benign mother of vulgarity of the
'nineties, amongst whose daughters must be counted the good
and great-hearted buxom wench who conceived me. It was
a mixed progeniture. I am to-day austere and also a man of
the world. One side of me despises intellectualism and the
rejection of the common streak which I believe is the salt of
art and life. The other side of me loathes triviality, insensibility, and the commonplace. I love the English ease and
geniality, the large companionship of the public-house. But
I despise English philistinism, the English middle-class ignorance of the first thing about culture; their complacency and
sentimentalism; their obsessions (in a normal peace-time)
with bridge parties and golf and motor cars; their use of the
theatre as a place in which to roar themselves silly, or gorge
themselves with chocolates. And I despise equally the not-so-
long-ago fashionable Bloomsbury-Chelsea highbrowism which
does not understand that genius is a miracle to be revered
whether in fashion or not.

There was no music in my home, not even an upright piano.
My father and his violin never entered Summer Place. But
I remember that my mother and my Aunt Beatrice would
sing me to sleep with melodies from *Norma*, which is a fact
significant of much in the general musical background of the
period; for the airs of Bellini and Donizetti were frequently
woven into the texture of the Christmas pantomimes. The
first part of *Babes in the Wood* was concluded once in Manchester by a rendering by the whole strength of the company
of the Hunting Chorus from *Freischütz*; that is how I first
came to know it. The Demon King and the Fairy Queen
defied one another to the strains of a duet from Balfe's
Satanella. These quotations from "grand opera" were freely
adapted to the dramatic exigencies recurrent in *Sinbad the
Sailor* or *The Forty Thieves* and the sources were not ac-
knowledged in the programme. The point is that producers
of this, the lowest nineteenth-century form of public entertainment, thought the public liked it all, and they did. Jimmy
Glover, in his overtures to the annual Drury Lane pantomimes,

drew boldly on Wagner; he even strengthened the brass parts. To-day crooning and "swing" have expelled not only Bellini and Gounod but Leslie Stuart as well. The cinema, and canned music—instead of the actual presence of a Dan Leno, a Vesta Tilley, a Marie Lloyd; the bulk of the people are now brought up on celluloid phantasms which nobody can come to know and love. Chaplin, the one lovable comic character known to the film, really belonged to the music hall of other years. Spontaneous combustion occurred every night in the old variety theatres. The people of England saw themselves transformed there by genius to rich types; they were (if I may use so strong a term, as Mr. Wititterly said) apotheosised. The English theatre has never excelled, for comprehensive presentation of the English character, the art of the music-hall as it was known in the 'nineties and Nineteen-hundreds.

In the theatre itself Irving held the stage in the grand manner, exactly as Maclaren held the crease in the grand manner on the cricket field. I attended a "farewell appearance" of Irving in the Manchester Theatre Royal (now devoted to films). He was about to leave England on a tour to America. At the end of the performance he came before the curtain and spoke to us in a sepulchral voice, bidding us "Good-bye." And the audience rose as one man and sang "God be With You Till We Meet Again." It was a good time in which to be alive and young. No doubt it was a simple period in ways. But there was the possibility of hero-worship. If it is argued that there was a splash of fustian charlatanism in our heroes, what of it? There must be a smack of fustian in all showmen. The age and generation that despises a show is a fool, especially if instead it prefers Hollywood.

Swinburne with his aureole and his roses of rapture and lilies of languor; maybe drying his socks over the fire at the Pines at Watts Dunton's in Putney, but he was alive yet. George Meredith at Box Hill, rug over his knees but the beard as ever a challenge; optimism in epigram, courage in tweeds, Phaeton in a wheel-chair. As a corrective there was Bernard Shaw not accepted and venerable as he is to-day: der Geist, der stets verneint; Mephisto—in Jaeger. Thomas Hardy was brooding upon dynasties down at Max Gate in Dorchester— Tess and Jude echoes of battles long ago. H. G. Wells was

already running round bursting into notions; also he was
creating Mr. Polly. Henry James, with his great head, his
eyes looking at us patiently, a little perplexed at times, but
taking hold of us at last, reassuringly saying "We must wait
for, and listen to, and as it were become aware of, *acutely*
aware of, whatever *happens*." From the Victorian years a
light fell on the new century. Groups of noble dames on the
lawns, stately homes mellowing like the peach on the wall.
Even Labour men and Trade Unionists, Wat Tylers in the
eyes of surviving Dedlocks, were not Officials but men: Keir
Hardie and John Burns, red ties and turned-down collars and
homespuns. Even the crooks once were artists. To-day they
bump off their victims without taste or good manners or
originality of technique. Charles Peace played the violin in
a Sunday School every week. Horatio Bottomley was beloved
by widows and orphans throughout the land. When the
enterprising burglar wasn't burgling, he listened to the
gentle village chime.

  .   .   .   .   .   .

I dwell on the England of my youth because I wish to
trace the course and background of my life from an uneducated
boy in an illiterate home to a man who became comfortably
off without once consciously working to make money; who
to-day without immodesty counts himself reasonably instructed
in all the arts and an expert in one of them. Temperament
from an unknown father, and experience of human nature
learned during impressionable years in a hard school which
knew the uses of laughter. These forces counted for nearly
all. But the times were good, I say, for such a boy. The
environment of my home sordid maybe, and unlettered and
unbeautiful. Outside, up and down the land, walked character
everywhere, extravagant and free; everywhere was the sense
of rich resources and of security at large. The world was
anybody's oyster, there to be opened, even if as in my case it
was opened by indirect means. I am not complacently looking
back on times that were in many ways terrible and disgraceful
in a city which was one of the wealthiest in an Empire rich
as any the world has known. If I eventually emerged from

the enormities, I do not forget them. I was a Socialist when
to be a Socialist meant something of a handicap to a member
of the working-classes. I am here saying no more than that
it was an age in which poverty and wealth alike went with
vitality of living. Humour kept breaking in. We wore our
rue with a difference.

.   .   .   .   .   .

Towards the close of the Nineteenth Century, I professionally entered the fine arts; I made, and I think I earned,
the first money of my life as a pavement artist. One day I
bought some substances from a house-decorator's shop, the
raw material of paint; slabs of colour soft to the touch. It
was Saturday afternoon, and I chose as my pitch the pavement
in a thoroughfare not far from Summer Place. I drew the
traditional pictures—a winter scene, with a robin redbreast
on a bough; a wreck at sea with decorative waves; a salmon
cut into halves; a dying soldier in the Egyptian desert giving
a last letter to his mother to a friend, both red-coated and
fixed in pathetic and eternal attitudes. It is necessary that the
pavement artist should select smooth stone on which to work,
and he must prepare a basic tone or texture by the application
of reds and whites and greens, which he blends by rubbing
with the palm of the hand. He wafts away the residuum
with a sweep of his cap. The more detailed work, outlines
and chiaroscuro, involves delicate caresses from the little
finger; this time he removes the superfluous dust by means
of a delicate puff of breath sideways. After he has finished
his exhibition he frames it in a border of fish-bones executed
in white chalk. Then with another sweep of the cap, the
pictures are rendered clean and clear and pre-Raphaelitish;
this is your varnishing day, so to speak. All is ready.

According to the custom, I printed at the head of my
collection the legend

ORIGAL WORK

Then I assumed the traditional position—erect against the
wall of the pavement, left leg bent backward, the sole of the

foot against the wall, my cap on the ground at the side of the masterpieces to receive the takings. A football match was about to begin, and in less than half an hour, my cap was full of coppers. Now and again an admirer would drop his coin on a picture in the middle of a sunset and I would in time, but not too hurriedly, remove it (also according to custom). I could scarcely cope with the halfpennies and pennies lavished on me. When I reached home I was flogged and sent to bed for disgracing the family. My aunt alone supported me, and next day she bought me a real box of paints, water-colours in tubes and real brushes. But in my heart I preferred the coloured stuffs from the house decorator; they were more accommodating to my technique, more yielding.

During this period I became an authority on foreign affairs, at least amongst boys of my age. I played no games, but secretly I acted over and over again, in remote corners and alleys, scenes from contemporary life and history. I am at a loss to account for the fact that my mind was for long alive with sensations of the Dreyfus case. The Battle of Omdurman naturally enough stimulated the imagination of a boy. But Dreyfus, Picquart, Major Henry, Zola and, of all things, the Bordereau! I looked the word up in a dictionary, and then I compiled one—it was probably like Mr. Dick's Memorial and as symbolical of my state of mind. I acted the trial with myself as Zola, and I borrowed my grandfather's eyeglasses and learned to say "Canaille," of which I did not understand the meaning. Once I built a house with my building-blocks, and I cut out of cardboard a stately figure of a man sitting on a chair. I put him inside the house, and retired to a distance and looked at him through the window. He was Cecil Rhodes; I was spying on him, and he didn't suspect it.

I can only suppose that I was inspired to all this mimicry of events by the fact that copies of the *Graphic* and the *Illustrated London News* somehow penetrated Summer Place; possibly they were given to the three girls by their various lovers in the hope that they would improve their minds. There were no books in the house as a rule, though I recollect references to Mrs. Henry Wood and Miss Braddon.

Terror overwhelmed me one day when I read in a newspaper that according to a German scientist named Professor

Falb, the end of the world would take place on November 13, 1899. Through all my infancy the idea of eternity had appalled me; I would lie in bed at night trying to imagine us all going on for ever and ever. I saw a small compressed space remote in the sky, a trap from which there was no escape. "For ever and ever and ever and ever and ever and ever," I would murmur to myself in the dark, thinking hard on the word "ever," until my mind became a piercing tunnel of terror reaching on without end. But Professor Falb and the Last Day were forgotten as the year went by. I joined in the excitement of the outbreak of the Boer War; I can see the day and the hour; dark and cold in a Manchester street and a newspaper announcing "Ultimatum to Kruger," which necessitated another reference to the Free Library and the dictionary. Professor Falb and his prophecy were forgotten. I wore all the patriotic buttons, General Buller and General French. We called him "Kroo-jer." There was Bugler Dunne blowing his bugle with his legs shattered at some battle or other; and the British Army, glorious in red coats, marching over the veld where they could be seen and shot at miles away. Dum-dum bullets; Queen Victoria's Christmas present to the troops, a packet of chocolate each. Little Englanders and Lloyd George one of them; and Kipling and Sullivan and "Pay! Pay! Pay!" The awful Black Week when we suffered terrible losses at Modder River, *hundreds* actually killed within a few days. . . .

Forty years ago the army was looked down upon even in Summer Place. My Aunt Beatrice never dreamed for a moment of going out with a soldier. Soldiers of the ranks in the late nineteenth century were common fellows who wore round caps on the side of the head, like modern lift boys, short coats and tremendously long trousers striped at the side. They swore and winked at girls and they carried canes with which they would severely smite themselves on the thighs. I once knew a Volunteer who lived next door to us in Summer Place. The Volunteers was a nineteenth-century institution; they were mainly middle-aged family men who on Saturday afternoons would put on a helmet with a spike sticking from the top; and they would go into the fields with rifles and practise marksmanship while stretched prone on the earth, legs sprawling outward; or for a change, they would lie on their backs upside down, knees up and they would fire ornamentally between them.

.   .   .   .   .   .

There are, of course, unhappy memories from those years, mingling with the happy ones. I was what was known as a delicate boy, subject to nervous debility. I read a description of the Siamese Twins, and the thought of them terrified me; neither of them able to do anything without the other present or joining in. The Siamese Twins ousted my vision of eternity for a while; and fresh nightmare persistently brought me screaming to the top of the stairs, where my Aunt Beatrice would come flying and take me and put me to bed again, and she would lie with me until I was asleep in her arms, which usually gave out a rather overpowering but, in my young nostrils, lovely scent.

I discovered Charles Dickens and went crazy. I borrowed *Copperfield* from the Municipal Lending Library and the ordinary universe became unreal, hardly there. I read at meals; I read in the streets; at night I would read under the lamps on my way to anywhere I happened to be going; I would read until I was frozen cold, then run like mad to the next lamp. I read in bed, surreptitiously and against the rules, using a tallow candle. I read myself to an acute state of myopia; but no boy was encouraged to wear glasses in this epoch of progress, and I actually arrived at the age of nineteen before I visited an optician, and saw for the first time the delicate tracery of a tree in the spring-time; the pulsations of the stars at night; the curve of a slow ball bowled by Rhodes; the brilliance of a stage-scene, with every feature of my beloved actors marvellously revealed to me.

I can write of this boy without self-consciousness. He happened so long ago. He might have been my son. I see him against the background of Manchester's streets; he did not know sea or mountain, did not travel a dozen miles beyond Manchester, until he was nearly out of his teens. When his home crashed and the family dispersed, he was still a boy more or less without companions, with an imagination fed on penny dreadfuls, and on Dickens, Irving, Maclaren, Trumper,

Gustave Doré (whose pictures of Dante he one day found in an old book). Later, he worked in various ways to earn a week's wages, pushing a builder's hand-cart, lending a hand with ladders, enjoying an occasional view of the city from the slates of the housetops, and vastly curious about the odd things to be found in the gutters of roofs.

I boiled type in a printer's works, a statement which may require elucidation. Type was set from the case by hand, and fixed into galleys. After the printing was done, the type was broken up and cleaned by boiling in a pan. This job occupied my time from seven in the morning until six at night. I did not like it, and decided to give it up as soon as I possibly could, without starving. One day another youth, also boiling type, said something that offended me. I put down my pan and struck him on the forehead with a fist which contained a square lump of lead type. He fell stiff as a rod, and as I ran from the building, never to go back, I had a horrible, if momentary, sensation that I was some pitiful hunted character out of Dickens, a fit subject for Cruikshank. I ran from Cross Street into Pitt Hardacre's Comedy Theatre in Peter Street (later to be known as Miss Horniman's Gaiety Theatre). I asked for a job as a seller of chocolates at a "penny a bar," and I got it. As I was afraid to tell my family that I had lost my connection with a "trade," I found myself obliged to continue getting up every morning in the freezing dawn and pretend I was still going to the printer's. (In those days the poor boy was supposed to be lost to the world if not "put to a trade.") So I spent the mornings in the Manchester Reference Library until the time of the beginning of the theatre. I would leave the house shortly after six in the black and ice of January, and I would walk three miles to the city, then keep walking until the reading-room opened at nine. The warm air from the bumping pipes already heating, the odour and taste of the rubber-mats, the long tables, the rows of books, the gathering traffic of Manchester outside, the deepening of the fog as the soot descended—and here I was in my Ivory Tower; nobody knew of it. I even incorrectly signed the card which you filled up to get a book: I called myself Frederick Wood; and I began tentatively to explore all schools of thought. And every afternoon and

evening, six days weekly at two and seven, until the end of
March, I ascended to the gallery of the Comedy Theatre with
my tray of chocolates strapped over my shoulder; and I saw
Eugene Stratton for more than a hundred consecutive times—
dancing as though with no weight in him, feet only brushing
the boards of the stage. The Comedy Theatre was closed in
1903 by the Watch Committee, guardians of morality in
Manchester. It had obtained the name of a bad house, though,
frankly, nothing out of the way came under my notice.

.   .   .   .   .   .

I reflect with compassion on young Cardus's gropings, his
vain hours spent on the wrong trail. I grow physically weary
as I look back on his travail, on his half-baked aspirations,
often so quickly blown to nothing—hours of despair, after
the first raptures of discovery in boyhood. First I read books
and listened to music and saw plays for the joy of it all; a
boy does not feel poverty. But the increase of years brings
consciousness of shabby things; nobody at the present time
will understand the humiliations to be endured in those days by
the down-and-outs; nobody, that is, who has not experienced
them. In the end I landed on my feet, after all; found the
kingdom without even setting out to look for donkeys. For
I have told you that I seldom if ever set myself to work for
advancement. My luck must have been in, as they say. Yet
though I must have wasted much and missed much, I cannot
for the life of me see how my curious complex of temperament
and talents, qualities with terrible snags in them, could have
been better suited than by the pragmatical education to which
in God's good time they were submitted. The training of the
imagination of a writer should begin in early boyhood, pro-
gressing in even ratio with his powers of understanding. It
is not possible to *learn* an art; you can only go through
experiences in art, each reaching to a subtler plane. I com-
prehended my penny-dreadfuls in boyhood, my melodramas,
my heroes on and off the stage; understanding and imagination went hand in hand. I would not have understood *King
Lear* or even *Julius Cœsar*; not as poetry and literature. I did
at least know what my penny-dreadfuls meant, and best of all

I enjoyed them. I was seventeen before I came to know Shakespeare, and I approached him through the theatre, and read him in later years, when I had something of the mind and culture and sense of life he needs. I know no foolishness greater than to suppose that Shakespeare can be introduced to the young at school. Shakespeare, part of a curriculum! I was luckier at Summer Place, for occasionally a relation connected with the theatre, probably behind the bar, would make an appearance at a family gathering, and let down her back-hair, like Miss Petowker of Drury Lane, and curdle my blood by seizing the bread-knife, crying out "Is this a dagger that I see before meh?" Beethoven is studied to-day in musical appreciation classes. There are academies of dramatic art. It wouldn't have suited young Cardus; for one thing he hated all sorts of teaching. Early in life he hit upon the profound truth that enjoyment and education are very nearly one and the same, that the first precedes the second, and that neither is of much use without inherited temperament, unless one sets out with no more aim in life than to be successful and wealthy.

.   .   .   .   .   .

I must etch with some light and shade the outlines of the picture I have drawn of our house in Summer Place; it was not all dirty—drab. In many ways it was like thousands of other homes of its class and period and economy—slatternly in some things, in others scrupulously observing honourable precedent. The word debt was terrible to my grandfather and grandmother, and to all of their station of life. They thought it was outside the pale to buy anything on credit; they had a contemptuous word for it—"tick." So it would frequently happen that one day Summer Place made shift with bread and dripping and "potato-ash," and next day would be heard by the neighbours feasting deep into the night, all according to the ways and favours of fortune. My grandmother never descended to buying bread in a shop; a certain day every week was devoted to baking; I delighted to watch the dough being moulded and massaged. No tinned meats were ever seen in the house. For there was a widespread pride in home-made things, and there was a time of the year for jam, and weeks before Christmas the plum pudding and mince pies were planned and discussed in detail. It was an age which scarcely knew that depression and sense of one's superfluity in the scheme of things which goes nowadays with poverty, and even with an economic competence. Radios and chain stores and canned everything; Heinz in his many varieties—there is a good case for all of them, I suppose. But these things, I believe, have taken away much from the people of England. Forty years ago there was an enjoyment of ordinary everyday activities and vistas not known now. My Aunt Beatrice and her sisters rebelled against their conditions not negatively but positively; they did not droop under hopelessness; it was not discontent that stirred them to action but a capacity to see visions and dream dreams. They were not unhappy at Summer Place and certainly not depressed. They were simply being kept down. And they were like many of the poor of England then; they were resilient.

·   ·   ·   ·   ·   ·

My mother withdraws to the wings as the more effulgent personality of my Aunt Beatrice commands the stage. Beatrice frankly joined the oldest of professions and became an adornment to it. All these things I did not know at the time, but I have gathered reliable material and evidence from which to make a picture here of a great and original girl. I well remember her face, her blue eyes, her lovely weak mouth without lipstick; red as a rose. She was tall and walked like one of the well-born of the earth. Her hair (when she dressed it) curled on her back; she had the husky voice of Mrs. Patrick Campbell, whom she took for her model. With a splendid disdain she rose above the scruples of her station in life. She also had no use for hole-in-corner irregularities; illegitimate children, after all, were the winked-at perquisite of the poor. Beatrice wanted purple and poise in *her* sin. There was little scope during her day for a girl's excess of imagination and vitality. Even in the theatre, which my aunt adored, women were always represented as chaste or domestic. There were villains, but not villainesses. I can't imagine why Beatrice did not go on the stage; nearly all her lovers came from the theatre. I retain my glee when she imitated Lady Isabel in *East Lynne*—"Dead, dead; and ne-hever called me Mother." When she worked in the laundry at home, she sometimes spoke with a Lancashire accent as though to be matey, as she would have said; she would slap her thighs, and scream with laughter as she beat Louie Frear at her own game of burlesque in *Sister Mary Jane's Top Note*. This riot of low comedy would break out while she was washing up, or in any of the day's dreariness. But after tea she would vanish upstairs and reappear hours later, full blown and aromatic, white fluff of boa, belladonna in eyes which looked out defiantly on Manchester's gathering nightfall.

My grandfather warned her of the wrath to come. There was a brawl one night. Beatrice flaunted a new fashion—something with gold braid, and a short Hungarian jacket called a Zouave. It was worn with a tight waist and a great outspreading of skirt; there was a collar with bone supports which made pink spots in the neck; then from her little toque came down in a V shape a spotted veil over the face, fastened under the chin in a knot tied by wetting the fingers and twisting the ends of the stuff round and round. Beatrix Esmond walking downstairs at Walcote House to greet Esmond could not possibly have made a sight more wondrous than my Aunt Beatrice coming down the steps into the kitchen of Summer Place, holding her skirts. But she did not trip, she descended. And my grandfather raised himself from his chair and clutched at the arm; I remember the intensity of his knuckles. He pointed a finger at her and he denounced her. "A daughter of mine! Anybody would take you for an actress." It was a hard saying in that period. To my amazement, Beatrice, instead of throwing a contemptuous remark at him over her shoulders and sailing out of the house, sat down and burst into tears, hysterical and hopeless. Her mother and her two sisters comforted her and my grandfather took refuge in silence. It was necessary for Beatrice to go upstairs and attend to her *décor* again.

She was charming to me always. She never spoke in her vernacular to me, but in her softest and most refined tone and accent. She called me "darling," and it was something of a term, was "darling," at Summer Place. She took me to my first theatre; it was called *The Swiss Express*, and what is more, I saw it from a box. It was a farce with the brothers Renard in it; they never spoke a word but acted in dumb-show.

Her greatest conquest, amongst many, was the Turkish Consul of Manchester. She arrived down to breakfast one morning in Summer Place and caused consternation by announcing that she was that week going to Paris. That, and the use of Turkish cigarettes, decided her character once and for all, not only to my grandfather but to the entire neighbourhood. To Paris she did go, and came back "all chic," to use her own triumphant term, dressed beyond compare; in her train was largesse of saucy hats and gowns and feather boas and lace stockings and bottles of perfume and pots of rouge, which even to me, a delighted child, were not only gorgeous but somehow fearful to contemplate. The sight of the cavalcade of two cabs outside the front door, one carrying the gold and frankincense and myrrh, attracted an attention in the Place which threw politeness to the winds. My grandfather once more and for the last time rose in his wrath and made allusions to Jezebel. But my aunt went straight to her bedroom and soon it was changed to a boudoir —or as a boudoir might have looked after a wind from Venusberg had disturbed it in passing. She brought me enormous boxes of chocolates. She laughed until tears filled her eyes as she mimicked herself and kicked her left leg backwards and upwards and put a finger to the side of her mouth and said, "La! La!"

To my mother she introduced one of her Consul's friends, another stout gentleman in a fez and gold spectacles. He fascinated me with his flapping heelless slippers; I could not understand how they kept on. My mother lived with him in a house outside the city, and I went to stay there from time to time and I had to learn a new phraseology and speak of a "drawing-room" and a "hall"—not and never a "lobby." I was enchanted by the dish-covers which hung on the wall in the kitchen, beginning tiny and getting one and one bigger and bigger. I lived for the most part in the kitchen with the cook. Now and then I was permitted to go into the dining-room after dinner, while my mother and the Turkish gentleman drank port and cracked nuts. He one afternoon surprised me when I was alone in the dining-room breathlessly gazing around. There was a dish of fruit on a gleaming sideboard and he benignly said to me "Eat melon and enjoice yourself," then he disappeared with some embarrassment.

The crash came when the Consul decided he had had enough. Beatrice, audacious and glorious, brought an action of breach of promise against him. She became a part of the news for a week. Her photograph appeared in the popular papers of Manchester and environs. The *Manchester Daily Dispatch* described her as "prepossessing," another word that I had to look up in the dictionary. I was credibly informed in later years that as soon as Beatrice went into the box she attempted to prejudice or corrupt the judge with a smile. The judge throughout the hearing was on her side obviously, and who wouldn't have been? Once he administered a rebuke to the counsel for the defendant for bullying her. Unhappily the judge's goodwill was changed to nought on a technical point. The case more or less collapsed; Beatrice was awarded £200 damages—and the Turkish Consul had offered to settle out of court for £3,000. My aunt was badly advised. But she revelled in her appearances in court, each time in a different and more expensive garb.

The day after the verdict she put £100 on a horse running in the Manchester races. It was beaten by a short head, and started at ten to one. Beatrice was brought home stiff and insensible from drink; and it had been champagne. She did not drink heavily as a rule. Next day she packed up and went to Blackpool, taking me with her. It was the summer during which Victor Trumper scored twelve centuries, mostly on "sticky" wickets. For a month I was as happy as a boy well can be. My aunt every morning would give me a shilling and send me to play on the sands or listen to the ventriloquists until the tide came in. Meanwhile Beatrice threw ambition to the winds and spent herself and her remaining money recklessly. She brought back to Summer Place a rather seedy little man in a stiff wing collar; he got on very well with the family for a while. Apparently, they thought, Beatrice was resigning herself to her alloted place in life. The seedy little man would sit and sip what he called "port wine" and at intervals he would say to my grandmother, "Just a little for the stomach's sake." He suddenly vanished from the scene.

A year or two after the breach of promise action, both my grandfather and grandmother were dead. The family broke up. Beatrice was compelled to live in a long mean street which was not even a Place; and I went with her. A house with a back yard, sordid beyond description. She tried to furnish it and introduce some gaiety. One night I entered the house and found two broker's men ensconced in the little living-room. My aunt explained to me that she had run into debt. She sent me out of the house; "Go and read in the Library." When I came home again fairly late, the broker's men had gone, and a genteel young man with watery eyes and a fair moustache sat in the middle of the room playing a flute at my aunt, with his legs crossed intensely. He made curious noises as he took in breath between the phrases. My aunt served my supper in the scullery and then asked me to go to bed. Next morning she gave me ten shillings for pocket money, and the genteel young man with the moustache and flute was never seen again by me or by my aunt.

Her life came to an end soon after in circumstances which may appear a little abject. She became inexplicably compassionate about an elderly man who for years had been the gardener at a house when she picked up a temporary job as laundress, deep down in the cellar, two days a week. She married him, kept him, and bore him a daughter and died at the age of twenty-eight. And that is my Aunt Beatrice as I shall always remember her.

.   .   .   .   .   .

Cricket will be a recurrent theme in this book, but I think I shall be able to develop it symphonically and weave it into the main texture. I hope to write of the game and its players as Hazlitt wrote of fives and Cavanagh. If I cannot interest the reader who knows little or nothing of cricket, I have made my book vainly. And if my life in music and amongst musicians does not win me the attention of those who know me as the author of *Days in the Sun*, equally have I wasted my time. I am not a man who is interested in sport. I have

attended only one race-meeting in my life. I have never seen
an English Cup Final. I have seldom known that it was
Derby Day until next morning's newspapers. I cannot play
any card games; I do not at first sight pick out a spade from
a diamond. I am a member of the Savage Club and have never
entered the billiard-room. And I have not once in my life
owned a single golf club and once only have I played golf—
at Criccieth for a week, and at my first attempt to drive from
a tee I landed on the green in one blow. I "holed" (if that is
the correct term) in about a dozen.

There was no cricket at the Board School I attended for a
few years. There were no fields attached to this establishment,
only a playground made of asphalt. I became interested in
cricket by chance, and as the game proved in after years the
knife with which I prized open my oyster, I will digress from
Summer Place to a June morning on which I found myself
outside the county cricket ground of Old Trafford. I was not
then in the habit of venturing as far from home as the six or
seven miles that separated Old Trafford from Summer Place.
Forty-seven years ago Queen Victoria was on the throne, the
Boer War had not yet impinged on the mind of the nation,
and there was comparatively little unemployment in the land,
except on principle. Electricity remained more or less in its
period of wonder and experiment; one of the most startling
advertisements in certain of the daily newspapers was of an
electrical belt which cured all human aches and pains if carried
round the body. The advertisement depicted a naked man
wearing one of these belts, with sparks flying out of him in
all directions. H. G. Wells and his war in the air suggested
for most folk the height of romance. Even the balloon
(employed in 1870 to convey food to besieged Paris) had come
to be regarded as a device employed to announce the presence
in the neighbourhood of a circus. The motor-car was a thing
of uncertain capacity and temper; owners of them exposed
themselves either to ridicule or contumely. A man with a
red flag preceded a traction engine in the streets, and he would
wave it to warn us to get out of the way at once. The cinema,
known as the bioscope, was the last turn on the programmes
of variety; it usually depicted the notabilities of Europe walking here and there at a great pace, exploding all over.

On this summer morning of June, in a remote England, I somehow found myself outside the Old Trafford county cricket ground. I had just passed my twelfth birthday and I doubt if I had read a book of any kind, except a penny dreadful. But I seem to remember that I had seen Irving in *The Bells* supposedly on a winter night and dusting imaginary snow from his boots and shivering and sending a blast of cold air through the theatre. The point relevant to this chapter is that I first saw Irving and A. C. Maclaren at much the same impressionable time of life; they wakened the incurable romantic in me which to this day will not be exorcised even by the cynicism which saves a grown man from foolishness, or should save him.

The boy that was young Cardus paid his sixpence; it was necessary for him to push hard with his stomach against the iron turnstile. So for the first time I entered the place where years afterwards I was to live through many happy days with the greenest grass in England before my eyes. The first cricketer I saw was A. C. Maclaren. Lancashire were beginning an innings when I sat down on a hard wooden seat. Maclaren drove a ball far to the distant boundary, straight and powerfully. I cannot remember the bowler's name; he has passed with all other details of the match into limbo, but I can still see the swing of Maclaren's bat, the great follow-through, finishing high and held there with the body poised as he himself contemplated the grandeur of the stroke and savoured it. Then the clouds over Old Trafford burst and rain fell in torrents. No further play occurred at Old Trafford that day. Absit omen! I waited for hours, sheltering in all sorts of holes and corners, praying for the sky to clear. The match was abandoned after lunch. This brief glimpse into the genius of cricket fired an imagination already stimulated by what in those years was called pernicious literature. This brief sight of Maclaren thrilled my blood, for it gave shape and reality to tilings I had till then only vaguely felt and dreamed about of romance. I went home happy, craving for more. I did not think of cricket; I knew next to nothing of the rules and technique. Without knowing it precisely, I had received the grace of art. From Maclaren to Wagner and the romantic gesture would henceforward be a sure and natural transition, as sure and natural as the transition from the enjoyment of Tom Hayward's serene and classic batsmanship to the music of Bach. No; I am not arguing in favour of an extreme æstheticism; I have never been able to afford anything of the kind. I am not suggesting that we should look for more than Maclaren in a Maclaren. I am all in favour of seeing the object as in itself it really is. But having looked as far and as closely at it as that, we are, or should be, beyond the surface. The external world probably exists only for a cat as a thing in itself. For human beings the essence of the object is the power consciously to perceive it—which is Bishop Berkeley for the millions. Maclaren was not just a cricketer any more than Wagner was just a composer; or any more than Phil May just drew comic pictures for *Punch*; or any more than Mr. Squeers's blind eye was to Dickens only a blind eye and not very much like a fanlight; or any more than the G Minor Symphony is nothing but a composition in the tonic and dominant of eighteenth-century music; or any more than Harry Tate was only a music-hall comedian when he came on to the stage, ostensibly a business man arriving at the office, and on asking the staff if there were any letters this morning and after being told there were not, replied, "Well, then, we must write some." In the *Comédie Humaine* of Balzac even the scullions are endowed with genius. We can each of us in our way endow the scullions in the *Comédie Humaine* of our own existence if not with genius at any rate with savour, if we bring to them an imaginative sense of the world in which men and things may constantly be felt breaking out surprisingly in all directions from the dreary routine of appearance. We may as well all die to-morrow if the wine of temperament we bring to the day's diet of sights and sounds does not go as well with the modest dishes as with those prepared by a recognised chef.

.   .   .   .   .   .

During the whole of the summer of 1902 I seem to have lived free as the wind watching and playing cricket; it was in this year that I saw Trumper score a century before lunch at Old Trafford in the Test match lost by England by three runs. To this day I find myself at times confused in my memories and feelings of high pleasure—I find impressions of the batsmanship of Victor Trumper getting themselves mixed up with the sensations derived from the leaping strings in a Straussian orchestra, from flights of seagulls, from roses that rear to spikes of great nobility. It was, of course, Beatrice who, with her last fling of extravagance, enabled me to take the longest holiday I have ever known in my life, a whole summer, and at the right age for it. Long days at the county ground, full length on the grass. And every evening we would go forth to the fields and play on bare dusty earth until the sun went down and you had to crouch at the stumps like Jessop to see the ball against the reddening sight-screen of the sky. Where are all the boys now that were my companions?—thin Smith, who bowled slow if he had that day been absent from school and had seen Johnny Briggs, or bowled fast and all over the place and beyond his powers if the destruction for Lancashire had been wreaked by Arthur Mold. Where is Thompson now, who was fat for his years and could never be trusted not to run us all out?

And where in the world between Australia and Summer Place is the boy who one day was given his first bat—Beatrice again!—a real bat, with a cane handle, as we used to say, to mark a notable distinction; the other kind had no splice at all visible to the naked eye, and it stung you all over the body if you made a stroke with the bottom of the bat. I can at any moment recapture the sensation of my fingers pressing the rubber handle along the splice, coaxing it to roll down and fit nearly; but often it would go too far and would have to be turned up at the bottom. The misgivings when the bat was first used were acute; what human boy has not stolen a glance at the edge—while nobody was looking—after the first stroke, and rubbed off the mark made by the ball?

We wore cricket belts which fastened with metal clips shaped like snakes or serpents; some of the more well-off amongst us even wore coloured ties. Famous cricketers of the 1900's wore ties when they were being photographed in groups, all in a row, some at the end looking out of the picture into the far east or far west; some sitting, perhaps on a chair with the back to the front, while they leaned forward over it confidentially; and to balance things, two of them reclining on the earth at the front. I doted on the old photos—and do still—signed "Elliott & Fry, Brighton and Hove." The camera was not yet sure of itself, any more than electricity was; it stood on three legs and a man would disappear under a black cloth and make helpless signs with his arm to the heroes about to be taken. Then he pulled a round black ball on a string, and emerged into the air again.

There were photographs of A. A. Lilley keeping wicket with, apparently, Niagara just behind him; there was an especially favourite one of Tom Richardson, most majestic of fast bowlers, holding his right arm aloft, fixed in eternal and obliging immobility.

In 1902 I was staying with my mother for a few weeks at the house of *her* Sultan, and on June 26th I set out from a suburban place called Timperley to go to Old Trafford; it was a morning of sunshine and blue sky; also it was a national holiday which should have commemorated the coronation of King Edward VII; appendicitis overwhelmed him at the last minute and the public celebration of the occasion could not be postponed, even though the word appendicitis terrified everybody and subsequently became a very fashionable illness. On this radiant day I set forth; my hero J. T. Tyldesley at the close of play on the previous evening had finished 36 not out. I had to walk six miles, for somehow I took a wrong turning, and found myself on the other side of a canal and I could not get over; so I ran on and on, terrified at the thought that Tyldesley was making brilliant strokes and I not there. Some men in a dirty coal barge cheered me as I ran—a pitiful object, but not, I think, untouched with grace before the Lord.

I received full and just consolation for my miseries and sweaty toil along the canal bank. When I reached the county cricket ground the crowd was enormous. I paid my sixpence and in panic I rushed through the gates and round the ring of the congested spectators, as I heard the roaring at some flashing play I couldn't see. At last I crawled through a hole in the multitude and obtained a place on the grass. Tyldesley was still not out and I saw him cut Tom Richardson for fours innumerable, crash bang against the pavilion rails until a line of white powder, dried paint, could be seen at their base, knocked off by Tyldesley's strokes, square and swift. Tyldesley scored 165, then his middle stump was sent spinning round and round by a breakback from Richardson. In a mirror and furnace of heat Richardson made a noble sight, swarthy and handsome and tall and supple and strong, a giant with black curly hair and a moustache; he ran to bowl in long swinging strides and just before his arm wheeled over he leapt upwards: it was like a wave going to a crest, then breaking.

Lancashire on that heavenly day scored hundreds of runs; even my appetite was satiated, and I was scornful as I saw D. L. A. Jephson sending down his underhands. The heat grew hotter; the crowd, tired of easy runs, began to amuse itself. It was the custom of Old Trafford crowds in those days to while away tedium by the singing of part songs. They would come to a lachrymose cadence—plagal, I think—whereat they would applaud themselves. They would single out a policeman as he marched protectively round the edge of the field, and at each of his strides they would chant in unison, "Left, right, left, right," and when the policeman ended his beat suddenly he would receive the applause of thousands. Old Trafford, June 26, 1902: a concourse on the sixpenny part of the ground of caps and bowler hats; here and there a straw "cadie" and few women. Away across the field was the pavilion and there the business men of Manchester sat in their tight trousers, coats buttoned at the top of the chest, high stiff collars and high hats. Outside the ground the cabs and hansoms waited. Not a cloud in the sky. . . .

I went home that evening tired, hungry and thirsty, with a full and contented heart. Part of my way I ran along the bank of the canal again, but now the barges were of burnished gold and in the sunset I saw the happy isles.

.   .   .   .   .   .

After the breaking-up of Summer Place and the passing of Beatrice I lived precariously for a while, usually in odd jobs ranging from a messenger-boy to driver of a joiner's and carpenter's hand-cart. I dwelt in a single back room in a Manchester lodging, so cold in the winter for want of a blanket that I collected newspapers and periodicals to pile on my bed

over my feet. There were loose boards in the uncarpeted bedroom floor. On a rickety table, called romantically a chest of
drawers, was placed a mirror that swung backwards and for-
wards; occasionally and unexpectedly, it turned completely
over, and round and round. It reflected in spots only. The
front of one of the drawers in this chest would sometimes
come loose into my hands when I pulled at the two knobs.
Much coaxing was necessary to fit it back into its proper place,
so that it might not offend the eye. I was a fastidious young
man.

I frequently changed my situation (a blessed word of the
epoch) as office boy, handy lad, or what not. Once or twice
I was discharged because of absent-mindedness. The years
went by and I didn't count a day of them. One summer evening,
I recall, I suddenly ran like mad down the street, impelled by
a strange ecstasy of happiness; there was no special cause for
this outburst, and I had not before known the like of it; it
was pure joy at the thought that I was alive and young. I
said to myself, as I stampeded along: "Ten-twenty-thirty-
forty years from now—before I am an old man!" An eternity
in which to do things. No boy really believes he will ever
grow old; he thinks he is going to be the first of mortals
never to die.

Another stroke of fortune befell me in December, 1904. I
was engaged by the Manchester agent of a marine insurance
company. His name was Hugh Fleming. He had a brother,
Christopher. They were charming and distinguished to look
at. Hugh resembled Edward Elgar; Christopher often wore
tight trousers and a cravat, a bowler hat, and gave the impression he was about to ride in Rotten Row. They exuded the
air and flavour of "county"; how they came to be associated
with insurance I cannot tell; but it was easy work then, with
Manchester trade burgeoning. I helped another clerk, a man
of middle years, to write out the policies; the Flemings would
not use the "new fangled" typewriting machine; probably it
was cheaper to employ clerks. I sat on a high-legged stool,
like Tim Linkinwater, and wrote in a copperplate hand sundry
details about bills of lading and the S. S. *Benares*, Liverpool to
Shanghai, 12 bales (tar) Cottons W.P.A. @ 6/3 %. There was
a phrase or clause in the policy which thrilled me: something

about "of the seas, storms, floods, pirates, jettison, letters of marque"—but I forget it; I forget the right rhythm and romantic cadence. I should have thought I would never forget it, so many times day after day for seven years did I see the phrase as I sat by the side of my senior clerk writing with a steel pen out of an inkwell ("They come as a boon and a blessing to men, the Pickwick, the Owl, and the Waverley Pen"). It was part of my job to make copies of the policies, a complicated operation involving a book with pages of absorbent tissue paper, and a press with a handle. It was important not to dampen the tissue paper too much with the broad brush used in the process. We had a telephone attached to the wall. To communicate with the Exchange you turned a handle. (It was the age of handles.) Sometimes it was possible to obtain a slight electrical shock, temporarily stiffening the finger joints.

My office hours were from half-past nine to five; and there was little to do until afternoon. Many times I was alone half the day. The Fleming brothers would go to Old Trafford to watch Maclaren and Spooner; or in the winter they would sit in the adjacent Constitutional Club, looking in at the office for the morning letters and returning in the evening to sign the answers. My colleague, the head clerk, went the rounds of the public-houses, not necessarily to drink. In the evenings he was engaged "professionally"; the public-houses of the period gave variety performances on the premises. My colleague made a profound impression on me, when first I met him, by showing me his card. It contained no allusion to insurance: it simply stated:

VINCENT ST. GEORGE
Entertainer

He lived in one of Manchester's most depressing barracks of back-streets. He dressed shabbily but as smartly as he could. He invariably wore a worried look, for he had a wife and two children to support. His income from insurance was thirty shillings weekly—I started at eight shillings weekly, and in the course of eight years, from 1904 to 1912, I advanced to a golden sovereign, by which time I had celebrated my twenty-first birthday. Yet the Flemings were as kindly and as friendly as any men I ever knew. It never occurred to them that a married man with two children might be finding it hard to subsist on thirty shillings weekly, even in 1904. As for myself, in my teens and unmarried, they probably wondered what on earth I did with my money at all. At Christmas, Hugh Fleming, senior of the firm, so to say, gave the head clerk and me a sovereign and a half-sovereign respectively. I imagined I had by grace of Providence met a reincarnation of the Cheeryble Brothers. One day every month we stayed late at the office balancing the month's returns. The Flemings would dine at the club, while the staff—the two of us—would search high or low for a missing item, usually a matter of sevenpence. As soon as we had found it we would telephone to the club and Hugh would come in, redolent of old brandy, cigar in mouth, and he would sign the completed document of accounts which I would post by registered letter from the G.P.O. He gave us overtime, of course—two shillings for his head clerk, a shilling for me; that was supposed to be money for our "dinner." I never spent it that way; for a shilling I could see a favourite actor from the pit of the Theatre Royal. A packet of chocolate and a glass of milk were sustenance enough, one night a month; usually my evening meal was included in my board and keep at my lodgings.

I am not writing ironically of the generosity of the Flemings. According to the custom of the times and the relative spheres occupied by employer and employee, the Flemings were, I insist, kindness itself. The office was, as they say, a happy family. The brothers called us by our Christian names, and behind their backs, of course, we called them affectionately "Hughie" and "Chrissie." Once or twice, during summer, Hugh would return from Old Trafford; he would look in the office and ask if we were busy: and if we were not. he would tell me to hurry at once to Old Trafford; Maclaren was not out at eighty. He would give me my tram fare and the price of admission to the ground, and I would leap down the stairs and dash along Bridge Street, terrified that Maclaren might get out before I got to the ground.

I fear I repaid him with a not too conscientious service. I unashamedly used the insurance office as my place for study and hard reading. I can recapture, as I write, the pleasure that came over me on a winter day, when I built up the fire between noon and two o'clock, the hours for lunch. The Flemings were at the club. Vincent St. George (better known as 'Arry Williams) had gone to talk to the "boys," or "pros," as he sometimes called them. I would brew a jug of tea (Nestlé's milk) and, without knowing it, chew some banana sandwiches, lost to everything except my books. The silence in the room; the rumble of Manchester outside; the dark November day; the fire smoking and spluttering so that I had to break a single coal with the poker. I would perhaps go from the clerks' small outer office and for a moment, just a moment, invade the austere calm of the private office of the Flemings. I would walk in softly, treading the rich carpet. The polished furniture and the deep leather chairs, a spacious desk, with blotters that rolled like a swing. One or two engravings on the wall— everything still and inviolate. Of course I often went into the private office when the Flemings were present and letters and policies had to be signed, or when I had to receive instructions. But in those days it was one thing to go into your principal's private office at his call or command; it was different—subtly and thrillingly different—when he wasn't there.

Often I forgot, during office hours, the existence of the insurance world. I delivered policies to the various firms in the afternoons, first taking them to the Inland Revenue for stamps. Usually there would be not more than six places of call, each near the other; the whole itinerary could be covered with time to spare in half an hour. I would race round; then go to the Manchester Reference Library. To do myself justice let me explain that always I intended to stay there only as long as the time I had gained in getting the policies delivered at breakneck speed. But more often than not, some writer or subject absorbed me—usually Newman and music—and I lost sense of where I was. I can always feel the sickening in my stomach as I at last came to my senses and looked at the clock and saw it was nearly five. Shamefacedly I would go back to the office. For some inexplicable reason I was seldom admonished. Mr. Hugh might say, "Been rather a long time, eh?" And privately, as man to man, the head clerk would say it wasn't fair. "After all, the hours are easy, lad." He always called me "lad."

On the way to the office in the mornings (and I was supposed to be there first at 9.30 to open the letters, the safe, and get the inkwells filled and so on), I was just as reckless. I could not resist a public reading-room on the way from my lodgings to the city. I was falling very much under the spell of Ernest Newman in the *Birmingham Post*; also, there was Walkley to read in *The Times*, as well as Montague and Agate in the *Manchester Guardian*. I could not to-day count the palpitating occasions I charged up the stairs of 64 Bridge Street, Manchester, to the first floor, and pressed against the double doors, heart in my mouth. If they resisted—ah! I was here first; when the clocks had struck ten I had seemed to be miles away. But if the double-doors gave to my pressure, and I did not at once see the head clerk in the outer office— then I knew that Hughie had arrived before me. I was not afraid of the sack, or of a stern reprimand; I feared a reproach. When I entered the office late I would hear him in his private room and he would call out, "That you, Cardus?" The head clerk did not come under this terrible risk of censure by kindliness; he was given a sort of licence to arrive late. It was understood that his labours as an entertainer were of no light order.

For seven years the office of the Flemings was my study, my school. I even used the "firm's" notepaper as manuscript when I began to learn to write English. I bless the names of the Flemings, as I bless many names in this book. I cannot imagine what would have happened to me if I had not been guided to the office of the Flemings. I could not have educated myself and at the same time worked for my living. Through all the years I remained with the Flemings only my week's emolument stood between me and destitution. You may argue that Fleming got me cheaply even if I did strain his

tolerance and patience. The truth is that I received the existing
standard wage. Fleming could have replaced me with profit
at any time. From the day I entered his service he must
have known I was a misfit. It was the first turning-point
in my life when I saw an advertisement in "Situations
Vacant" in the *Manchester Evening News*; "Wanted Smart
Respectable Youth for Insurance Office. Hours 9.30 to 5.
Apply personally with references to Hugh Fleming, 64 Bridge
Street." For as long as I needed them the Flemings kept up
the fiction that I was "smart" as well as respectable. Looking
back on myself as I then was, I should choose different words;
I was, I think, quiet, imaginative, sensitive and easily hurt.
Doubtful qualifications for anybody in the shrewd Manchester
of 1904-1912.

One day, also in office hours, I wrote a song for Vincent
St. George, words and music. He was an artist in a style
known as "serio-comic," which meant that a certain heaviness
of vocalism was employed here and there, as a contrast to a
more hearty approach to the audience. Two lines from my
song remain in my mind: "For the breezes fan an Englishman,
In the homeland of his pride." I was too young to go to hear
Vincent St. George sing my song in the Stretford Arms, with
a piano accompaniment of vamped six-four chords; but he
informed me that it was a terrific success, and for a long time
afterwards he would refer to it as one of his favourite
"numbers." He paid me ten shillings for the exclusive rights
of public performance; and with part of this, the first royalty
I ever received, I saw Forbes-Robertson as Hamlet, and
next day had the temerity to differ from the general high
opinion of this actor in the part. I thought he was elderly,
a   cautionary-tale-finger-wagging-oracular   Hamlet;   rather
like a university extension lecturer; a Hamlet in invisible
pince-nez.

I edited from the insurance office a Review of Art and
Literature and called it (in despair) *As You Like It*. I wrote it
in my best policy handwriting in a large exercise book, a
hundred pages, and published it once a month: in other
words, I lent it to those of my few companions I thought
equal to it. I pretended that my most distinguished con-
tributors lived in London: my music critic was a beautiful

and imaginary girl whom I—God knows why—named Doris Wallace. I copied essays and articles from journals which I knew my readers would not see; old numbers of the *Athenæum*, for example. Sometimes I borrowed from Ernest Newman and the *Birmingham* Post, and I ascribed his wittiest sayings to D. W. I fell in love with her, wrote letters to myself from her, not amorous, but full of quotations from the best writers. She lived—I decided—in St. John's Wood, in Hall Road. I had of course never been near London then. Edward German lived in Hall Road; during this period, as I shall presently explain, he had a curious effect upon my dormant musical mind and nature; I looked him up in *Who's Who*, and made D. W. one of his neighbours.

At this time I met a boy named Seddon; at once he became my Steerforth. His influence on me, I see now, was considerable. He introduced me to Shaw and to the Fabian essays. He was also a handsome creature, dark and aquiline, but a dwarf, though of perfect physical proportions. He worshipped the human body and followed a certain Bernarr MacFadden, who conducted a School of Health and Beauty. I often wondered what was going to happen to Seddon; he grew from eighteen to twenty-six and time could not touch him or his exquisite youthfulness. I could not understand how nature was ever to drag him under the general law of mortal change and perishability. Illness apparently was beyond him. In the foullest of Manchester winters, in rain, fog and snow, he went without hat or overcoat, or umbrella, and he would fast one day each month. I have seen him lost to sight in a cloud of steam as he—like, and entirely unlike Dr. Johnson in the *Journey to the Hebrides*—dried himself in front of a fire. In his twenty-seventh year he journeyed to Brighton to spend a holiday in August at MacFadden's summer school. This was against a lifetime's principles, for he loathed crowds and seaside resorts, and cities; he belonged to the fresh-air movement and was commonly known as a crank. I did not share all his views but I went so far as to discard a hat, thus we were as nudists of the period, and wherever we walked people turned round and looked at us. Seddon, to get a sight of his one and only god, Bernarr MacFadden, journeyed to Brighton in August, 1913; he was drowned while bathing, the day after he arrived there.

During one stage of our friendship I could not bear him out of my sight. He was learning to be an engineer's draughtsman and his firm was situated miles from my place in Bridge Street. Often he worked late at night and I would go to wait for him, walking up and down the pavement, round the corner from his office. I would keep my eyes on this corner, praying for him to appear. Or I would read a book in the light of a shop window and when I heard somebody approaching I would not look up, but would will with all my strength that he was about to greet me. Once I stayed in my miserable lodgings a whole week-end and did not see Seddon—a terrible deprivation. I explained to him that I was spending a few days in London at the home of my music critic in St. John's Wood. When Tuesday evening at last came round I saw Seddon at once and casually told him of my visit; I spoke of a handsome room with french windows opening on a garden, with a fountain sending up a delicate spray. I spoke of the gathering London twilight and the way "D. W." sat at the piano and played the mazurkas of Chopin while I listened and saw the flickering shadows on the ceiling, thrown by the first of autumn's woodfires. I have not since heard the mazurkas of Chopin played with the poise, touch and aristocratic ardour which were imparted to them by "D. W." in those halycon times, in Hall Road, St. John's Wood. Years afterwards, when I went to Lord's for cricket, I would walk down Hall Road and look for the house of my adolescent stirrings. It had been taken down long ago. I never discovered whether Seddon suspected that "D. W." and her home in Hall Road were a creation of my own. As time went on, I had to drop her, naturally. I even married her to a German musician and sent her to live in Dresden. Seddon said nothing when I ceased to mention "D. W.," though he had listened to my talk, my adoring talk of her, for years.

With Seddon and "D. W." out of my life my fantasies came to an end. I had no awareness of sex, no curiosity about it. I never had those bright visions of beautiful women which came before the eyes of the young Mr. Wells. My "D. W." was a symbol and symptom of an awakening æsthetic; she represented the life I wished to live. I had no "preoccupations with my virginity"; I never thought of my body except as something to feed and occasionally to wash. The history of my sex life could be interestingly and comprehensively told on a post-card, like that of most men, English or other.

All sorts of foods and substances went into the stock-pot of my mind between the years of 1907-1912, as I emerged from the teens to the twenties. Seddon was a zealous Shavian—another term that dates us. He tried to make a Socialist of me, which was not difficult because of my admiration for Shaw. I joined the Independent Labour Party, but I think they found me disappointing. On the face of it I should have been splendid propaganda for them: an example of the new generation breaking free from poverty; the "underdog" of Robert Blatchford in the flesh—and not too much of flesh. But I could never work myself into the proper state of indignation. Like any human being, I loathe the social injustice that winks at starvation in a world of plenty. Something may be done about it some day. But I lost sympathy with Socialists the more I met them. Their creed or system was obviously not to be a means to an end but an end in itself; I could not discover what manner of rich, imaginative life they were planning for the world after poverty had been abolished. More and more Socialism, apparently. They seemed to me arid folk with an ethic and economy the result not of abstract thinking but of personal experiences of an uncomfortable kind. Few of them, as a fact, had ever lived as near to the bone as I. I could not see the use of class-consciousness, and when in the course of time they applied their labels to the arts, dividing works of the imagination into proletarian sheep and bourgeois goats, I lost interest for ever in doctrinaire politics and economics. We are bound, of course, to admit the phenomenon of the external universe; we have physically to subsist in it, and so the more justly it is balanced the better it will be for introvert and extrovert alike. But I suspect that whatever the condition of material things, whether peace or war, plenty or want, the proportion of happy and unhappy folk all over the earth remains much the same. The planners of the future invariably forget that in their new world or "order" the old familiar human family will persist, most of them bored for want of instruction in the art of living imaginatively.

When Miss Horniman bought Pitt Hardacre's Comedy Theatre (where I had sold chocolates six or seven years ago) she bought it at the right time for me; my mind was exactly ready for Galsworthy, Shaw, Sudermann, Rostand—and more important, ready for the dramatic criticism of C. E. Montague, A. N. Monkhouse and James Agate, columns of it and them in the *Manchester Guardian* every Tuesday, three great phalanxes. Miss Horniman, a delightful spinster who openly smoked cigarettes in the lounge of the Midland Hotel, gave me and countless other young men of Manchester our first contact with the "play of ideas," as we called it, bless us. And the *Manchester Guardian* sniffed at the "commercial theatre," and at the actor-manager who every autumn came North in an opulent cavalcade, actor-manager's wife and all, and more often than not better as manager than actress. An outbreak of the Manchester School of Drama set in—Houghton, Brighouse and Monkhouse. The action of their plays usually began in a drawing-room in the Eccles New Road; the son and heir of old Seth Northcote—Manchester Home Trade— had got Jessie, one of the maids, with child. One of Brighouse's plays even conquered London; Monkhouse was a finer thinker: his theme was the skeleton in the suburb; he tried to dramatise the inhibitions and evasions of the social class in which he anachronistically lived and died.

The intelligentsia of Manchester, shepherded by Montague, went knowingly and in droves to these dreary slices of life; the same people attended surreptitiously on Beerbohm Tree across the way at the Theatre Royal; perhaps like myself they kept to themselves their feeling that after all there is something to be said for personality.

What with music and musical criticism and Miss Horniman's first nights, and Montague and Agate; what with my Schema of Culture, my Review of Literature and Art, and the insurance policies, and what with cricket in the summer appealing to me more and more as a way out of the rut sooner or later, I was a busy youth. But there was no conscious egoism about me; I emulated my authors as I emulated my cricketers with not a thought of fame and fortune even as a remote possibility of the future. I wished simply to obtain in good time leisure and income enough to learn to write for the joy of writing. For by now I had made up my mind: I would one day live by my pen or perish. I was not yet sure what my subject was to be—literature, theatre, music or leader-writing. I never dreamed of condescending to a novel, and if anybody had told me I was destined one day to make a reputation as a writer on cricket I should have felt hurt.

I practised my pen with Newman my model in music criticism, with Shaw and Montague and Agate my models in theatre criticism. I believed in a *Manchester Guardian* style and I set myself diligently to acquire it. Years later, when I had established myself as one of the *Manchester Guardian* staff, I had deliberately to set about ridding myself of this style. But I am straining the leash of my book once more. These things will be told as they occur, in the proper sequence of my life.

I owed much to Agate in my nonage. I did not meet him until years later, but he had already gained the reputation for gusto that still dogs him even now he has come to mellowness and some lovableness; it was a gusto that refreshingly disturbed and fluttered the gem-like flame of Montague's austerity. I liked Agate's way of dealing once with a pantomime at the Theatre Royal—a huge column in leaded minion, beginning or ending "Et in Arcadia"; he scarcely alluded to a performance, and he never tried to disguise that he went to the theatre most times with his notices in his pocket already written and brilliantly re-written. Agate did not begin his life work as dramatic critic with the *Guardian*; he served a slight and diverting apprenticeship on the staff of the *Manchester Daily Dispatch*, a paper noted at the time mainly for its racing news. Agate was eventually asked to resign, when in the course of a notice of a French farce he uspd in the *Daily Dispatch* the word "hypergelast," borrowed (I take it) from George Meredith's Essay on Comedy, and denoting the loud vacant laughers. I am told that while Agate represented the *Daily Dispatch* at the theatre, the door attendant frequently regarded him with an unusual deference, for he dressed in a style that led the uninformed to mistake him for "Carlton," who was the racing tipster of the paper. Then there were his ponies, which to the uninitiate of the period came under one and the same generic head—they were just "horses."

Manchester was good for a young man to live in during the years before the 1914-1918 war. The Germans had given the place a solid culture; they came to Manchester for trade and brought their music with them. Richter had played on the staircase on Christmas morning when the Siegfried Idyll wakened Cosima as no other woman before or since has been wakened; at the Royal Manchester College of Music Brodsky was the Principal; friend of Tchaikovsky and Brahms. The Continental Restaurant was München in Lancashire. I one night saw Brodsky, Richter and Strauss going in there together. I remember a week in Manchester when a new play by Galsworthy was given at the Gaiety Theatre on Monday; on Tuesday there was a concert of the Brodsky Quartet; on Wednesday a matinee by Réjane; on Thursday a Hallé Concert, with Richter and Busoni, and on Friday a production of Ibsen's *Ghosts*, connived in camera; for *Ghosts* was then a banned play in England. At the other theatres the same week, I have no doubt, the despised commercials were producing themselves—probably George Alexander in a Pinero play. All these exciting events were written upon in the *Manchester Guardian*; Montague almost breaking shins over his own wit and pregnant with metaphor; Agate already full of Sarah and the Goncourt brothers; while Allan Monkhouse, who grew to look more like Dante every day, kept the balance in prose as cool and judicious as any in the land. No city has known the equal of the *Manchester Guardian* as an influence for acute living. A little austere, maybe, but a passionate Puritanism. I often wondered who read it except the Jews and the Germans and the self-educated denizens of the hinterland of Lancashire.

At Manchester University there was Professor Herford, a lean don of literature, with a skin of parchment and a ghostly beard and small powerful lenses in his spectacles. He translated Ibsen into English. One night *A Doll's House* was given at the Theatre Royal by a company directed by Leigh Lovell, a forgotten pioneer of Ibsen in England, who acted with his wife. The *Guardian* asked Herford to write the notice. He covered two columns, roughly two thousand five hundred words, all about Ibsen. He forgot to make mention of the performance and the performers, and had to be rung up from

THE HOUSE WHERE I WAS BORN
2, Summer Place, Rusholme—the end house
Photo by William Whitaker, Marple

the office to his home. It took some time to explain the omission from his essay. Then he said in his vague throaty voice: "Oh—ah—yes, I see: the performance? Very capable, and up to a point—ah—er—very—ah—intelligent." On the University staff was also Professor Samuel Alexander, greatest of contemporary metaphysicians, a figure out of the Old Testament, a more genial Moses, with savour of wit in his wisdom, so absent-minded that he once went upstairs at a friend's house to dress for dinner; he had come straight from a lecture late in the evening and he brought his clothes and black tie in a suitcase; he was shown to his room, where a fire warmed the winter damp and cold, and after divesting himself of his everyday garb, he got into bed, as a consequence of long habit, and was found there sleeping peacefully hours later. One of the few enlightened deeds done for culture by a British Government in recent years was the awarding of the O. M. to Alexander.

I attended free lectures at Manchester University. I heard Bernard Bosanquet give a discourse on Hegelianism—The Distinction between Mind and Object—with no notes; hands grasping the lapels of his coat—flashing his beard and words about like arrows. I followed his argument for ten minutes; then something snapped in my brain and I became a little mad. Professor Herford was the chairman, and apparently he settled himself down to sleep; most times he appeared to sleep when in the chair. Bosanquet at last finished his lecture, and the audience was, like myself, reduced by now to an idiocy of mystification. Herford raised himself to his feet, and in his high throaty donnish voice said: "Well, gentlemen, I'm sure you'll agree that Professor Bosanquet has made everything perfectly cle-arr to all of us."

.   .   .   .   .   .

It must have been round about 1908 that I often performed a ritual known only to myself. I would go and stand, fairly late on Monday nights, on the pavement at the corner of Cross Street and Market Street, opposite the *Manchester Guardian* building. I would look at the lighted windows and imagine that behind any one of them Montague was at work on a dramatic notice; that Agate was adding a finishing touch; that Samuel Langford, greatest of all writers on music, was meditating on Brahms over his desk. I began to send out articles to newspapers, nervously, modestly. I posted one to the *Captain*, a boy's paper. It was returned. Everything I wrote for years came back, and I consoled myself by keeping the printed rejection slips—"The Editor regrets . . ." It was not possible to get into print in those days if you could not write good English. "Can you write?" was the first thing asked by editors of young men when they were being interviewed after applying for a job as a junior reporter. To-day, editors as a rule do not raise this question.

I nearly went to London to call on Barrie. My plan was to invade his rooms, exactly as Sentimental Tommy invades Pym's rooms, and not leave until he had given me a job as a secretary. But my courage failed; I did not even begin the journey. When in time I came to know Barrie, and I sat in his high flat looking on the Embankment, I told him of the project, and he confessed he would no doubt have fallen for me had I persisted. "I was too shy," I said. And he said: "And so should I have been—no, not shy, but terrified."

It was 1910 before I got into print for the first time; I was then twenty years old. The article appeared in *Musical Opinion*, and it was entitled "Bantock and Style in Music." I wish I could reproduce it here; it was written in the scholarly manner of the rationalist school presided over by J. M. Robertson and Newman. It contained footnotes and was copious in allusions. I could almost have indexed it, beginning with Alembert and ending with Zukunftsmusik. The merit of the article (or, as I should have preferred then to call it, essay) was that it noted the fact that Bantock was a derivative composer, with no style of his own. I called him synthetic, and by quotation and musical notation I revealed how he skilfully assembled the latest current idioms. This was not a common view of Bantock in 1910, obvious as it is to-day. Newman and Langford discussed Bantock for a while as an important and creative figure in English music; he was ranked with Elgar or only a little lower. I have a high regard for the pioneer work done by Bantock in a period when our music was as dowdy as a pew-opener. But as a composer with things to say, he was not more important than William Wallace, another clever synthetic composer, who wrote the first British symphonic poem.

The prominence given by *Musical Opinion* to my article raised expectations in me that were not immediately satisfied; I thought of throwing up my job at Flemings and devoting myself to free-lance journalism. But a postal order for seven and sixpence in payment of my Bantock essay rendered me discreet for another year or so.

I shall write at length in another chapter on Samuel Langford. He was a great man, simple and subtle. He was of the soil and he made himself a man of wide humane culture. He succeeded Ernest Newman as music critic of the *Manchester Guardian* in 1905. Newman went to Birmingham in consequence of a row with Richter, who conducted a work by Berlioz at a Hallé Concert—*Roméo*, I fancy. Richter was the All-Father of English music in 1904, and Newman was thirty-six. He began his notice of the performance of *Roméo* by saying that Richter obviously had not known the score. Years afterwards Newman came one winter evening from Birmingham to give a lecture in Manchester. I was one of the audience, at the back of the hall. At the end of the lecture Newman and Langford came out of the hall together and walked slowly along the pavement to the Midland Hotel round the corner from Albert Square. Unknown to them, I followed at their heels, crossed the street behind them; then they passed through the hotel's portal. I could not enter there. Langford's shuffle as he walked and Newman's elegant poise—I doted on them and tried to catch the wonderful words which surely were issuing out of their mouths. Twenty years later, or thereabouts, C. P. Scott appointed me to the post of music critic of the *Manchester Guardian*, and so I succeeded to the line and dynasty of Newman and Langford. The unknown youth who dogged their footsteps that night was ready all the time to hasten by, head down, if either had chanced to look round.

.   .   .   .   .   .

In 1905 I knew no music except a few tunes picked up much

as the butcher boy picks up his whistling repertory. The
"Soldiers' Chorus" from *Faust*, tunes from *Norma*, and from
San Toy, *The Geisha*, and Gilbert and Sullivan. The names of
Mozart, Bach, Beethoven, Wagner were to me only names—
so many rather forbidding nouns substantive belonging to
the German language.

In 1908 on December 3rd, I stood at the back of the Free
Trade Hall in Manchester and heard the first performance of
the A Flat Symphony of Elgar; I was one of many who
listened with excitement as the broad and long opening
melody marched before us, treading its way over a slow
steady bass, broad as the broad back of Hans Richter, then
conductor of the Hallé Orchestra. I was by this time informed
enough about music to say to myself, with nearly every
musician in the audience: "What a long first subject!" and
to wonder how Elgar was going to cope with it.

I cannot account for my sudden awakening. In three years,
from the age of fifteen to eighteen, I acquired a background
of music and a sense of the shapes and forms of music; more
inexplicable still, I was arriving at some understanding of
music, the association values of it, so that a symphony was
not merely a symphony for me: on this foggy December
night in 1908 I did not listen to a composition in A flat; I
entered the world of it; became absorbed more or less into
the substance that was Elgar himself. I *tasted* him and from
now onward I knew him at sight or rather at first hearing;
the sound of any chord by Elgar, played at random and overheard by chance, would bring to my mind the living image
of the man. The point of my conversion is that this grace
descended on me without a conscious seeking for it on my
part; I did not study the notation or technique of music
until years after, by which time I knew by ear, literally by
ear, a considerable number of the standard works and knew
them pretty thoroughly.

The miracle—I can describe it by no other word—occurred
in April 1907. I remember the precise date, the seventh. I
went to the Prince's Theatre in Manchester to see the production of a light opera called *Tom Jones*. I was not aware
that it was a work by Edward German; I was engrossed in
Henry Fielding's novel, which I was reading for the first time

of many. I had fallen in love with Sophia—as much in love
with her as Fielding himself; and when I saw her in the
entrancing guise of Ruth Vincent, I was more than satisfied.
The tone of her voice, her pretty petulance, was exactly right
when she said, "Tis an odious muff." But while I doted on
her and on Hayden Coffin as Tom Jones, rather Wardour
Street-ish in garb and accent, the music of Edward German
got past my ears and entered my mind behind my back so to
say. Next morning I heard over and over again, in my head,
most of the melodies; also I savoured the orchestration, the
changes of atmosphere from act to act. I could not have put
into words then what I now know I was feeling. In this
glorified musical comedy Edward German scored for orchestra
with a warmth of blended instrumental colour uncommon
in English "light" music; also, as the three settings of the
stage action changed, I was vaguely aware that the flavour
of the music changed too—open-air in the autumn at the
country estate of Squire Western; the antique off-the-highway
inn at Upton; and last, the stately nocturne of Ranelagh. By
obvious enough devices, conventional "olde-shoppe" idioms,
German woke me up musically; that is the simple truth and
to this day I am unable to explain why it should have been
left to Edward German—of all composers—to release the
flood. I returned to *Tom Jones* night after night; I sold
several of my precious books to obtain admission to the pit.
To my amazement and delight, I discovered from now on
that I could remember music without effort; my mind
retained music as the kidneys secrete water. To this day I am
not a quick reader of a score, but I have met nobody with a
more retentive memory than mine, or one that absorbs music
as quickly. This phenomenon baffles me the more because
I am not usually quick at remembering poetry; I am obliged
consciously to learn a poem line by line; and if I do not go
over it frequently in my memory, it soon slips out. I never
forget music. All of which may not be an experience of much
psychological interest to anybody but myself, though to say
the truth I have not heard the like of it.

I state these facts free of qualms about immodesty. I am
trying with detachment to render an account of myself. I
cannot, I say, explain the sudden unwilled (for there is the

point of it all) urge which in 1907 swept me into the seven
seas of music, not once to be in danger of drowning, though
overwhelmed here and there by enormous and unexpected
waves. I was a swimmer by grace. My first attempt at
Tannhäuser floored me (as Dick Swiveller would say) when I
heard it given by the Carl Rosa Opera Company round about
1908. A year afterwards, my mind was playing most of the
score over and over again whenever I wished, usually just
after I had gone to bed at night; for I would imagine I was
conducting the opera *from memory*. This is a practice I have
persisted in to the present time—first to read for a while
stretched free and relaxed between the sheets, with the
world forgot and well away—this is one of the few unstaling
pleasures of life; then until sleep comes I hear at choice a
performance of any one of a store of compositions gathered
in nearly forty years of listening to music. A musical score
for me is as a map; I can read it vividly only after I have
been there many times. I distrust the man who tells me
he is able to "hear" music by score-reading alone. To such
a man I would offer the menu if I took him out to dinner.
"Read it," I would say (perhaps), "savour the association
values of choice juices and meats and fruits and vintage.
Taste them not from material performance here and now in
phenomenal Time and Space; partake of them *sub specie
aeternitatis*, from the Noumenon of the Score, or rather, the
Bill of Fare."

I fancy I learned the language of music much as Wagner
learned it. At the age of eighteen or so I took lessons in singing
for a year and less. I have received no other professional
instruction in music. I once copied great tracts of the piano
score of *Tristan*, note by note; I wished to search out for
myself the secret of Wagner's harmony. I was never a pianist.
I am one of the three worst pianists in the world at the present
time. The others are James Agate and somebody whose
name I am not at liberty to mention—he is a very famous
pianist.

I compiled a cultural scheme when I was veering towards
the twenties, a plan of campaign; so many hours a week to
that subject, so many hours to this. I decided that as knowledge
was one and indivisible, each subject would need to be studied

in relation to all or most others; Synthesis (said I to myself) was the thing. I came upon the works of J. M. Robertson, also once a poor boy who by self-education had made himself informed and critical far beyond the scope of most of the dons at the universities. Possibly in his Scottish zeal he went too far; he took all knowledge for his province, and in the course of a mortally-spanned life achieved two unprecedented feats of criticism. He attacked and exposed, by deductive and inductive reasoning, the historical authenticity of

(*a*) Jesus Christ
and
(*b*) Shakespeare.

But he was stimulating, and his books served as my encyclopædia. I owe much to him; his *Essays towards a Critical Method* and his *Evolution of States* were for long my constant bed-books, with Wisden and the Lieder of Hugo Wolf. Thanks to Ernest Newman I discovered Wolf almost coincidently with my twenty-first birthday, which I celebrated by going to see Forbes-Robertson as Hamlet. My Schema was drawn up so comprehensively that it involved metaphysics, with ethics and æsthetics correlated; sociology, economics, comparative religion and all literature. But the interesting fact about this vast five-year cultural plan is that I did not think of including music. The truth is I did not regard music as a subject which called for deliberate and persistent study; I took it for granted and learned it by absorbedly and un-selfconsciously living in it, out of school, as it were. The language of music I learned exactly as a boy learns his everyday speech; not until I understood the vocabulary and syntax by ear and instinct did I look into the grammar, the forms and the technical rationale; by which time I was sufficiently advanced in understanding to realise that the text-book forms are so many abstractions; that no two composers use the same form alike; that the average music college curriculum has little or nothing to do with music as a matter of personal imagination; and that apart from practical and executive musicianship, it teaches only a sort of philology of sound to young people who have not yet learned the living vocabulary of music. It is as though prosody were to be expounded to a mind not yet acquainted with a sense of poetry.

I did not keep rigorously to the Schema, for one day I picked up a copy of Samuel Butler's Note Books and read the following: "Never try to learn anything until the not knowing it has come to be a nuisance to you for some time . . . A boy should never be made to learn anything until it is obvious that he cannot get on without it. . . ." I have ever since acted more or less upon that wise saying. The older I grow the more it seems to me that miscellaneous education for the young is dangerous; it merely clutters up the untrained mind with information. Information can always be found in reference books.

Music, I say again, came to me by grace. A man is not boasting when he claims to have received grace. The things that we are praised for in this world, our "successes," are exactly the things for which we do not deserve credit; successes are easy, they come by grace. It is our failures that go sadly by without recognition of the effort and talent we have put into them; single-handed we hammered them out, but inspiration left us in the lurch. A few years ago, I saw Richard Strauss in an audience at the Salzburg Festival, after the curtain had fallen on the last act of his opera *Die Frau ohne Schatten*. He was applauding vigorously. I spoke to him of the work. His cheeks were still pink with pleasure and he said, "Mein Meisterwerk." I hadn't the heart to tell him he was deceiving himself; he had "born" the opera after terrible labour; it was perhaps a poor thing but 'twas his very own, owing little to inspiration. The truth is that it was easier for Gibbon to write *his* autobiography than for me to write mine. I think that in all my life I have made a good and thorough job of only one thing—listening to music. But I can claim no credit for it, any more than I can claim credit for my satisfactory machinery of respiration. When I get to heaven I shall produce on my behalf, in hope of salvation after all, my stock of failures and frustrations; my attempts to become a leader-writer on the *Manchester Guardian*; my attempts to sing the Abschied of Wotan; my attempts to understand Hegel; my attempts to spin a fast ball from the leg to the off-stump.

My luck was indeed with me through thick and thin. Had I been able to give my singing master just a shade more of satisfaction in 1910 I should certainly have gone on with my studies and in time would have taken my place as one more amongst thousands of competent, unnecessary vocalists. My voice was not unbeautiful but it was almost inaudible.

From the moment I gave up ambitions towards executive ability in music, I was free to cultivate the art of listening— which is an art *sui generis*. The executant cannot hope often to listen to music and hear it in the absolute—as an aesthetic Thing in itself. The player in him, the performer, whether conductor, fiddler, pianist, or singer, will interfere with the processes of reception. The violinist will attend to the violin as much as he attends to the Brahms concerto; the pianist will hear more of Horowitz than Chopin; the orchestral player, if orchestral players listen to music at all, will give most of his mind to his particular instrument or group. Everybody knows how hopeless it is to get an æsthetic judgment from an instrumentalist or vocalist. Try as he will to prevent it, the technical equation will creep in. And of course the creative artist is in even a worse case; in so far as he is possessed by a personal and original daemon is he unable to live for a moment with another and different and most times alien daemon. I have listened to my music without a single technical or pedagogic axe to grind; I have never been prejudiced, as nearly all executants are, for or against a composition because of some bias, conscious or subconscious, the result of discomfort suffered by technical set-backs or frustrations. I have known pianists, for instance, who think they dislike Brahms; but analysis and cross-examination have nailed them down to the fact that they have found Brahms ungrateful to the fingers.

Pure listening involves a special training of a special faculty. I am not referring to ear-tests, appreciation classes and all that stuff. It is a matter of an imaginative and non-egoistical reception of music. But I hope to develop this idea later during my book—which is running ahead; not that I have wished at any time to tighten the rein. During the course of an autobiography it is as well now and then to hint at the shapes and significances of things to come. Upon this

important point of listening to music as an art and study in
itself, I wish at the moment only to emphasise that luck was
again on my side. For the critic of music should be the most
enlightened and unprejudiced listener; it is his job, his full-
time job, to hear and to receive music with a highly sensitised
mind, governed by psychological and aesthetic insight. He is
an artist with experiences in music his material. The art of
the enlightened listener became my main musical study from
the day my singing teacher turned me down. It took me
nearly twenty years to learn to listen to music so absorbedly
and with so much enlightenment that people began to pay me
—actually pay me!—to go to concerts, to hear Toscanini, to
go to Vienna and Salzburg, and to live the life I wanted most
of all.

   .   .   .   .   .

In 1911 I arrived at the age of twenty-one. My income was
one pound weekly from marine insurance. Once only, so far,
had more than twenty shillings come my way in one and the
same week; that was when *Musical Opinion* paid me for my
Bantock article. My subsequent attempts as a free-lance writer
were intermittent and futile. I aimed loftily: the manuscripts
I posted to editors were invariably intellectual or cerebral. I
had few powers of observation of ordinary life and no sense
of journalism. I vaguely knew that my time as a writer was
not yet at hand. I had read enough—too much—but I was
gauche; I needed a finishing process. My education had
advanced far enough to make me realise, of a sudden one day,
that I was a provincial, that even Manchester was a provincial city. The beginning of education sets in, I imagine,
when one realises that one's ego and one's orbit do not comprise
the whole of the world.

One night I walked along the Palatine Road which goes
southwards from Manchester, and with my imagination's
vision I saw the glow of London, saw it as young Jude saw
Christminster in the distance. How to get there—not yet,
but in the long run? I knew I was unripe for London; it was
a dream of a future day. My immediate problem was how to
escape from the tragi-comic dilemma of my connection with

the Flemings. The years had gone quickly by; to my consternation and amazement I had grown up. I couldn't go on
being an office-boy at twenty-one. My position in the office
indeed was now an embarrassment to Fleming as well as to
myself. Once or twice I was asked by Hugh, and asked
delicately, what I intended to do—"You don't really want to
go into insurance seriously, do you?" To my dismay, I found
myself rather at a loss to give a convincing answer; for
though I had long since made up my mind to become a
writer of some sort I did not at the moment feel confident
enough about it to commit myself, so to say, to a public
statement.

How could I come by my finishing process? I wanted to
learn how to turn my reading into experience and salt it with
some savour of life. I was tired of the prison of Manchester's
streets; four narrow walls of the Flemings' office were stifling
me at last. The fledgling was anxious to leave the nest. How?
I had no visible means of support.

As usual whenever I have been stranded at cross-roads,
with no signposts to help an instinctive feeling of the way, a
miracle happened. One day, I picked up a sporting newspaper
called the *Athletic News*; I did not ever read sporting periodicals
and I don't think I had ever seen this particular journal until,
one Monday morning in January 1912, I somehow found
myself turning its pages and hit upon an advertisement:
"Wanted assistant Cricket Coach at Shrewsbury School. Must
be good bowler. Apply with testimonials, etc."

I was then a fairly good bowler, slow to medium, with an
off-break. I applied for the job. Weeks went by and no reply
came. I forgot all about it. One night I went to hear *Tristan
and Isolde* at the Theatre Royal in Manchester; I climbed up
a Piranesi stairway to the high gallery and the music came
to me like the sound of a rising sea. I walked home to my
lodgings; four miles through dank and squalor, my mind
and heart aching with Isolde's "So bange Tage." When I got
into the house and turned on the light (everybody was asleep),
I saw a letter for me on the chest of drawers. It bore the
Shrewsbury crest and motto: Intus Si Recte Ne Labora. I was
offered the post of assistant professional coach at the salary
of two pounds ten weekly; and the term would begin in the

first week of May and extend to the last week of July. I at once glimpsed that the chance of my life had come. I could live at Shrewsbury on a pound a week and put the rest into the post office savings bank. By the end of the term I would have accumulated at least £18. I would have capital on which to fall back when summer had gone and I had to return to Manchester. Why, with £18 I would safely be able to launch into literature and music as a full-time winter study and occupation!

You can measure from this decision of young Cardus what bliss it was to be alive then; the very thought of £18 in my possession in one lump sum, for which you could if you chose receive golden sovereigns, was strength and fortification. Yet to this day I am surprised that I was bold enough to venture into a strange world. Remember, I had never journeyed far beyond Manchester and I was one of the shyest and most self-conscious of youths, one of those who when they went into a Lyons café (I never aspired to restaurants) sat down on the seat nearest the door; if a waitress looked at me as I was peering into the café I would not dare to enter at all. Mr. Kipps was like that. To-day I regard my decision to uproot myself from Manchester, to break with the environment and habits of a groping lifetime, to go alone into a new social habitat "amongst the nobs" (as the socialists told me they would be: also they said I was backsliding), to face the critical gaze of an English public school and, most awful of all, to have my work inspected by a famous All-England cricketer who would be my boss—here were faith and foolhardiness to which I am sure I could not rise at the present time, in the same circumstances.

.   .   .   .   .   .

On May the 1st, 1912, I went to London Road Station, Manchester, and entered a third-class compartment in the afternoon train bound for Shrewsbury, a lazy county town then. My only luggage was an old black and dented tin box tied round and round for security's sake with a rope. The lock, if I remember, would not lock. Inside this box were a few garments, a suit of cricket flannels, and a hundred books and more, mainly volumes of the new Everyman Library, or the Home University Library, which you could buy at a shilling each. Amongst these volumes was Grote's *History of Greece*, and Walter Bagehot's *Literary Studies*; also there was Descartes' *Discourse on Method* ("Cogito ergo sum"). In this tin trunk, as it lay on the platform of London Road Station, waiting to be put into the luggage van by a porter, reposed all my goods and chattels except the clothes I had on my back, some odd shillings, a pocket comb and two pairs of spectacles, each six and a half diopters strong, for myopia; one pair of which I wore from the moment I opened my eyes in the morning until I closed them at night. The other pair I had procured in case of accidents on the field of play at Shrewsbury. I don't believe that any youth has set forth on a career as a professional cricketer more curiously equipped than this.

I remember opening the door of a third-class compartment after I had seen the tin box safely stowed away. The carriage was unoccupied, only recently out of a siding, where it had stood in the warmth of the day for hours with the windows closed. The compartment was overpowering with that odour of stuffed seats and padding which is peculiar to railways. I remember the refreshment of air when I pulled a leather strap and let down a pane on which was printed "Non-Smoker."

At four o'clock, or thereabouts, the train moved out of the station; I still had the compartment to myself. We passed under the bricks and mortar of Manchester, through a Nibelheim of clanking noises; then we emerged into the sunshine of May day, yellow slanting gleams piercing the miasma of smoke and grime. Looking down through the window in my solitude I saw from the height of a bridge—I saw like one of God's spies—the Manchester that had nurtured me since I was born; rows and rows of dismal houses, with back yards full of old cans and bedsteads and torn oilcloth; long vistas of streets with lamp-posts and corner shops. I saw a council school with an asphalt playground and spiked railings. I was leaving it all; to-night I would sleep out of Manchester, not in a house in one of those endless streets that stretched away in a static lean dreary hopelessness. I was on the way to Shrewsbury, an old town with a market-place in it.

Out of Manchester into Cheshire ambled the train, and my anxiety about this new life was shot through and through with a sensation strange to me: I was shaking myself free of habit: I didn't know what was about to happen to me. I did not know exactly what setting awaited me in Shrewsbury; I had not even seen a photograph of the place. My life had been bounded by an eggshell; except for a few week-end rambles in Derbyshire, my twenty-one years had been spent within a radius of three and a half miles of bricks and mortar; for the first time in my life I was able in physical fact to run alongside my imagination.

The evening light fell on cows standing still in the meadows. The train came to a halt with an escape of steam, then silence. I stuck my head out of the window and saw the gleaming railway lines, the immaculate tidiness of the per-manent way as it stretched and pointed to a distance of green and wooded futurity. I was journeying not the mere fifty miles or so that divide Manchester from Shrewsbury; I was shedding a skin.

When the train reached Crewe I left my compartment and from an unobserved point of vantage watched the porters hauling bags and cases and crates and noisy milk-cans out of the luggage van; I was afraid my old tin trunk might be mixed up with them and lost for ever, even though I had stuck addressed labels on it. Several boys were sitting in the carriage when I returned. They were on the way to Shrewsbury. The new term began next day. They disconcerted me as I sat in my corner pretending to read; I feared they would penetrate to my secret, that I also was travelling to Shrewsbury and was the new "pro." I was aware that I did not look the part at all; I lacked the expected masculinity. I was the thinnest professional cricketer that ever lived, and I fancy I must have resembled Traddles. The charming accents of the speech of these boys gave me my first taste of the good days to come.

.   .   .   .   .   .

But these days did not offer themselves at all fulsomely. A crisis was sw iftly approaching; it nearly killed me. I did not suspect as I left Shrewsbury station on the balmy evening of May the Ist, 1912, and walked up the hill past the old timbered shops and chambers (Palins and their Shrewsbury Cake), past the Library with the Darwin statue outside, past the drooping lilac tree—I did not suspect that within forty-eight hours I should have to fight as severe a battle for my future as ever happened in all my days from my cradle to the present moment of writing. The head professional was none other than Attewell, who years ago had played for Nottinghamshire, and had made history at Lord's for the Players, and also had crossed the seas to Australia in a period when people talked of Australia as a place "down under." I had decided to share my Shrewsbury diggings with him; we slept in the same bedroom, and I soon got used to his snoring. He was a plain simple character, lazy in the Midland counties way of the nineteenth century; much journeying about the land and several voyages to Australia had not in the slightest sophisticated him. As soon as he saw me when I reached 14 Cross Hill (next to a printer's, whenever I wish I can hear the low throb of the presses) he looked at me like a father and said: "There's not much of thi, mi lad."

Next day he took me up to the School; we passed the quiet residences in Quarry Place with doctors' polished brass, and flower-beds on the window-sills; we walked down the avenue of tall lime trees; we came to the ferry which has to be crossed before you can climb the zigzag path leading to the little gate under the shadows of rich foliage, next to the chapel. If the ferry were on the other side of the Severn, and nobody about, it was necessary to make a funnel of your two hands and call "Bo-at; Bo-at; Bo-at." Then the boatman would come and propel the ferry by tugging at the rope stretched across the river.

When the gate has been closed behind you and you have passed the School House on your left and the Speech Hall, you see the most beautiful playing-fields in the world, spreading and imperceptibly mingling with the pasture land of Shropshire. There is (or was) a little wooden cricket pavilion with the Tuck Shop underneath. The "pro's" dressing-room was to the right of the balcony. On the afternoon of my second day at Shrewsbury the first practice took place; I was given an outside net, and the captain of the school batted against me; two other boys shared the bowling. William took charge of the middle net and his comfortable accents sounded rather cruelly assured in my ears as he gave his instructions. "Coom for'ard, sir, left leg for'ard." I tried to utter advice of the same sort but my tongue clave to the roof of my mouth. Then I was put off by sudden shouts of "Heads! Heads!" when somebody in another net had skied a ball into the air. You would see people ducking and shielding their skulls—and the ball nowhere near.

A small crowd of boys congregated behind my net to inspect the new "pro." Panic abruptly seized me. I bowled a ball that hit the side of the net; then I bowled a ball that went over the top of the back-net. I heard a guffaw that filled me with shame.

That night I could not sleep for anxiety. I expected the sack already. What then? I could not ask Fleming for the place I had thrown up. Besides, after I had got out of it all, the muck and the routine, after I had seen my Pisgah sight, my mirage if you like, I could not go back. I prayed hard. No; I was not a Christian, I was an atheist; but sometimes the atheist in his extremities will turn to Christ. William did his best to reassure me. "Ya're a reight bowler," he said, rhyming with "howler"; "doan't worrit; all'l coom reight. But yo wants a few steaks in you, lad," which was very true.

Next day, a Saturday, was for me more awful still. After I had crossed the river again with William and come to the cricket pavilion, I read an announcement on the notice-board; that afternoon the first XI (including William) would play the next XV (including me). For a moment I lost nerve and contemplated flight. After all I would vanish from the scene. I thought of gently withdrawing myself from Shrewsbury. I could repack my tin box and go away, out of the country altogether, where my failure and cowardice would not follow. I could go to Labrador, for example, or Rio. But I recovered in time; besides it was easier to face the music of a "trial" with the "next XV" in the presence of a critical English public school; in the presence of William, wearing his International cap, in the presence of the Head, the Rev. Cyril

SHREWSBURY PLAYING FIELDS

Alington, soon to become headmaster of Eton, than crawl back to Manchester, or anywhere else, defeated.

In later years I learned that the captain of the school suffered torments equal to mine on that far-off Saturday afternoon, thirty or more years ago. It was the custom at Shrewsbury for the cricket captain to choose the professionals and give them their engagements on his own responsibility. He had engaged me without a trial, on the strength of my bowling averages in Manchester club cricket. He was naturally as anxious as I that I should do well. He opened the innings for the first XI, when the match began. I opened the bowling. Normally I exploited, as I have told you, slow to medium-paced stuff, with off-breaks. The school captain was in form; he drove and pulled my off-breaks all over the place. The better he batted, the worse I bowled. In one over he smote me for four fours, then while the field was changing positions he came down the wicket and whispered: "For the Lord's sake, what's the matter? You can bowl better than this, surely?" He was really in a predicament; the more he chastised me the more he made it a necessary duty for him to sack me. Desperation possessed my soul and body. I saw this green and lovely Shrewsbury being taken away from me after I had miraculously found it.

I spoke to the captain of the XV. I told him I wanted four slips and a third man fine and deep. I didn't want anybody in front of the wicket on the on-side but I'd like two short-legs. I was going to bowl fast—it was a gamble. I did not as a rule bowl anything like fast. But a man can do all sorts of things when the world is at stake. My world was certainly at stake on this glowering day at Shrewsbury. I shall always see the scene and the hour: a darkening sky with rain-clouds sullen over the Wrekin. I measured out a long run, then I began. I tore along the earth; I hurled myself at the wicket. The first ball, a full-toss, exploded on the top of the bails while the astonished captain of the school fled. Sheer need impelled me on to more and more fury—full-tosses, long-hops, wides, no-balls, spinning stumps, and consternated batsmen. I bowled until my back seemed ready to break. And all the time a single dread vision was before my mind: the endless squalor of Manchester and myself sacked from Shrews-

bury, an outcast and a paltry waster of opportunity. After
a few overs I was spent, broken-winded. I took my sweater
from the umpire and hobbled from the field. In half an hour
I had overwhelmed six batsmen for about a dozen runs. I
never bowled fast again, and next day I was obliged to consult
a doctor in Quarry Place and have my shoulder-blades
massaged. The doctor's name was Whincup, and to this day
I owe him ten and sixpence.

Old William was vastly tickled. "Tha's got thi job here
all reight!" he said that evening, as again we sat down to
dinner, "but tha'd better get that steak into thi reight now
while t' jooce is in it. Tha young devil—hey, bah goom, Ah
allus suspects you quiet 'uns. Thee and thi spectacles and
books! And thee and thi six wickets! Why, lad, Ah never
see'd thi bowlin' 'it t' floor once all afternoon!"

Shrewsbury School and William and the playing-fields
over the river Severn; richness in the open air of England;
trees and the murmur of summer in the distance. Crack of
bat against ball. You'll have more of it in these pages before
I finish. The gentle tinkle of the little bell in the church tower
under the elms, as the quarter-hours passed from one o'clock
to two; then all the boys would go indoors for lunch. And
the fields of Shrewsbury are vacant in the heat, while William
and I sit and rest on the wooden balcony of the pavilion, after
our scorching work in the nets. To have lived at Shrewsbury
in those days and known cricket there is to have lived in a
heaven down here below.

.   .   .   .   .   .

William had worked in a factory when he was a boy; then
out of obscurity he was taken far and wide by cricket. He
belonged to a world gone for ever, I think; industrialism in
Nottingham in the nineteenth century did not harden
humanity, as it did in Lancashire. Lace is different from
cotton. The Midlands in the nineteenth century remained
suburban near the cities, even rural. William's village was not
ten miles from Nottingham, where they held an annual goose
fair. To his last days he spoke with a cadence almost scriptural;
he had the soil in him and without the slightest loss of dignity

he would raise a forefinger to his head and say "Mornin', sir,"
to any boy at Shrewsbury School, senior or junior, whom he
chanced to meet on a walk. His speech was flavoured with
ancient saws and idioms. We would take an evening walk on
Sundays over the fields. He would talk of the weather, and
quote some old rhyme about a red sky at morning's a sailor's
warning, a red sky at night is a shepherd's delight. He was
not a great reader, but once when he picked up one of my
"Everyman" editions, *Paradise Lost*, he put his forefinger on
the first page and following every word with it he intoned,
for the first time in his life, these words in monosyllables,
coming to a full stop at the end of each line. Thus:

> "Of Man's first dis-o-bed-i-ence and the Fruit.
> Of that For-bid-den Tree, whose mortal taste."

One of his objections to poetry was that there was not enough
"readin'" on a page. Every Sunday he performed his weekly
task of writing a letter home to his wife and family. He went
about the undertaking thoroughly. He cleared the table in
our sitting-room; he produced a bottle of ink and a pen and
showed much respect to both. For an hour he would write
with pursed lips, murmuring words to himself. From time
to time he contemplated the ceiling as though counting flies
on it. He would watch me as I wrote in my fluent clerkly
hand. "Gow!" he would ejaculate—meaning God; but he
was evasive. (Also he substituted "Gow dall it" for "God
damn it.") "Gow!" he would say, "Ah'd give all mi cricket
to write like you." He was not referring to the substance of
whatever I was committing to paper, but to the act of calli-
graphy itself. Each Sabbath after our midday meal he put on
a hard stiff collar. I recollect his struggles with it. "Cuss
it," he would protest, "but Ah *mun* do it; it's the Lord's
Day."

The duties at Shrewsbury were not heavy. There was
usually an hour's net practice from a quarter to one till a
quarter to two; and house matches from four to half-past
six. Sometimes Attewell and I umpired in these games; also
each morning I helped Attewell to prepare the wickets. I
carried a frame and marked the batting and bowling creases

with whitewash. At close of play every evening after the boys
had vanished to their houses, the field stood empty and I
would walk over the grass gathering the stumps from a dozen
pitches; and I would carry them in sheaves in my arms, a
solitary reaper in the evening sunshine.

After dinner at my lodgings—eggs and stewed fruit, for
I was virtually a vegetarian for economy's sake: in spite of
William's injunction, I rarely ate a steak—I returned to the
playing-fields. Hardly ever in all my five summers at Shrewsbury, unless the weather were wet, when I went into the
Library near the Castle—hardly ever on a fine evening did I
go into the little town. I sat under a great tree, with a book,
until the twilight came and the little chapel huddled itself
in the deepening shades, and the rooks came flapping by
overhead to their high nests. Now and again a boy or a
master in cap and gown would walk along the side-path,
waking echoes for a while. Sometimes I would take out a
hose-pipe and water a parched stretch of turf. The last gleams
of light coming from the setting sun rainbowed the falling
spray, which made a delicious sound as it fell on the earth,
and the grass softened to a deeper green. Such peace I have
seldom known since, nor has anybody, anywhere.

.   .   .   .   .   .

Our lodgings at Shrewsbury were conducted by a Mrs.
Rodenhurst, who for six days a week was harassed and pale
and gaunt, but not unlovely, in spite of her steel spectacles
which sometimes needed some wadding under the bridge to
prevent them from hurting her nose. But on Sundays she
achieved translation; after a morning of sweaty work in the
kitchen, when she prepared for us the one symphonic meal of
the week, she would go upstairs for rest and come down at
tea-time clad in some extremely tight shiny stuff, with chains
and bangles, her hair coiled on her neck, and the steel spectacles
supplanted by gold-framed ones—at any rate, rolled-gold. Her
husband was nebulous; he seemed to do little but sit about
the front lobby and stairs in his shirt-sleeves.

Mrs. Rodenhurst's main guests all the year round were, as
she would proudly inform me, "theatricals." I bear in mind

that *A Royal Divorce* occupied nearly all her rooms. I saw Augereau enter the house one night with a quart-pot; next morning I saw Josephine in the butcher's shop up the street; she was choosing a nice piece of brisket. On another occasion I came into the house late at night and saw, lying on the floor of the lobby, a confusion of bedding, pillows, sheets. The table in the kitchen still held the debris of a meal; beer bottles and glasses and the remnants of cold viands. *A Royal Divorce* had been jousting; as I lay in bed I heard the stairs creaking and caught a scuffle and a titter. I could never find out from William whether these nocturnal escapades came under his notice. He was a peaceful sleeper.

I wasted none of the leisure offered to me by my work at the school. My reading left the original Schema far behind. Now and again, of course, I had to take short cuts; for instance, I could not possibly go through every metaphysician from Thales onward, so I learned almost by heart George Henry Lewes's *History of Philosophy*. But I tackled Kant, with an English translation alongside the original. I recall that once, in the middle of the night, I understood for a brief ecstatic moment what the *Ding an sich* was, and had a vision of the categories. For some reason which has slipped my memory, I also read the Koran during my first summer at Shrewsbury.

I tried my hand at one or two essays and sent them to the *Speaker* and the *English Review*, still without success. I had no style of my own; I emulated my different mentors; on music I aped Ernest Newman; on literature I vacillated from Bagehot to Montague, Agate and Dixon Scott. It never once even yet occurred to me to write about cricket. I came to know the editor of the *Shrewsbury Advertiser*, the first of all editors I ever met. This was the age before syndicates swallowed district newspapers and destroyed their splendid parochialism. The editor of the *Shrewsbury Advertiser* took himself very seriously. He was thin and tall, with a neck so long and thick that his collar was the most massive I have ever seen. He wrote the leader in the *Advertiser* every week; and you could see it coming for days. He would walk the streets with something clearly on his mind. He would gaze blankly at me and pass me by. Each Wednesday evening he retired to his room —"My sanctum," he called it. Nothing more was heard of

him until towards eleven o'clock; then he went out for air
to cool his brow; he walked up and down the avenue of limes.
Frequently I met him, fresh from labour. And he would tell
me what had this week been the burden of his discourse. An
attack on the Department of Public Highways. Somebody
had proposed the removal of the horse-trough at the junction
of roads near the market; the motor-car was invading
Shrewsbury's narrow thoroughfares, and the progressivists
claimed that the horse-trough was an obstacle, not to say an
anachronism. The editor of the *Advertiser* chastised the vandals;
also, he virtually wrote an Essay on the Horse. His peroration
came to a mordant close with an allusion to "these obscurely
and hastily gotten progeny of the velocipede." One night as
we perambulated between the lime trees, with the flowing
Severn at the end of the avenue like a silver chain in the moonlight, he experienced a moment of doubt. "Perhaps I have
been too brutal," he said. But no; he would withdraw nothing;
besides, the paper had been put to bed by now; he was prepared
to abide by the consequences.

The *Advertiser* came out on Fridays. The title was printed
in Gothic characters at the top of the front page, full of
advertisements about live-stock, and messuages; underneath,
in smaller Roman type, appeared this lovely sequence of
names: Circulating in Broselely, Wenlock, Hadlow, Knowle,
Cudleigh, Wem. Every Friday at lunch Mr. Watt (that was
his name) took his glass of milk and plate of ham and salad in
Morris's Café, and now you would see a much relieved man
temporarily in social touch with the town, brow unclouded.
But by Monday gestation had set in again. He was with
leader. He ran a Poets' Corner and I actually contributed to
it once, at his request. This was my only appearance in print
as a writer of verse; I have forgotten what I composed for
him, something about something or other coming down the
tremulous dawn secret and unseen. "We don't, of course, pay
for poetry," he said, "but we allow a signature." The rest of
the literary matter in the paper observed a dignified anonymity.
Mr. Watt had been known to attend Monday evenings at the
Theatre Royal as critic of drama. He discussed the historical
sources of *A Royal Divorce* ironically, and concluded a notice
with a Parthian shot: "We assume that Friday evening will,

according to long and unstaled custom, be devoted to the
benefit of Miss Hortense Ste. Cloud, whose affecting presentation of Josephine is too well-known to Thespians of Shrewsbury
and environs to need further encomiums here." The last
time I saw a copy of the *Advertiser* I scarcely recognised it.
There was a column supplied from London about the Ivy
Restaurant and night clubs. There was a comic strip. The
leading article did not extend beyond a third of a column,
and it contained no allusion to life in Shrewsbury. Mr. Watt,
on principle, cast *his* leaders into the classical three long
paragraphs. "As a musician," he would say to me, "you will
understand the form: exposition, development and recapitulation." The passing of the country newspapers of England
was a harbinger of ill days and things to come. I visited
Shrewsbury in 1938 for the first time since 1916. The Theatre
Royal no longer had a little foyer of a rock garden and bull-
rushes and gold-fish, with old play-bills on the wall, one of
them announcing a performance of"Bellini's sublime opera
Norma." No manager in squash hat and faded dinner jacket
met in person his "patrons" at the main entrance. No; a
commissionaire in gold and scarlet announced, out of the side
of his mouth, that some Hollywood drama of love and intrigue
was now showing; and the place was gilded and pretentious.
I preferred Augereau and Napoleon in the flesh—the same
flesh that next morning at opening time I would watch as
they disappeared into the vaults of the Crown Hotel.

I suppose the Severn still flows its course, and the School
stands on the hill, and on a June afternoon the chimes tell
the hours, tell them no faster and no noisier than in the years
when—how many times?—I put my hands to my mouth and
shouted "Boat," and crossed the river in the ferry, then
ascended into heaven.

.   .   .   .   .   .

I see my five Shrewsbury summers to-day as a continuous
tissue of memory and I shall write of them here with little
or no mention of the interrupting winters. I worked hard
all day and half through the night preparing for the writer's
trade; the £18 I saved at Shrewsbury in twelve weeks was

increased to £25 by perquisites and tips, which was equivalent
to six months' income from the Flemings. The shoe pinched
—especially at Christmas—and I had sometimes to hunt for
a job as a clerk; but on the whole I was happy and confident
that sooner or later I would learn to play on the music critic's
most necessary instrument, which is the English language.

When I went back to Shrewsbury in 1913, I suffered
a loss. I entered the house of Mrs. Rodenhurst and at once
asked whether Attewell had arrived yet. "No," said Mrs.
Rodenhurst; "No, Mr. Attewell wasn't coming again to
Shrewsbury; another gentleman had come instead, a Mr.
Wainwright from Sheffield; he was to be the cricket instructor
now, with, of course, you, Mr. Neville." She'd heard that the
School had told Mr. Attewell that they were engaging
somebody else.

It was true. Poor William—his left-leg for'ard had become
out of date. I had felt an anxiety about the old man's future
at Shrewsbury as soon as I had myself settled down and found
time to look around. For, one day in the nets, a boy drove a
ball over the fives courts nearly into the river, and William
had shouted down the pitch: "Hey, sir, yo' mustn't play that
stroake that way, sir," and the boy had apologetically answered:
"But, Attewell, I c-couldn't h-hit it any farther, you know."

Wainwright, of Yorkshire and All-England, was of the
modern school. "Pla-ay back; get thi legs reight." He was
at the extreme to Attewell; he belonged to a period that marked
a transition in the development of the social life of the English
professional cricketer; he was a bridge from the simple and
dignified forelock-touching William to the Hammonds and
the Sutcliffes, who burnish their hair and go to Savile Row
for their clothes.

When Mrs. Rodenhurst told me of the advent to Shrewsbury of Wainwright, I asked her if he was in his room, or
where. "No," she said, "he went out about an hour ago. I
think you'll find him in the King's Arms." I went to the
King's Arms and made my very first appearance in the bar-
parlour of a public-house. The room was empty save for one
man, dressed in blue serge, with a shrewd lean face. I recognised him. I had seen him playing for Yorkshire at Old
Trafford. I introduced myself. "I'm the assistant pro.," I

explained. "Art thou?" he replied, "well, then 'ave a drink wi' me." I told him I didn't drink—only ginger ale. "Christ," he said, "tha'rt a reight bloody cricketer." He was a tall man, who walked as though he didn't care a damn for anybody. There was something sinister about him. Every night he got drunk as a matter of course, quietly and masterfully. One day he backed a winner at a glorious price, and towards eleven o'clock that night he and the drill-sergeant of the school arrived arm-in-arm (supporting one another) in the sitting-room of our lodgings. Very gravely Ted introduced me to the drill-sergeant, whom of course I knew very well. The drill-sergeant as gravely introduced Ted to me, then taking my arm, he whispered rather noisily in my ear, "I'm 'fraid 'e's a l'il drunk, so I've jus' bror him h-home." Whereupon Ted dissolved into helpless laughter and said, "My dear ser-sergeant, don't be 'diculous. . . . Bror me. home? Why, you ole fool, it's me that's bror you 'ome." Then (aside), "'E's jus' a l'il drunk, so I've bror him home." The sergeant hooted with glee. "Bless m' soul," he said, "Ted; jus' lis'en t'me. If you'd bror me home, this would be my lodgin's, see? I would be 'ome, not you. See? But this is your lodgin's—so I mus' 'ave bror you 'ome. See?"

The syllogism was too much for Ted. He collapsed and fell on his umbrella which, though the night was hot, he had carried with him for hours neatly rolled up, and he broke it into two equal halves. We then, the sergeant and I, put him to bed, the sergeant all the time solicitously muttering, "I bror 'im home. Jus' a l'il drunk, tha's all, pore f'ler." Next morning Ted came down to breakfast fresh as a daisy and saw the broken halves of his umbrella which Mrs. Rodenhurst had carefully laid on the sofa. "What the 'ell," said Ted blankly. I told him what had occurred the night before. Ted reflected; "Ah remember as far as commin' out of t' King's Arms wi' t' sergeant and gettin' as far as t' Royal Oak, An' Ah remembers nowt else."

One Friday he came to me and asked if I would like to make an "extra pound or two." Yes, I said, providing they could more or less honestly be come by. "Well," he continued, "there's a match to-morrow in t' Sunday School League at a village in Salop about thirty miles away. A team called Belvedere gets t 'championship if they can win, an' they asked me and thee if we'll play for 'em." "But," I said, "we are not members of any Belvedere." "That's aw reight—we've got to call oursel's Thompson and Smith or some such-like. We're to play as new members, and we 'aven't to let on as we're t' pros from Shrewsbury School. Nobody'll know us away down t' Salop village." It seemed "fishy" to me, but I agreed. "But wait a minute, lad," proceeded Tom. "Tha must understand that in this class o' cricket eighty all out or so is a record score. Pitches are bloody awful. Now, Ah doant suppose tha'll be able to mek many runs, but in case tha feels like it, let me tell thi tha mus' do nowt of t' soart—tha must get out as soon as thi gets double figures, if tha can get that far at all. We mustn't give t' game away. Remember tha'll be Thompson, and Ah s'll be Smith."

We journeyed to the Salop village on Saturday according to schedule. Our team won the toss and Wainwright, answering to the name of Smith, went in first. The ground was rough; but Ted hit a six at once to square-leg. In next to no time four wickets fell for less than a dozen, nearly all scored by Wainwright, who was not out when I joined him. The first ball bowled at me nearly decapitated me; the second ball shot and hit me on the toe. Wainwright laughed at me sardonically and hit two sixes one after the other. Then he hit two more. I decided that he had done enough. So I went down the wicket and said, "You must get out now—what about your instructions to me? You must have scored thirty and more. We'll be giving the game away, you know." And Ted simply replied, "Tha can get out thi bloody self, if tha likes. This is the first time Ah 'ad a bat in mi 'ands since I stopped playin' for Yorkshire more'n ten years ago. And hey by goom—Ah'm enjoyin' it, lad, Ah'm enjoyin' it!"

The point of the story is that at an English public school the cricket coaches never are given an innings, either at net or match practice—at least, such delights never came our way at Shrewsbury. Our job was to bowl. The wine rushed to Wainwright's head, the sensation of willow thumping leather. He made eighty or so, then he bowled out the opposition neck and heels, taking six or seven wickets in two or three overs.

We were paid our fee. We were back in Shrewsbury before nine o'clock. Ted was disgusted because I would not "celebrate." "Tha'rt a reight bloody cricketer, thou art, and Ah've often toold thi so." Ted took all his cronies of Shrewsbury to one public-house after another; they walked in uneven processions from the Crown to the King's Arms and then, after a while, back to the Crown. The truth came out, of course. Such magnificent hitting as Ted's could not very well have gone by without a notice in a quiet village of Salop. Belvedere was severely chastised by the officials of the Sunday School League. The team had all their points deducted and were reduced to the bottom of the championship table for playing "two ineligible men." To do Ted justice, he was contrite when he heard of the severe punishment meted out to Belvedere. "Ah shouldn't ah done it. Ah should a' kept to t' contract. But Ah couldn't 'elp it, lad. Never 'ad a bat in me 'ands for years. It all coom back to me, lad. Ah'm sorry, reight sorry—hey, but bah goom, Ah did enjoy mesel'. Christ, Ah did."

Wainwright could not persuade me to drink; but he introduced me to the Dunhill pipe (seven shillings and sixpence each in those days) and to Edgeworth tobacco, which I bought at a shop curiously called Pelican Snelsen, opposite Shrewsbury market. He revolutionised cricket at the school; he taught the "new" technique of batsmanship—a play back or drive. Also, he declined to go round the playing-fields marking the pitches, nor would he allow me to perform this menial labour; we were bloody cricketers, he said, not plasterers and house decorators. The School, at his command, employed a ground-boy to do the job.

There was at Shrewsbury, as there will be in paradise itself, one unpleasant person. On the first day of Wainwright's engagement he walked importantly into our dressing-room in the cricket pavilion.

"Mr. Wainwright?" he asked.

"Aye," said Ted, looking him up and down.

"Well, my name's Jenkins. I'm in charge of the ground and I just want to let you know that if there's anything I can do for you, please let me know."

"Aye," said Ted.

"And, of course, you'll always come to me first, if you require any materials."

"Materials," said Ted, who was not only head "pro" but controlled the sales of cricket bats and balls and so on. "Materials? What dost t'mean?"

"Well, you see," explained Jenkins, "there's the whitewash and buckets, for instance."

"Whitewash and what?" said Ted, rhyming "what" with "hat."

"Yes, buckets, and the whitewash. You'll come to me for them. Just as a matter of form, y' know. They're always in the shed, of course, but everything you'll require will go through me. That is the procedure. Just a matter of form, y' know."

Wainwright looked at his pipe.

"So tha supplies th' whitewash?"

"Yes, Wainwright; only too glad to help any time."

"And tha supplies t' buckets, eh?"

"Yes, but you'll always come to me personally for them, won't you? Point of order. Only a matter of form. . . . still. . . ."

After another look at his pipe, Wainwright, who was sitting on a table dangling his legs, closed the subject for ever.

"Tha can tek one of thi buckets," he said, in the most friendly way he could manage, "and fill it full o' whitewash to t'top. Then stick thi yed in it."

One wet afternoon we were sitting in the "pro's" dressing-room at Shrewsbury, looking over the misty green fields. Suddenly the Headmaster rode straight across the sacred turf on a bicycle. Wainwright leaped to his feet, flung open the dressing-room window, stuck out his head, put two fingers into his mouth, emitted a piercing whistle, then shouted, "What the 'ell dost t' think tha doin'? Get off t' grass, tha bloody-looking foo-il." And he w waved the Headmaster of Shrewsbury to a by-path; the Reverend Cyril Alington abruptly and docilely veered to it and disappeared round a corner, most humbled. I was horrified. "Good lord, Ted," I said, "that was the Headmaster." "Ah don't give a —— who he was. Ought to have more sense. Ridin''is bloody bicycle over t' turf on a day like this! T'ell wi' 'im."

Alington was contrite. When I saw him next morning he

was entirely apologetic. "I don't know what I was thinking about. I'd just come from a Governors' meeting; my mind was preoccupied. Wainwright was quite right to order me off the wet turf; quite right. I should have known better." Then, after a pause, "But I do think he might have admonished me in language a little less—er—less drastic."

.   .   .   .   .   .

Wainwright removed himself from Cross Hill, next door to the local printer, who set up posters about Auctions and Flower Shows inarticulate with full stops. Wainwright, a man of means and of the larger world, took a cottage across the river, not far from the School's playing-fields. On Sunday mornings certain of the older and more knowing boys visited him in secret, and there were cigarettes and, I suspect, drink.

I was at last alone in a room of my own. I could stretch out my legs at will and smoke my pipe and read; if I was certain Mrs. Rodenhurst was not in, I could put my feet on the mantelshelf, like Macaulay. I bought a tobacco jar from Pelican Snelsen, and two or three cheap briars to keep company with my Dunhill. I bought a pipe-rack. In short, I was a growing young man of the period. And there has never been a period so good for a young man to live in.

As the atmosphere of Shrewsbury School more and more became my element, I strengthened in self-assurance. Not at once, though. One morning, Mrs. Rodenhurst brought my breakfast to my sitting-room as usual. The teapot's spout had been damaged and an india-rubber substitute was stuck on to the broken stump. It revolted me. But, I thought, it is probably a temporary measure. To-morrow she would surely give me a new teapot. But no; next day and the day after, the india-rubber attachment again sickened me. I decided to take Mrs. Rodenhurst to task. For three consecutive mornings she served my breakfast with the phallic-spouted teapot, and now my blood was up. I waited until she had left the room. Then I made my decision. I would call her back. I would go to the door of my sitting-room, fling it open, and shout down the corridor, "Mrs. Rodenhurst!" Just like that;

peremptorily, even angrily. And when she answered the summons, I would reprimand her, and insist on a new teapot, a wholesome teapot, here and now.

This, I say, was my resolved purpose. But, I thought, I had better rehearse calling her name down the corridor to see how it sounded. I gently opened the door and shouted, so quietly to begin with, that I could scarcely hear it myself:

"Mrs. Rodenhurst."

Then, a little louder:

"MRS. RODENHURST."

The tension severely increased. I tried again, mezzo-forte. Then in the excitement I lost control of my voice, and it bellowed full force down the corridor:

"MRS. RODENHURST!!!"

I was petrified. Suppose she had heard it? I pulled my head back into my sitting-room, silently closed the door and sat down, pretending I was reading the morning newspaper. Fortunately Mrs. Rodenhurst had been out all the time, across the street at the grocer's. Nobody was in the house except myself. I put up with the india-rubber spout until Mrs. Rodenhurst of her own free will bought a new teapot for me, months afterwards.

I was at first perplexed at Shrewsbury by the following procedure. Attewell invariably addressed each boy, junior or senior, as "Sir." And they called him Attewell. But for a while they addressed me "Sir"; but I was not—obviously was not—expected to "Sir" them. The paradox was that Attewell, not I, was the favoured one in this subtle etiquette of address. Not for a year did the boys address me by my surname. But when Wainwright took Attewell's place they at once called him "Sir" and seldom called him by his surname during the two or three years he remained at the School. What is more, they privately resented that he as freely used their surnames as I did. The fine shades in the hierachy of manners in pre-1914 England defied the most cunning social spectroscope.

One day a little science-master at Shrewsbury wanted half an hour's batting practice. His name was Richmond, and he was small, with grey hair and crow's feet around his eyes. As neither Wainwright nor myself was available at the moment to bowl at him, I recommended Bates, one of the gardeners. "He's quite quick and he can turn them from the off," I said. Next day I asked Richmond if he had enjoyed his net. "Yes, indeed," was the reply, "as you told me, he's very good. Once he missed my leg-stump by an inch. I was certain the ball had pitched off the wicket, so I asked him, 'What did that ball do, Bates?' and he replied, 'It bloody near bowled you, sir.'" Richmond, a martinet for the "done thing," would not have liked it if Wainwright had spoken to him in this way; while if I had even said "damned near," I should have been taking a liberty most reprehensible and not to be thought of.

When Alington appointed me his secretary, my star again shone, and, as usual, at the right moment. I had so far met nobody of experience in the art of living. I had grown up amongst people with little time for it, with utilitarians who bought in the cheapest markets and sold in the dearest. I knew from my books, from Henry James in particular, that poise and awareness to all things, with an ironic eye steadily on one's ego—this I already guessed was one of the ways towards enjoying life.

I sensed Alington as soon as I saw him walking the playing-fields at Shrewsbury, too handsome for any parson or peda-gogue, with a longish face and a good jaw and quizzical eyes, and a twist to his mouth. He was tall and slender, with a slight stoop. For some reason hard to explain, I always felt he had stepped out of a novel by George Meredith. Through the sunshine from the west he would walk over the cricket field from game to game, in his grey clericals. It was possible to play a dozen matches simultaneously at Shrewsbury, cheek by jowl, with cover-point in one engagement and square-leg in another back to back. A dozen matches flashing their white over the green; thuds of pursuing fieldsmen under your very nose; cricket balls whizzing through the air or volleying over

the earth, menace to skull or shin. And Alington walked here
and there, carrying his straw hat under his arm and chewing
a daisy, the stalk in his mouth, with his black entanglement
of wool called Bogey running ahead, a red tongue and nothing
else telling you it was a dog. He moved like a man who saw
and savoured himself as he moved. His voice fascinated me
because of its suave inflections. One day I sat under the great
cotton tree which dropped its white fleece on the field near
the Chapel. I was reading Gilbert Murray's version of the
Medea of Euripides, and Alington came by and stopped as he
saw me; until now he had not spoken to me, except as one of the
cricket professionals. He asked me what was my book; I told
him, venturing at the same time one or two remarks (while
my heart pounded away) in praise of the translation—and I
knew not a word of Greek. Alington, in his most aromatic tones,
gently said, "Ah, yes, Murray is a most ingenious fellow."
It was my first living taste of irony. Irony in grey clericals
at that! This was new to me. So far, I had seen only the
dowdy side of religion; I was taught Scripture (as they called
it) at Sunday School, by females who did not obviously feel
an inward glow of any sort, holy or other; I was expected to
seek God in unlovely tabernacles, outward manifestations of
the minds of the people who worshipped in them. When I
went to Shrewsbury, I was mouthing Nietzsche's "Slave
morality." "The only Christian died on the Cross." I was,
and I remain to this day, incapable of an anthropomorphic
belief in God or in a hereafter. I never discussed religion
with Alington, though I often was tempted to open the subject. But I felt that he would have respected my scepticism
and not have patronised it as a young man's callowness.

I am, of course, drawing riskily on impressions received
from Alington thirty years ago; maybe I dramatised him; I
do not gather from the books he has written in recent years
that he has ever had in his nature any acid likely to bite into
the conventional culture of an English divine and gentleman
of the Edwardian high noon. He was only forty-two years
old when I came into his ken, and I was twenty-five and
extremely youthful and impressionable for my age. I write
only of the effect he made on me; it was important and I do
not think he suspected for a minute that I was getting far

more out of him than any of his favourite and most gifted students were. I saw *décor* in him, and irony. When he was appointed Headmaster of Eton, telegrams of congratulation were sent to him to Shrewsbury from all parts and from all ranks of society. He had them heaped like rose leaves in a bowl on the table of his library. He would come again and again into the room as the pile or *potpourri* grew from hour to hour, and he buried his hand in the orange envelopes and tissues and let them flutter like petals down to the bowl again. He could laugh at himself, and I think it is as well that all earnest young men should be brought into close and frank touch with somebody who *can* laugh at himself. Alington, I imagine, understood that the pride which is vain and goeth before a fall is one thing, and that aesthetic pride is another. I saw him as the artist who would be readier to interest himself in a boy's temperament than in the most successfully negotiated examination paper. He was, for me, an influence that inspired and corrected at one and the same time; not by precept but by example. It is given to few—even to few Doctors of Divinity—to preach a belief in God and not sound omniscient or metaphysically untrained. It was Alington's indirect influence that compelled me to overhaul my disbelief, much to my annoyance; a young man's scepticism towards all revealed religion could be mightily dogmatic a quarter of a century ago. If Alington's influence did not convert me, it persuaded me at least to thank *God* that I was an atheist. As I say, he worked his charms on me unwittingly; it will astonish him to learn that in an important way he affected my sense of life, stimulated my antennae to subtler vibrations of things and presences. Because of Alington, I call myself to-day an old Salopian.

.   .   .   .   .   .

When the war broke out in August 1914, I immediately offered myself to the army and, not to my surprise or dismay, was rejected because of shortsightedness. Alington's secretary at Shrewsbury rushed to the colours, with thousands of other young idealists; and at Alington's invitation I took his place. I gave up hours of my cricket regretfully, and when

I heard the crack of the bat on June days outside the Head-master's study, while I tried to transcribe my own improvised shorthand, I felt sorry for myself. I did not believe that Alington really thought I could be useful to him as a secretary; he acted, I guessed, out of consideration for my age and position at the school: a young man, physically fit enough to play cricket professionally and a war on; better use him sedentarily; a vacancy had conveniently turned up; he was not illiterate, and there'd be no additional expense. But Alington at once made me comfortable; he led me to think that I was the most confidential and necessary secretary in the world. He talked to me as if I had been with him for years.

My little room, next to Alington's library, was at the front of School House not far from the main steps. It looked on the School square, with smooth lawns and two great trees. There was ivy on the walls outside my window, and often I heard a whir of wings, almost in my room. The sun fell on my desk in the mornings through the leaves of the trees and dappled the polished wood of the surface with changing light and shade. Sometimes I was obliged to draw the curtain, and now all the noises of the outside world came to me in varying waves of sounds; near, not so near, detached and somehow symbolical. A gardener clipping a hedge; a sudden resonance of voices, a crunching of feet on gravel as at eleven o'clock the boys changed from class-room to class-room. Now stillness again, broken by the hurried crunching of a boy late, as the bell in the tower ceased its ringing, ceased slowly as though giving the dilatory scholar a fair chance. Then silence all the more peaceful because I could hear again the sound of the gardener clipping the hedge.

I went on with my work, perhaps making a catalogue of the books in the library. One day I found *Das Kapital* of Karl Marx on a shelf next to Jowett's Plato, crushed to death in a corner. I began at once to read it, standing on a ladder. "Congealed labour"; "surplus value"; a strange fellow for Jowett, in a public-school of those years! I wondered how it came to be there, then I saw in a corner of the fly-leaf Alington's signature dated the late 'nineties.

I tried to work a typewriter and write down Alington's letters from his own peripatetic dictation. He walked in and out of his library and my room, suiting the action to the word and enjoying lots of sarcasm for the fun of it, afterwards saying, "But don't put that in." He dictated a letter to a parent thus: "'Your boy's progress this term has been so remarkable that already I see in him a Prime Minister of England, of the near or distant future'—you know him, Cardus, don't you?—a complete fool—but don't put that in; begin again, 'I am happy to report that your boy is not losing ground in his work this term. There is a distinct improvement in his off-break, which he is now bowling at a decent length' —no, don't put that last sentence in; finish at 'work this term.' I'll sign it with the other letters after lunch." All this was spoken with relish; it was an education in the manifestation of the comic spirit in an unexpected place.

The typewriter was never conquered by me. I worked it with two fingers; the first on each hand. No matter how much I practised on the machine I could seldom find the letters readily, not all of them. Sometimes I was prepared to swear it was a typewriter that did not possess a letter P, or, on another occasion, a letter Z. But by expenditure of much thought, and there was no vulgar hurry at Shrewsbury, I contrived to present Alington with a neat enough correspondence, which he would sign with a sort of broken-backed Daddy-long-legs, supposed to represent C. A. Alington. For hours and hours I worked at my own studies; I do not believe there was a more diligent student in the school than myself. Georg Brandes —and Croce, and *Also sprach Zarathustra.* I recollect these additions to my culture decorations of 1915; it was, I think, one of Croce's first translations into English, a study of Marxian economics. One day Alington was visited by Lord Milner; the occasion a Speech Day no doubt. They both came out of Alington's dining-room across the hall and were passing through my room to the library, when Alington paused in his walk and directed Milner's attention to me. "My secretary," he said, "rather subversive, even dangerously so." That was my first introduction to an English lord. I thought he looked as though rather cut-off from mankind.

After a month or two in Alington's service, even though he seldom spoke to me except in the way of everyday routine, I was alive on a side of my character dormant more or less

until now. I began to produce and assert myself. I began
with Mrs. Rodenhurst. I gave her notice in no unambiguous
voice at one attempt. And I did it with such sweetness in
my firmness, that she affectionately sniffed as I departed to a
higher social plane in Shrewsbury apartments (not lodgings)
in a road called a Crescent.

·   ·   ·   ·   ·   ·

My Shrewsbury bubble burst abruptly. Even now, more
than a quarter of a century after, it is hard to bear the memory
of the disillusionment, the sickening suddenness of the
reversal of fortune I suffered. Without warning, without a
chance to look over my clear sky for a coming cloud—for I
never really trusted my fine weather—I was reduced to a
deplorable state of things. It all began when Alington was
chosen for the Headmastership of Eton. I was as pleased as
Alington himself when the news came to Shrewsbury in the
summer of 1916. I basked in reflected glory. I have told how
he entered his library and made the gesture with the heaped-up
telegrams in the bowl. Let me confess here that once, when
nobody was looking, I too went into the library and let the
rose petals of congratulations flutter from my hand.

Alington asked me to go with him to Eton as his private
secretary. I trod the air. But the last days of the 1916 Shrewsbury term were sad; I was leaving a place where for five
summers I had lived happily. I wandered about the playing-
fields on the last evening I was destined to know at Shrewsbury.
The term was over; the school was nearly vacant. Not a
human sound was to be heard as the red streaks of the sunset
barred the sky. But in the high nests the rooks were noisy
as ever, indifferent to aches or regret, unconcerned whether
this was the first of May at Shrewsbury or a dying summer
and a leave-taking. They cawed and fluttered, then they would
settle down until a solitary rook, out late, came deliberately
but comfortably winging his way home, and a racket and
disturbance began again, the air above the tree-tops black
as though with the embers of a fire suddenly poked. At last,
silence and stillness while the dusk deepened.

I took my last glance over the fields. The grass might have

held some juice from me for ever, some sweat, some touch of the feet or body—for how many hours had I run and walked here; how many times had I lain on this earth on a hot day, giving myself to the luxury of release and recumbence, while I stared straight into the sky? I turned away, walked past the Speech Hall where a week ago I had, unknown to anybody but myself, joined in the Shrewsbury School song, at breaking-up: "Floreat Salopia!" I walked for the last time from the lawns of School House, and as the ferry over the Severn was closed for the night, I went across Kingsland Bridge into the town. Next day I left for Manchester, still sad at heart, though my mind was thrilling with the new life before me. Where would it take me, where was I heading for now? Eton? Secretly I nursed the thought that not far from Eton was— London.

.   .   .   .   .   .

A few days after my farewell to Shrewsbury, I received a letter from Alington, already at Eton. He wished to know if my position was clear and final with the military authorities. Rejected men were being called up for re-examination; a "comb-out" was in progress—to use the elegant language of the newspapers of the period, as though we were all so many lice, those of us not already dead or maimed. This was the period in which old men regretted they had not a third or fourth son to mourn; it was also the period in which Siegfried Sassoon spat his bitterness into his poems.

Alington naturally did not want to enter into his work at Eton with a secretary liable to be taken away from him at any moment. I went to the Military Board (as they named it) and explained my position and need. Would they re-examine me now, accept or reject me, so that I might let the Head-master of Eton know where I, or he, stood? Oh no, they couldn't possibly do that: my "class of rejects" was not yet on the lists for re-examination. I *could be* called up to-morrow or next week, but perhaps not for months. I argued in vain. I mentioned the name of Alington to the Chief of the Military Board without awakening a glint of recognition in his failing eye. I mentioned Eton, my trump card; and he

spoke to another red-capped septuagenarian about it: "Eton
College" they called it, every time. I was left in the air, and
I was unable to go to Eton; and not only that, I was unable
to obtain any other regular employment; for nobody in
Manchester or elsewhere would offer a job to a young man
who could not give an assurance that he would be at liberty
and out of the army for a week. I became a casual labourer,
and in time I tasted a poverty and humiliation which I hope
to describe with no more exaggeration or self-pity than will
appeal to me as a writer telling a good and true story.

For a brief space I received some consolation for the loss
of Eton and Alington. Out-of-work again, with no prospect
of a re-engagement at Shrewsbury, I saw my little stocking
of earnings grow less and less as the cost of living in war-time
mounted higher and higher. I applied for a job as music
critic on the *Daily Citizen*, the first Labour newspaper in
England; they opened a Manchester office and published a
"Northern Edition." The editor in Manchester was Frank
Dilnot and he asked me to call and see him. This was my
first entrance into the holy of holies of a newspaper office.
Dilnot was friendly but, I thought, very powerful as he sat
at his desk and leaned back in his chair and talked to me. I
sat facing him bolt upright on the edge of my chair. He
offered me a cigarette and I, with much presence of mind,
said "No, if you don't mind I'll have a pipe, thanks." He was
favourably inclined to my proposition, which was to cover
music for the *Citizen* in Manchester and the North of England;
but unfortunately the paper had not so far received a single
press-ticket from an important concert—or musical association;
there was still an idea in England that a Labour paper was
written and read by illiterate and socially undesirable persons.
I guaranteed that I would persuade the concerts committees
to send me press-tickets. To get a footing in music criticism,
I was even prepared to pay at the door myself and stand at the
back; this was my job in life, better than any Eton, now the
chance had come. Dilnot accepted and offered me pay at the
rate of a penny a line. Though here was a set-back, I did not
hesitate. And so did I begin my life as a music critic, my only
condition being that I should sign my notices with my initials.
This was a departure from the period's rule of anonymity

in nearly all sorts of newspaper criticism. Even the football and racing correspondents did not sign with their names or initials; they used pseudonyms of a rather metaphorical, not to say metaphysical, order, such as Vigilant, Augur, Solon, Man on the Spot.

A penny a line! And I received, at the first asking, a set of "swell" tickets for the Hallé Concerts, sent to me personally by Michael Balling, then the conductor of the greatest orchestra in England. Also I demonstrated, but not so easily, that the *Daily Citizen* might decently be admitted to the "celebrity" concerts directed by a Mr. Percy Harrison, one of the last of the Victorian line of entrepreneurs; he looked like a Minister for Foreign Affairs, dressed with an un-English fastidiousness, and his hair was white as though powdered. He, in person, would lead on to the platform the great female virtuosi of the day, holding them gently by the hand and guiding them through pitfalls of chairs, fiddle-stands, fern and shrubbery. "A Labour paper?" he said, as I gave him a specimen copy, which he held at a distance to begin with, then surveyed at closer quarters through a double-eyeglass, retained to his person by a broad ribbon. He compromised— and alloted to me a season-ticket to the three-and-sixpenny seats, amongst the lower-middle classes.

My first music notice, the first of thousands, was of a Hallé Concert; the programme included Elgar's symphonic study "Falstaff," and I thought I was being very witty when I said that Elgar had given us a Falstaff in C minor, more devoted to psalm singing than to sitting on benches after noon. I wrote eighty lines or thereabouts, and went to my cold bed that night happy in the belief that I had not only made at last my debut in music criticism, but had earned roughly six and eightpence; a lawyer's fee, to say the least. I awoke early next morning and leaped downstairs in my pyjamas when I heard the newspapers pushed under the door. I could scarcely open the pages of the *Citizen*, and for a while I could not find anything faintly resembling a criticism of music. I ran it to earth on a page devoted to market reports and advertisements of baby-linen. The notice comprised exactly twenty-two lines; the sub-editors had cut me down to one and tenpence.

So it went on; at the end of my first month my payments amounted approximately to thirty shillings—ten concerts at round about three shillings each, and no expenses allowed. Sharpened by need, inspiration descended on me. I worked out a style of writing in which each sentence was related to and dependent on the next and to its predecessor, not to be disturbed or eliminated at peril to the entire prose structure or edifice. I began every sentence with a "Therefore," a "Consequently," a "Moreover," a "But," an "And," an "And so," or an "It follows, then." My idea was to make the texture of my notices so homogeneous that any sub-editor, no matter how lost to all sense of literary style, would late at night let his blue pencil hover for long in vain above my copy, unable to perform a single excision which would not involve him in a labour of rewriting or recasting; in despair, so I imagined, he would say "Oh, to hell with it!" and send up the article to the composing-room and catch his last train, tram or 'bus home. I would, by this resourceful device, be sure of a fair income at a penny a line each notice, three or four a week.

I overrated in my innocence the sense of literary consequence and continuity amongst sub-editors. The blue pencil came down just the same after approximately every thirtieth line, came down like a guillotine once and for all, sometimes in the middle of an apostrophe. There were misprints, too, which appeared above my initials, bringing the blush of shame to my cheeks. Thus, when some Italian tenor appeared at one of Percy Harrison's concerts, I was made next morning to announce that he had sung "Una furtiva lagrima" from Donizetti's "L'Eliza d'Amore." This remains one of my favourite misprints, though the best of all that ever appeared in an article by me appeared in the *Manchester Guardian*; I had written of Verdi's *Otello* with a brief reference to what I described as the "banal duet" which surprisingly breaks out at the end of Act II, a sudden atavistic return to Verdi's crudest period. Next day this phrase appeared in the *Guardian* as the "canal duel"—the Grand Canal, one had to assume.

.   .   .   .   .   .

My connection with the *Daily Citizen* lasted less than three months. Smaller daily papers, because of the scarcity of news-print, rendered music criticism a luxury round about 1916, especially in the columns of a journal intended for the workers of the North of England. And still the army would not make up its mind whether to draft me into the forces or reject me again; I and thousands of other young men remained liable to re-examination at forty-eight hours' notice. I could not have returned to the Flemings, even if my pride had let me beg of them to take me back; for the anxieties of marine insurance in war-time had persuaded the brothers into a dignified retirement.

I was reduced to appalling shifts. I was driven to the worst of the period's resorts for the down-and-out respectables —I became an agent for a Burial Society which specialised in policies covering funeral expenses amongst the poor, in places where the main ostensible problem was to keep alive. A herd of us was assembled each morning on the filthy pavements of All Saints, Manchester; and a superintendent with a waxed moustache bullied us to get "new business"—poor devil, like the rest of us, he depended on "commission." We were each given what was known as a "book," which meant a district and round of calls. First, we had to collect the weekly premiums for "business" already on the books; and we were each of us expected to increase the "business" day by day— in other words, to persuade more and more denizens of the slum areas of the city to consider and prepare themselves for the most important and expensive event of their lives. Birth was cheap in comparison; death amongst the poor of the North of England called for a funeral that the neighbourhood could be proud of and admire from behind drawn blinds.

I descended into the underworlds of Gorton and Salford and Hulme; my "territory" was back-to-back tenements, inheritances from the wealthy radicals of the nineteenth-century Manchester school. I knocked at hovels opening sheer upon rooms in which children, like kittens, urined the floors, mainly choosing the corners. A harassed woman usually came cautiously to the door. "Ah," she would breathe in manifest relief, "the Insurance!" Then she would give me the week's "contributions" and I entered the amount in a book and initialled it. Or she would, and often she did, declare an inability to pay at all. If she allowed the "arrears" to go beyond a certain point she lost all that she had paid out. I was supposed to coerce her into stricter economy, and if possible into increasing the amount insured by the policy. Sometimes the lord and master of the house appeared before me, without a coat, shirt-sleeves rolled up and no collar; many times he would advise me to get myself to hell or he'd knock my bloody face in. He thought, of course, that I symbolised or personified the company, the managing director and the shareholders.

I not only couldn't obtain new business; I was not equal to keeping down arrears. Often I knocked at doors, then walked away, trying to look as though I had never been there and was somebody else. The irony of it all was that my sympathy with these derelicts was wasted; they were as a rule much easier in mind than I, if a policy ran out through arrears and they lost all their instalments. As a result of these experiences amongst the poor I have seldom mixed up sentiment with strong views on the necessity of social reform in England.

One night in Oldham in the middle of December, a deluge and a gale finished my connection for ever with the insurance world. I had to walk three miles over a blasted heath to collect one of the few reliable contributions on my list. The night was black as a pit, and I was soaked to the skin. When I reached my journey's end the house was in darkness, the tenants had "shot the moon," decamped to bilk the rent-collector and all creditors whatsoever, myself not the most important. I returned to Manchester with ague seizing me, and in a Lyons tea-shop I arrived at a last-gap decision. I still did not feel ready to apply to the *Manchester Guardian* for a job as a writer; the standards of the greatest of newspapers held me in awe, not less but more than ever. But I was ship-wrecked and sinking, so next day I posted a letter to C. P. Scott asking for work in the counting-house; if I could only get some sort of a footing on the *Guardian*, I thought, I might later be able to glide imperceptibly on to the reporting or editorial staff. The way to music criticism was barred by the vast bulk of Samuel Langford. For my vanity's sake, I sent to Scott, with my modest application for a clerk's job, one or two specimens of my writing. One of them was the essay on Bantock. The others (in manuscript) were entitled: "Bergson and Laughter" and "A Survey of Metaphysics"—the latter paper emphasising the relativity of systems of philosophy and ending with a quotation from Browning's *Bishop Blougram's Apology*:

> We call the checkboard white,
> We call it black. . . .

C. P. Scott replied by return of post, inviting me to come to see him at his house—The Firs in Fallowfield. Would any other editor, alive or dead, have discerned new material for his staff in specimen-writings so austere and far-reaching?

.   .   .   .   .   .

But the gods had not yet finished their sport with me. Before I found myself truly placed on the main thoroughfare of my life, an "M. G." man once and for ever, the President of the Immortals played me a last dirty trick, then relented. On a winter morning near Christmas 1916, I walked along the drive to The Firs at Fallowfield and I saw the white house in which dwelt the most famous editor of the day. I was shown into a room decorated in the period of William Morris, The spacious windows let in a white light thrown from the snow which covered the lawn outside; no fire or any heating at all warmed the room, which was stone cold. I regretted I had given my overcoat to the maid. The furniture was austere, and on the wall were two paintings by Francis Dodd of Scott's sons, Lawrence and Edward. Lawrence had died years ago, and Edward was at the war; years afterwards he succeeded his father as editor of the *Guardian* and was drowned on holiday in Lake Windermere, one of the severest losses ever sustained in English journalism and public life. In a bookcase I saw a collection of Lamartine; I opened a volume and its pages were uncut. Scott, I discovered later, was not a man likely to read Lamartine.

I waited and waited and became colder and colder. Nearly

an hour passed and no Scott appeared. I wondered if I had been forgotten—should I ring a bell or what? The door was suddenly flung open and Scott entered wearing thick tweeds, and a soft turned-down collar and a coloured tie. I knew him by sight of course; I had seen him riding the streets of Manchester on his bicycle; and I had seen him making a political speech in the Free Trade Hall, an inaudible speech which prompted a man at the back to call out "Speak oop, owd Scott!" But this was the first time I saw him at close quarters. I thought I had never before seen such a clean old man. His white whiskers went away to two scimitars right and left. He stooped sideways, and his eyes were uncomfortably piercing. I was told in later years that one of them was glass, and I can well believe it. But he was charming on this morning of my ordeal. As we sat in the cold drawing-room, he led me on to talk of many things. A sort of *viva voce*! He extracted from me one or two facts of my education, then he went off at a tangent to discuss Bernard Shaw. He had run into him in Whitehall only the other week. And then Scott said to me, "He's beginning to look old at last—don't you think so?"— exquisitely implying that I knew Shaw and that we all lived on the same intellectual and social plane, don't you know. He asked me one or two questions about the *Guardian*; what did I like best in it, and so on. After a half an hour, during which I received the impression that he had invited me to lunch just as an old friend but had forgotten all about it, he abruptly wished me good morning, and I left the room which opened on the hall and I assisted myself into my overcoat and silently withdrew from the premises.

Next day he wrote to me suggesting that I might help him in a "semi-secretarial" way; would I call at The Firs each morning at about eleven? For a month I waited on him, and he gave me books and periodicals of which he said he wanted verbal summaries the next day. I almost learned each précis by heart, but invariably when the next day arrived he was not interested. I dutifully presented myself each morning at The Firs, came away with a pile of books and papers, digested any likely article in them, and returned to-morrow to Scott, and as delicately as I could I jogged his memory. Now and again, I swear, he did not thoroughly grasp my identity. No word was mentioned of remuneration due to me, weekly or monthly. At the end of a few weeks, another letter from Scott came to my lodgings, and it flattened me out. "My dear Cardus," he wrote, "It would seem that I am congenitally incapable of using a secretary. I fear then that I am wasting your time." He concluded with the hope that I would be able to find "some suitable channel through which to develop my literary tastes, etc." And that was that. The door of the "M. G." had been opened for me by fate. I had got my foot into the main temple. I had begun with the great Scott himself, not an underling! And—crash, bang; the door was closed against me and I was back once more in the gutter. Chance does not come twice to a man in the same direction. Here was the most unkindest cut of all. I did not receive a cheque or a penny's pay for my month's devoted if merely formal performance of secretarial duties to Scott. But I thought little or nothing of that; the terrible fact was that fortune had granted me a lifetime's wish—the chance to touch, simply to get near, the ladder of the "M. G." I had missed it; Scott obviously had thought I was, for his purpose, entirely hopeless.

From the end of January to March 1917, I eked out a sub-sistence wage and went on with as good heart as I could with my studies. But doubt was gathering and strengthening in my heart and, worst of all, cynicism. My twenty-seventh birthday was due. Too late, now, too late! Then, in the middle of March 1917, came another letter decisive and out of the dead past, as I thought—a letter from Scott. A vacancy had occurred on the reporting staff of the *Manchester Guardian*; would I call at the office in Cross Street next Monday and ask to see Mr. Haslam Mills? In all my life I have never known excitement such as electrified me as I read this letter. Haslam Mills—the most picturesque figure in Manchester! We had all read his theatre notices, usually of variety artists and the lighter forms of entertainment, written with rare savour of words and of things seen. I duly called on Mills and he en-gaged me, on behalf of Scott, as a member of the reporters' room.

In after years I came to know Scott more or less intimately. He was a man who once he had made a decision, or cast an event or person from his mind, never or seldom returned to it or him or her. To this day I cannot explain why ten weeks after my brief and shadowy association with him as a "semi-secretary," he should have given a second thought to me or communicated my name to Mills at the crucial moment. At this time Scott was directing single-handed the "M. G." in a period of severe responsibility, running up and down the land between Manchester and London, talking with Lloyd George and God knows who, an anonymous but influential force, a thousand urgent things on his mind. Yet one day he broke the habit of a lifetime, looked back, and reviewed a decision—and by doing so settled the shape of my career and my life at the moment when I, for all my romantic dreamings from boyhood onward, was withdrawing in the secret places of my heart, defeated, after an unequal battle.

.   .   .   .   .   .

On the second Monday of March 1917, I walked to Manchester three miles from my apartment in Fallowfield, and all the way I rehearsed every situation and contingency I could imagine likely to emerge from my interview with Haslam Mills. When I reached the office of the *Manchester Guardian* I crossed the street and stood for a moment on the corner, from where as a boy years back I had so often looked at the windows of the great building opposite and imagined Montague and the other mighty ones at work. Then I took in a great breath, said a prayer to whatever gods there be, asked at the inquiry office for Mr. Haslam Mills, and was shown into his little lair adjoining the reporters' room—was shown by a boy who had so little understanding of where he was leading me, to what a fateful cross-road, that he actually whistled on the way.

Mills rose from his desk and shook me by the hand and greeted me in his intimate and friendly voice, "Ah, Cardus, sit down, if you can find a comfortable chair." I wish I could draw a picture of him. He was tall and elegant and thin; grey hair was brushed straight back from his fine but not too high forehead; his eyes were deep-set, and when he spoke sitting down, his chin would tend to sink to his shirt-front, and then his eyes gleamed at you upwards. They were sensitive eyes which seemed to look not only at whoever was with him, but inward at himself; and I always felt they were observant less of one's appearance and movements than of one's choice of words. His face was deathly white and his mouth was keen, but not hard, and two deep lines were graven down each cheek. He was almost spectacularly handsome and he wore his clothes perfectly, with the right looseness. He favoured a soft striped collar and a bow; somehow he so arranged his neck-wear that it suggested a cravat. His fingers were long and feminine, and his voice and his English were not less alluring than Alington's. There was no stiffness, not an angle, about him; he was all curves. None the less he never gave a hint of a casual attitude or a low temperature; he relaxed as though with a feline reserve-power of suppleness and springiness.

He began the interview obviously savouring his part in it without stinting himself. He first of all explained that the *Guardian* as a place for a young writer (he did not call me a young journalist, oh dear no: "a young writer") was less a newspaper office than an Academy almost in an Athenian sense. He pressed his thumbs together and carefully made the apex of a triangle with the tips of the forefingers. After a forensic pause, he put the following question: "Now, Cardus, tell me—have you any private life?" I naturally evinced some bewilderment, and he inflected his tone so that I could not possibly suffer embarrassment. "What I mean is, are you married, or engaged to be married?" I told him I wasn't. "Good," he remarked; "it is advisable when one joins the staff of the *Manchester Guardian* to have no private life for at least six months."

"Do you command shorthand?" he asked. Nervously I confessed I did not, and quickly he dispelled my fears.

"It does not really matter on the 'M. G.,'" he said, "besides, Cardus, I am of the opinion that some men are born to short-hand, others achieve shorthand, while others have shorthand thrust upon them."

My wonder increased.

"The reporters' room on the 'M. G.,'" continued Haslam Mills, "is not as reporters' rooms elsewhere. At least, so I am credibly informed. I have myself never been in any reporters 'room other than this of the' M. G.,' though once I peered at the reporters' room of the *Daily Mail* through a small window in a door covered with green baize. I did not like what I saw in a necessarily brief glance." "On the *Guardian*," Mills proceeded, "we have our masters of Pitman—our old masters. We have also one or two iconoclast exponents of the more recent system of Gregg. But this newspaper, as you doubtless know, is not only a newspaper, a chronicler of events and occurrences; it is interested in the fine arts and in ideas, and in—let us say—the general scene. We can be decorative at times; we can even be amusing. Here, possibly, you will find scope."

He played with a paperweight for a moment and began again.

"What," he asked, "are your expectations about or *in re* salary?"

I told him I had no expectations at all.

"Good," he remarked, "that provides us with a reasonably broad basis for negotiation. The emoluments which accrue on the *Manchester Guardian* are not large. Would you, or could you, consider the idea of thirty shillings weekly, which is Mr. Scott's tentative and preliminary proposal—plus ten shillings for expenses, also payable weekly?" I accepted unconditionally. Mills got up from his chair. I could hear voices outside his door. "Come," he said, "it is half-past twelve, and my staff assembles. I'll introduce you to them. But do not let old Shovelton become garrulous with you, or let him take hold of the lapel of your coat when he talks to you. And on no account let him make his conversational points by tapping you on the chest with his pince-nez."

He led me to the adjacent long room, with tables and chairs and not a typewriter anywhere, visible or invisible. A bookcase with a glass window was situated at one end, a fireplace (empty) at the other. Mills called together everybody present and with paternal and embracing gestures he distributed me. He announced me as though I already were permanently one of them, then retired to his own room to compile the diary of the day's engagements.

They were all there—or nearly all: the various and gifted

C. P. SCOTT
Pencil drawing by F. W. Schmidt, Manchester

company who soon wove themselves into the tissue of my being and environment. Howard Spring was in France, also A. V. Cookman; but they both came back in good time, and with them I became known as one of Mills' young men. It was our job to *write*. We attended the variety theatres; or composed columns about the crowds at Blackpool and the Isle of Man at holiday times. Even though we belonged to the reporters' room, across the bridge as it were from the editorial mainland, we knew that Scott and the tribunes kept their eyes more or less on us. George Leach was one of the first to welcome me; he was Mills's deputy and the finest Irish correspondent in England during the dire years of 1916-1920. With Mills he had been called to the Bar and had lived in the Temple. One night when he was returning late to his home in Rochdale, he slipped between the carriage and the railway platform, and was so badly injured that his left arm had to be amputated. He was Irish, tall, and terribly independent-minded, with an upward tilt of his chin which brooked no nonsense; and a cruel mouth. But he was superb to look at. Occasionally and abruptly he would on certain days stick a monocle into an eye; but nobody was ever able to discover on what principle these certain days came and went. When he shook hands with me and introduced himself personally, I chanced to be gazing at a large portrait on the wall of the reporters' staff as it was constituted before 1914. "Ah," said Leach, "there's been some changes there. He's dead; he's at the war. So is he." He then indicated himself, seated next to Mills in the middle of the group, two hands resting on a silver-mounted walking-stick. "And," he added, "there have been structural alterations there."

Shovelton immediately seized hold of me and, as Mills had feared, gripped the lapels of my coat. It was his custom; by this means he riveted attention on his discourses, which could be lengthy and prone to wander. He was portly and venerable and not unlike Edward VII. He was a sidesman in Manchester Cathedral on Sundays; on week days he attended meetings of divers Manchester Corporation committees for the "M. G." He wore a tail coat and a top hat. When he spoke to you— usually of some experience connected with his many sojourns at spas or watering-places—he would go into patient and

unmerciful detail. "The tariff was unsatisfactory," he would
narrate, "and the towel-rack in the bathroom insecure." He
would apparently forget the towel-rack and modulate to a
point or key in his story from which you thought in your
despair that you could see the journey's end. But no; after
digression Shovelton would pause, clear his throat, grip the
lapel of your coat tighter, and begin again—"Now, reverting
to the towel-rack. . . ."

It was Shovelton who, early one Saturday afternoon, found
himself alone at the office performing what was known as
week-end duty, most times a formal job; for nothing happened in those days at week-ends which could not be attended
to by the Press Association. "Saturday duty" meant that some
reporter stayed in the office and read the newspapers from two
until five o'clock. Nobody else was in the building. One
Saturday, though, tidings came to Shovelton of a railway
accident in the North of Scotland. He packed up a black
portmanteau and, like a man, caught a train and departed to
the scene of the disaster, leaving a note to that effect to the
News Editor. No message or copy whatever had arrived from
Shovelton when the sub-editors and printers began on Sunday
night to get ready the first editions. The morning papers had
displayed accounts of the accident signed by "special correspondents." The News Editor of the "M. G." tore his hair.
"Any copy from Shovelton?" Not a word. They had to
make shift with agency stuff and the lists of killed and injured.
At last, just after Sunday midnight, a telegram came to hand.
It was opened by the News Editor, now squinting with misery
and self-pity. It read:

ARRIVED SAFELY SNOWING HARD
SHOVELTON

Under Haslam Mills, the reporters' room of the *Manchester
Guardian* was the most gifted and resourceful in the world.
I often thought—and I believe it yet—that if the editorial
staff of the paper, from Scott and Montague downwards,
had been killed one day in a catastrophe of some sort, the
"M. G." would have appeared just the same next morning.
Nobody would have detected any considerable falling-away of

knowledge, understanding and English in leaders written by George Leach, Haslam Mills, Hedley Lockett, A. P. Wadsworth (now Editor of the "M. G."), J. V. Ratcliffe (now a leader-writer on *The Titnes*), and H. Boardman. Dramatic and literary criticism would have come in spate from Howard Spring and A. V. Cookman. I myself would have answered for the music criticism.

In an autobiographical sketch, Howard Spring seems to deplore that his colleagues in the reporters' room of the *Guardian* wasted their talents, frittered them away, and came to little or nothing in the end. None of us, it is true, achieved fame as a novelist. The truth is that it was in itself the ambition of a large part of one's lifetime to get on the *Manchester Guardian* staff at all; once we had attained that eminence, we were tempted to chant Nunc Dimittis. You don't essay another Himalaya after climbing to the top of one. To keep a footing amongst the quality on the "M. G." was no easy task week by week. Howard Spring wrote, after he had left the paper, one of the finest of English novels. *Fame is the Spur* contains strokes of genius and its spacious canvas is unfolded with an acute sense of the irony of the passage of time. None the less, if I were Howard Spring, author of *Fame is the Spur*, and I were to find myself suddenly on my deathbed and aware of it, I should with my last breath instruct that my epitaph contain the following major and penulti-mate sentence—to avoid any misunderstanding of essentials:

IN SPITE OF ALL TEMPTATIONS
HE REMAINED A
"MANCHESTER GUARDOAN" MAN

. . . . . .

I began work with the *Manchester Guardian* on Monday, March 26, 1917, and my first job was to report a lecture by Mrs. H. M. Swanwick on "Population and Militarism." I have consulted the files of the paper and find a reasonably accurate summary, seeing that I "commanded" no shorthand, Pitman, Gregg, or other. It is possible that I asked Mrs. Swanwick for her manuscript, though I doubt if I could have had the

courage to approach her. During the lecture she suffered one
of those lapses of memory to which the best of us are prone.
Wishing to quote an authority she forgot his name, and while
she groped in the air with her right hand, she looked from the
platform to the reporters' table. "Perhaps," she beseeched,
"one of the Press will help me—I'm sure the *Manchester Guardian*
will know. . . ." With as much tone of voice as I could muster,
and conscious that my colleagues of the other papers w ere
gazing hard at me, I said: "Malthus." And, of course,
it was—an easy one. Still, Mrs. Swanwick appeared somewhat
impressed, and I heard subsequently that she told C. P. Scott
that one of his clever young men had come to her assistance
without a moment's hesitation. The reporters on the other
Manchester newspapers, men expert in shorthand but strictly
impersonal in their approach to all public lectures and talks,
regarded me askance. It is not customary for the Press to
recognise the objective reality of public speakers. Once only
did a reporter depart from an impersonal attitude at a Manchester public meeting. He was from the *Daily Dispatch*,
young and a stranger to the city, fresh from Tooting or
some such place. An arts and crafts exhibition was being
opened by Professor Samuel Alexander, O.M., professor of
philosophy and æsthetics, author of *Time, Space and Deity*.
Alexander, in his address, related the arts and crafts to his
own theory of aesthetic Idealism. In the middle of one of his
profounder sentences, the young man from the *Daily Dispatch*
turned to the *Manchester Guardian* representative at the press-
table and whispered, "The old boy's rather getting out of his
depth, isn't he?"

I was dismayed, when I arrived at the reporters 'room on
the morrow of the beginning of my new life, to learn that
my name was not entered in the diary of engagements. Had
I begun as badly as all that? But Mills came to me and
explained: "I have left you off the book to-day; but don't
go home, please. Remain in or about the office—and" (he
spoke the words in capitals) "ABSORB THE ATMOSPHERE." I
remained in the reporters' room all day with short intervals
for sustenance, and well into the night, and I respirated as
self-consciously as a man masticates with new dentures. It
was fascinating. I could not take my eyes off Haslam Mills.

The way he relished words and phrases was education and amusement. One of the older reporters described some trouble which was happening to the potato, a plague or something. In his article he found himself in difficulties; he had used "potato" twice in one sentence and it was necessary emphatically to end with much the same word. So he thought he could solve the problem like this . . . "the something, something of the potato, and so-and-so-and-so-and-so of the potato, involving the something and so-and-so of the tuber." Haslam Mills walked round the reporters' room (the guilty one had gone home) mouthing the word, over and over again: "Tuber; the something and so-and-so of the TUBER!!" He affected hysteria.

Towards seven o'clock the giants of the editorial staff arrived; it was called the "Corridor," a term denoting the long passage occupied by the great. But nobody occupied Montague's room next to Scott's while he was at the war; when he returned the lamp burning behind the frosted glass was as constant and as reassuring as the Eddystone Lighthouse. From the reporters' room it was possible to look across the landing to the "Corridor," and in its glow I caught my first sight of Herbert Sidebotham, a fleeting glimpse as he went from Scott's room back to his own. James Agate has described once and for all how Sidebotham walked with a forward nodding movement of the head and upper part of the body, like a horse. His appearance put me in mind of a reincarnation of Bacchus or Nero; I could see vine leaves in his hair, and a toga draped about him. He and Arthur Wallace were equal to maintaining original sin and humanity on the "Corridor" of the *Manchester Guardian*; they even came into the reporters' room from time to time, calling upon us on the way downstairs to the adjacent "Thatched House," inviting us to follow.

But it was easy to get wrong ideas about human nature on the "M. G." editorial staff. Austerity concealed a few, if not a multitude, of common failings. I once heard C. P. Scott belch, with no effort to stop it, as he handed me a proof over his table. I once heard Montague curse during a cricket match when he was bowled middle-stump, attempting a six over mid-on's head and as far as the sunset. When he was taking off his pads, he said: "I love this game, Cardus, love it—but I'm damned if I can play it."

.   .   .   .   .

The general opinion to this day is that the *Manchester Guardian* is a newspaper a little too fine and good for human nature's daily food. As I have already written, I often wondered what the average Manchester man thought of us. For one thing it is the only newspaper in the English-speaking world that publishes no racing news or information. But our style of studied aloofness from the crowd was misleading. The truth is that compared with the "M. G.," *The Times* has always been as Mount Olympus to the Mermaid Tavern. I swear that during the Mills-Montague period—both in Scott's time—there was usually a laugh a paragraph in every signed article appearing in the paper. (Montague once began a leading article with these words: "The Home Secretary is gradually becoming a menace to the civil peace.") Mills encouraged ribaldry in our notices of music-halls; they were, in Arnold Bennett's opinion, as brilliant as anything in English journalism. Mills invented the tone and manner. For instance, he would write of two "cross-talk" comedians that "they went to work on the kindly but mistaken assumption that we were all stone deaf." Here is an extract from one of Mills's notices of a Manchester pantomime:

December 24th, 1917.
    The last train on the Bowdon line had combed out the stalls and dress-circle on Saturday night before the pantomime came to an end, and it finally finished in the presence only of the faithful who live along the Palatine Road. Towards the conclusion it had degenerated into an almost unabashed rehearsal, and one suspected angry tempers and unfortunate words behind the scenes. At any rate, it is certain that honest working men were brought to the surface every now and then as the curtain came up suddenly, and only just got back out of the net into their element; and that the Demon King, having sung both verses of the "Bedouin Love Song," stood with his heels visible in anxious

consultation with someone in the wings, and then obliged
with an encore rather noticeably after we had surrendered
our desire that he should do so. We do not mean this in
any sense as a complaint. It is as it should be. There are
many reasons connected with the nature of pantomime, and
probably arising out of the personal character of pantomime, why it should always happen thus on the first night.
But by far the best reason for saying that it is as it should
be is that it always has been. It is part of the ritual of our
temple. Nor is the pantomime going to last no longer than
one's wife's hats that it need be lifted, so to speak, out of
a band-box. This is a thing which is going to last; to last
so long that we shall probably come out of a matinée of it
and see the daylight lingering bitterly in Peter Street as the
earth turns round. It hath its seasons; its beginning and
meridian and end. It shares the dignity of things which
are going to reign, and finally, to abdicate. Pantomimes,
at any rate, used to last as long as that, and the "pantomime
at the Royal," was like the Sunday after Trinity in the
rubric of our devout youth about town. We knew a man
who used to make it his first business to book his seat after
he came back from his holidays at Rhos-on-Sea—the front
row of the stalls, but not the seat on which, as he knew by
annoying experience, the bass-fiddle was apt to get in the
way. A great strategist. But shall we be like that again?
We know now that terrible things are going to happen to
us after the war. How that we are all going to go to one
kind of church on Sunday; and all belong to one party, the
Conservative one; and all going to be strong, silent men,
with lean jaws and limited vocabularies. It is to be hoped
the pantomime at the Royal will never be reconstructed out
of existence. . .

After I had reported annual meetings and what-not for a
fortnight, Mills asked me to attend a Manchester music-hall,
a secondary affair, outside the city. But it meant that next
day my initials would be printed in the *Manchester Guardian*—
that is, if the notice got in the paper at all. The occasion was
a programme at the Ardwick Empire, headed by a fat comedian
named Ernie Mayne. I went to the "first house" and arrived

back at the office at nine o'clock, and set to work at once, isolating myself in an office fastness called the "library." I wrote three hundred words, and I took three hours over them. I was so late with my copy that Arthur Wallace, who that night was editing the theatre notices, missed his last tram home and had to take a taxi. He passed the notice without a "cut" or the disturbance of a comma. It began: "Mr. Ernie Mayne is indigenous to the music-hall." A more authentic *Guardian* touch was this: "Two individuals, whose names we cannot remember, did an astonishing variety of things with a violin and a piano—did everything, in fact, except play on them." The notice pleased Mills and it won me my spurs; but on looking back at it I blush. I think it was crudely imitative, and I suspect that Mills was a victim of indirect flattery. A week or two later Mills came to me one Friday evening. "You are off duty to-morrow, aren't you? It's your free week-end," he said. I replied that it was. "Well," he continued, "on Monday, Little Tich appears at the Manchester Hippodrome, and I shall put you down to write about him." He paused to note the effect on me. "But," he went on, "I want you to spend to-morrow in suitable preparation. Go into the country. Take a long walk. But take it alone. And meditate upon Little Tich." I followed the instructions to the letter.

Another instance of what young lions we were in the Mills circus: a certain Max Erard came to the Manchester Hippodrome. He played an organ in coloured electric light, and he advertised that it weighed eight tons. My notice jumped at the obvious opportunity for satire. He retaliated with a strong letter to the Editor, threatening horse-whipping. A few weeks afterwards he was back at the Manchester Hippodrome, top of the bill—"Return of the Great Max Erard." Mills again sent me to write of him; but as I thought it might seem cheap to go over the same ground, I omitted mention of Erard at all, concentrating on some more or less anonymous first turn of the show. As it happened, Sidebotham was this time taking (that is, editing) the music-hall notices, and I had attended a Monday matinée. Just before six o'clock Sidebotham came into the reporters' room and touched me gently on the arm. "You've not discussed Erard and his organ,"he said. I explained that I could add nothing to my notice of a month earlier. "But," persisted Sidebotham, "if you don't mention him again he'll think his threatening letter has dismayed us." He took me below to the Thatched House and stood me the first whisky and soda of my life. It flew to my head, and I went back to my Manchester Hippodrome notice and added, "Max Erard returns this week with his organ. It still weighs eight tons." Whether the remark is funny to-day I doubt; it was a great success in 1917. I was credibly informed that Scott himself smiled at it, after a comprehensive explanation had been given to him of all the antecedents—which must nearly have involved somebody in a short history of the British music-hall.

A remarkable sight occurred when Haslam Mills came back to the office from a theatre. He would divest himself of his beautiful white muffler and overcoat, and vanish into the depths of the office, returning with a freshly filled water-bottle and a glass, which he would place on the little desk in his room. Also he would remove his wrist-watch and lay it in front of him. He would lock himself in, not on any account to be disturbed. I calculate that on the average a notice by Mills of four hundred words occupied him an hour and a half. He was particular about the tidiness of his copy, which he wrote in green ink. "Take care always," he told his young men, "over the material appearance of your writings." (He always called them "writings.") If he had covered a page to the bottom and was then obliged to make a single alteration compelling an untidy erasure, he would re-write the page in full.

He was greatly concerned with the first sentence. "Your first sentence settles all; your first sentence determines the subsequent direction and quality of the rest."

One night after he had taken an unusually long time over a notice, and after he had gone home, I entered his room with a letter to be laid on his desk. I was performing late-duty in the reporters' room. On the floor at the base of Mills's desk I saw many crumpled balls of copy-paper. "Ah," I thought, "here are his frustrated attempts. If I study them I may learn much. I will see how the wheels go round—and how sometimes they don't go round." I picked up all the crumpled papers, unrolled them, straightened them out, and studied them. There were at least a dozen, and each contained no other words, *with not a single erasure*, than (neatly written as ever)

PALACE OF VARIETIES

Inspiration had not visited him after he had written down the heading. Very well, then. He had thrown the thing away and started fresh.

The "M. G." was a great but dangerous school for young journalists. It made us so word and phrase conscious that sometimes we suffered the embarrassment of the centipede which one day became aware of the complexity and delicacy of its muscular organization and reduced itself more or less to permanent immobility by wondering which foot to put forward next. It is no doubt true that the style is the man; it is another thing altogether that the style should be the *Manchester Guardian*. But some rare qualities came from this perhaps defective education of its writers. I do not agree with Samuel Butler's remark, "I never knew a writer yet who took the smallest pains with his style and was at the same time readable." I would amend this saying: nobody ever wrote well who at some time or other *did not* take pains with his style. In fact, until writing has by thought and practice become unselfconscious, it cannot achieve style—and by style I mean a natural easy expression which is not anonymous. The *Manchester Guardian* taught us conscience in the use of the English language, no matter whether we were writing a leader or a report of a street accident. We were not encouraged to consider our readers. "Let them educate themselves up to us," said C. P. Scott one night when I asked his advice about a paragraph sent in for the Miscellany column, which I was editing at the time—a paragraph from the Master of Balliol containing a quotation in Greek. This was the paragraph which impelled Mr. Flanagan of the composing-room to come down below one evening to see me, wearing his clean white apron, all ready for the evening's work. "I'm sorry, Mr. Cardus," he said, "but we can't set that classical quotation in the copy you've sent up to-night. You see, some years ago we stopped using Greek type. I don't know why, but we broke up the fount; there's none left." I expressed my regret and told him I would see about a translation after all. He was about to leave the room but paused and turned round to me once more, "I hope you understand, sir," he said, with a note of real anxiety in his voice, "we could have set it all right if we'd kept the Greek fount, like in the old days." He did not wish me to harbour doubts about classical culture in the composing-room of the *Manchester Guardian*.

There is a legend that the young men of the "M. G." were hypnotised at their pen-nibs' ends by the prose of C. E. Montague. The truth is that his influence on us was entirely personal; none of us dreamed of imitating him. Mills was our model; and he took an active interest in our work. Montague never altered a word of our copy. The legend would have it that he thought of the one word the writer had vainly sought, and inserted it into the article. On the contrary, he allowed many a poorly chosen adjective to pass him by. He frankly was not interested in any writer's chances of salvation except his own. But he was generous in his praise of good work done off—as he would say—your own bat. Merely to know that he was in the office, cloistered in the sanctuary with the frosted pane illuminated as though with the dry keen light of his own mind—this was ample inspiration, the better because, like the blessed sun, it fell on all of us alike, whether young bloods of writers or old drones of verbatim men.

There were the scoffers, of course. William Longden, nearly the oldest of reporters on the "M. G." or anywhere else, spoke blasphemy to me on the very first day Montague resumed office after his return from the war. "The hind's let loose again," he profaned. Longden lived and died in the belief that the art of writing consisted in as few words as possible, arranged in the simplest and most traditional order. Even Scott could not break Longden from a long habit of reporting that some event or other had taken place "under the auspices of." For several years Scott represented a Lancashire division in Parliament, and Longden, in an account of an election meeting, described him as "that sapient statesman." But after many years of unavailing instructions to the various chiefs of staff to discharge Longden, Scott lost heart and bowed to the inevitable; nobody had either the unfriendliness or the lack of humour to get rid of William Longden, who himself was always prepared to review drastically his technical value to the paper in his declining years, and even his claims to the sack on a small pension. Following an impartial scrutiny of the facts, he would say, "I'm sorry, but it can't be done." He and Shovel ton and Biggs combined in themselves about one hundred and fifty years of experience as shorthand reporters for the *Manchester Guardian*. Through their ears and by the way of their lead pencils, the policies of some of the greatest of our statesmen became known to a public which subscribed to the most influential newspaper in the Liberal stronghold of the land in a period when the electorate as a whole took the House of Commons seriously. Gladstone, Rosebery, Salisbury, Balfour, Chamberlain, Campbell-Bannerman, Asquith, Lloyd George—they were all at the mercy of the receiving sets of Shovelton, Longden and Biggs, as far as the North of England was concerned; and not one of them had cause to complain that the slightest nuance (to a comma) was ever distorted, let alone misrepresented, in the countless thousands of words taken down from them in all sorts of circumstances of confusion and heat, physical and controversial, and transcribed with enough speed to satisfy the composing-rooms of those years, when every word of type printed in the vast array of columns devoted to political speeches by the great newspapers was set letter by letter, each picked out of a case by hand.

Walter Biggs was a dapper little man with a pointed beard; he somehow looked like a French master out of the school stories read by boys once on a time. He wore eyeglasses askew and insecure, and invariably took them off to read. He was fond of telling us how ages ago when he worked in the South of England for a country newspaper it was his job one morning to print in bold letters on a sheet of brown paper, using a paint-brush, the following announcement:

DEATH OF CHARLES DICKENS

Then he stuck the poster in the office window. Like Shovelton, he assisted each Sunday in his parish church as sidesman or something. He had about him none of Shovelton's air of the world; he kept himself aloof from the reporters' room generally, yet without suggesting in the slightest that he was not one of us, down to the brightest newcomers. He frankly did not approve of C. P. Scott's attitude during the "Hang the Kaiser" delirium. He was all for smashing Germany to smithereens. One day Hedley Lockett said to him, "But, Biggs, don't you think that in these things, the question of vengeance should be left to the Almighty?" Biggs, with a far-reaching gesture of disgust, made a noise like "Pah!" and walked away. We shall never know what in their secret hearts was thought by Shovelton, Biggs and Longden of the young men of the "M. G.": those of us who were permitted so far to break the dignified traditions of anonymity in journalism as to sign our initials to our essays (always printed in "leads" to give an appearance of distinction); how did they abide us as we performed our tricks like a lot of puppies, writing not as *they* wrote, for the service and benefit of the public, but for ourselves? We were, though we did not know it, the beginning of the end of the classic age of journalism. It was one thing to encourage a young man to flash a virtuoso pen with Scott and Montague there to see that he stocked his mind all the time and tried to "see the object as in itself it really is." But it is another, and vastly different thing, to let a half-baked opportunist run loose, splashing his name at the head of the most piffling paragraphs, publicity blowing him out in a night to a reputation not pure enough to be called bubble. It would be a sign of a return to decency and integrity if newspapers on the whole went back occasionally to the anonymity which was Shovelton's and Biggs's and Longden's. C. P. Scott never once allowed his name or initials to appear in the paper attached to an article written by him. He was, of course, the Ultimate Essence, therefore not to be named. But I am wrong; the initials of C. P. Scott did appear in his paper on a memorable occasion, at the head of a main leader of his own lucid composition. I bought an early edition of the "M. G." in Sheffield one day: at the beginning of the long leader, majestic in three paragraphs—exposition, development and recapitulation—appeared this astonishing inscription: "Proof to C. P. S."

To my sorrow Scott removed me from the reporters' room after I had absorbed its atmosphere for less than a year. He called me into his room one night and, taking me by the shoulder and calling me his dear fellow, sat me down. Every "M. G." man trembled in his bowels whenever Scott did that and said that to him. He explained to me that he was short-handed in the Corridor; would I take charge of the Miscellany column and the back-page article and write a fourth leader now and again? He asked me as though I would be granting him a favour if I assented.

The Corridor in the "M. G."! This was a consummation beyond all dreams of mortal young man not under the influence of hashish. I do not know to this day whether Scott promoted me for merit or because my work in the reporters' room was persistently too decorative even for the uses of Haslam Mills. I entirely lacked interest in news, and though the "M. G." never desired that happenings in the external universe should become an obsession, it did like a reporter to admit now and then that the external universe existed, even if only as phenomena.

So in 1918 I mixed with the elect of the *Manchester Guardian*. I was given a little room at the end of the Corridor, opposite Harry Sacher. It was not truly a room of my own; it opened on a landing; one of the doors was a back entrance to the building, and every time it opened a cold blast of air withered me in winter. It was as though I were working in a public thoroughfare, especially when Powell arrived with his bicycle. Powell attended to Letters to the Editor, and he had bumps on his head just like my grandfather's; but nobody ever found out how they had come to be there. One evening, he arrived at the office very late and the bumps were gone. Side-botham endeavoured by deductive logic to account for their disappearance; but it all ended in conjecture.

Scott did not increase my stipend when he promoted me. I have explained how the reporters were granted so much a week for expenses in town during the day, lunches, teas and so on. As the editorial staff did not begin work at the office until six o'clock in the evening, no "in-town" expenses were incurred. I lost ten shillings weekly by my elevation to the Corridor of the *Manchester Guardian*. . . . I began my work as one of Scott's illustrious company, in charge of two important daily columns in his paper. The back-page article was one of the Blue Ribands of journalism, demanding experienced literary taste and judgment from its editor; and I contributed short leaders, and on Monday nights wrote theatre notices, and in my spare time I once again assisted Scott as a semi-secretary—all for two pounds sterling a week, less fourpence for National Insurance. It was well worth it.

.   .   .   .   .   .

My life became strenuous now in work, stir of life and nervous strain. C. P. Scott was unsparing in his demands on all of us, beginning with himself. But most of the Corridor had in the course of years achieved some autonomy, some measure of self-determination. I was taken possession of, body and soul; Scott in his zeal did not hesitate to use indirect coercion on a slave who was willing enough to forge his own shackles. There was scarcely a moment from waking to sleeping when something was not on my mind. I walked the Manchester streets by pure instinct; I snatched meals anyhow, and developed a dyspepsia which I tried to assuage by charcoal biscuits and bismuth. One day in my preoccupations I walked down a public lavatory in Albert Square and discovered myself in the Ladies' reserve; and an old woman who was in charge threw up her hands at the sight of me and "shoo'd" me out saying, "Get away from here, you impudent young rascal!" A more unjust suspicion than this has never been levelled at anybody since the world began.

Each day challenged wit and presence of mind. To call on Scott at The Firs most mornings was in itself an education in self-reliance and nerve. He must have reconsidered his decision that he was "congenitally incapable" of using a secretary. He gave me awkward letters to answer, including one from a Welsh parson who wrote at length drawing Scott's attention to the fact that all, or nearly all, the warring nations were calling upon the same heavenly Power for protection and aid. "Now," wrote the Welsh parson, "now, Sir, you will realise that this state of affairs places God in an extremely difficult position."

I cannot believe that any *Guardian* man ever knocked at a door behind which Scott waited for him and did not feel a need to pull himself together. Not that he was at all like the legend created around him by people who, because he did not like them, were never allowed to approach him. Or rather, I should say, because he did not like their opinions. Scott was not so much interested in people as in principles, and though he was a master of honest compromise, his adjustments did not go as far as a broadening of human sympathies. He could respect a principle at war with his own, and he could admire those who held it. But I doubt if he could like them. He was of the "what is rational is real" school. He had no dramatic sense; I mean that he could not see a human being as mixed in the elements, not to be judged entirely from standards of social good. He had humour of a kind, but at bottom it was critical. He had no patience at all for a gesture; he even prohibited the use of the word in the columns of the *Manchester Guardian*. I once tried a gesture in a scene with him that arose out of a question of English usage. In my hurry one night to send up the Miscellany column to the composing-room, I allowed a contributed paragraph to get into print with "from thence" in it. As soon as I saw the paper next morning I knew I was, as they say, "for it." Scott went through every column lynx-eyed, all excepting the market reports. Sure as death, he tackled me without delay. His whiskers clove the air when I entered his room. "You should know by now," he said with infinite charm and menace, "that the term 'from thence' is not English and is therefore banned from the *Manchester Guardian*. A man might as well say 'to thither.'"

With the bravery of the young I retaliated. I knew as well as Scott himself that "from thence" is vile, but some devil took hold of me, and I pointed out to him that there were precedents for the use of "from thence" in the works of accredited masters of English literature.

"Really?" he queried, aiming an arrow at me from his eye, "and pray where?"

HASLAM MILLS
Photo by F. W. Schmidt, Manchester

"In Henry Fielding in general, and *Tom Jones* in particular," I brazenly replied.

Without hesitation he said, with a delicacy of accent that froze my marrow, "Really? Well, my dear fellow, all I can say is that Mr. Fielding would not use' from thence' twice on my newspaper. Good-night." I got out of the room as abruptly as I could without falling down.

I am, during this period, dramatic critic at a first night of an Arnold Bennett play in Liverpool; I am contributing short leaders regularly; I am all the time getting through the routine of my job, still preparing the material for Miscellany. (Gordon Phillips had not yet returned from France.) Once I was compelled to compose the whole of this column between five o'clock and seven, because a breakdown in the Christmas post left me barren of outside contributions. The back-page article involved a careful selection from a mass of material supplied by aspirants to fame in the column from all over the country, known and unknown. This part of my work was watched over by Arthur Wallace with his own fatherly and humorous eye. Like a ghost out of the past, Arthur Symons sent an essay. I had included his *Studies in Seven Arts* in my Schema years before. I have an uneasy feeling that it was not worthy of him and that I had to reject it. When Montague returned, he gave himself up to leader-writing and private authorship. He seldom went to the theatre—which of course had lost quality during the war, especially in Manchester. Miss Horniman sold her control of the Gaiety Theatre and it was turned into a cinema. It was round about this time that Ellen Terry, an old lady now, a little deaf and a little blind, and of graciousness unparalleled, was obliged by need to appear at this cinema that once was Miss Horniman's famous theatre of the intellectual drama. Twice nightly Ellen Terry tried to recite from Shakespeare, but her mind was likely to wander and forget; and an audience to whom she was a legend listened respectfully to her. I spoke with Ellen Terry after one of these performances for the first and only time in my life—spoke to the heroine I had seen from the gallery at the Theatre Royal across the road, when I was a boy making my living by selling chocolates in Pitt Hardacre's Comedy Theatre, now this same lose temple of repertory

showing Mary Pickford and a fat American comic called
John Bunny, Ellen Terry thrown in.

.   .   .   .   .

With Montague out of action as dramatic critic, and Allan
Monkhouse being nobly ravaged by illness and Arthur Wallace
away in America on some mission, I was entrusted with the
dramatic criticism of the "M. G."—another curious turn in
my wheel. Langford was swallowing all the music, and
there was a lot of it in 1919, the heyday of the Beecham seasons
at the Opera House, seasons extending to months, two matinées
every week, and Hallé Concerts and Promenade Concerts, and
chamber concerts unending. Langford went to all of them,
even to midday organ recitals. I naturally thought he was
grudging not to give me a chance; he knew that I was preparing myself, when time and opportunity should occur, for
music criticism. (For all my divided labours, I maintained a
two-hour daily study of music or the literature of music.) I
discovered later that Langford, for all his greatness of mind,
suffered from a sense of inferiority; he was actually afraid
of losing his job. Scott did not understand him and could
not like a man as natural and as unbuttoned in speech and
dress as Langford.

But I was not particularly anxious to enter music criticism
under the shadow of Langford; at any rate not until I had
come to some confidence in myself as a writer working more
or less a seam of my own. Nobody respects a deputy. Dramatic
criticism on the "M. G." still counted for something. Each
Tuesday, whole columns were reserved for it. And Montague
watched over every word. For weeks after he had returned
from the war he looked at me as we passed in the Corridor, as
shy as myself, no doubt. The glances he cast at me, as though
from the inside of a prison of thick-ribbed ice, were encourag-
ing; he *conveyed* approval of me. He sent me to Liverpool
when Arnold Bennett visited the Repertory Theatre there for
the production of a stage version of his novel *Sacred and Profane
Love*. Between the acts I saw Bennett, a pouter-pigeon of
crinkled shirt-front and tails. He was glad to meet a young
man from the "M. G.," though he asked where was Montague.

He asked me what I thought of the play, and I confessed I was disappointed. He indicated the chattering people in the foyer by a sideways cock of his top-knot. In his jerky high voice, he said:

"But th-th-*they* seem to be l-l-lapping it up, all right, d-d-don't they?"

He inquired what were my ideas about a career, so I asked him if it was possible for a writer to live for long in the provinces and come to anything. He doubted it, and as the bell rang calling us back for another act, he said: "But d-don't c-c-consider leaving the *M-Manchester* Guardian for j-j-just a few p-pounds extra. M-Money is n-no use, my boy, except in l-l-l—(then, with a high explosion)—LARGE quantities."

Dramatic critic until after midnight, and humble factotum to Scott at ten o'clock next morning! Nobody dared complain of weariness to Scott. Illness he could not understand, though he tried sympathetically to get one's point of view. He himself was never tired; and he conquered ailments to the flesh as never Spartan before. Every night, or early morning, after the first edition was off the machines, he put a muffler round his neck—no overcoat despite the terrible Manchester winter—and he rode home four miles on his push-bicycle. Often I left the office a little in advance of him, missing the last tram and unable to afford a taxi. I would see him go by me head down, pedalling patiently, snow and wind in the face. Next morning he was at his desk at The Firs, fresh as eternal vigilance.

One midnight he skidded on his bicycle in the slush of Albert Square. A policeman came to his rescue, picked him up and after seeing that no bones were broken, said: "You ought not to be out as late as this, sir—in this weather."

Scott told him he had been working late.

"Gawd!" said the policeman, "at your time of life? And if I may ask, sir, who do you work for?"

"The *Manchester Guardian*," replied Scott.

"Well, all as I can say is this, sir," said the policeman, "the *Manchester Guardian* ought to be bloody well ashamed of itself keeping an old man like you out this time of the night."

Scott, it was vowed, circulated this story himself next day, and for the rest of his life, with surprising gusto.

But it was risky to try to be funny with him. He sent me late one evening a flimsy Press Association report about damage done by coast erosion at some South of England seaside resort, and asked me to write a short leader about it. My views on coast erosion were not abundant enough to run even to four hundred words, so in despair I attempted brightness. I was pleased when, by inspiration, I imagined the esplanade at Southend ravaged by the encroaching waters; I drew a picture of the town council sadly contemplating the ruined prospect, and I concluded with these lines:

> They wept like anything to see
> Such quantities of sand.

Pleased as Punch with myself I took the leader in to Scott and waited confidently for the proof. After half an hour, Scott sent for me.

"Your 'short,'" he said: "I don't see the point of the quotation,' they wept like anything to see such quantities of sand.'"

I explained that it was a quotation from Lewis Carroll.

"And why did they weep?" asked Scott.

I could not give a satisfactory explanation, whereupon Scott sternly rebuked me. "Never," he said, "employ any quotation of which you do not understand the meaning." He dismissed me, and next day the paper came out with the shortest of all short leaders on record. It simply stated the facts: the encroaching sea was causing anxiety on certain points of the coast. "What," concluded the leader, "are our engineers going to do about it?" Never again did I try to be flippant in a *Manchester Guardian* leader, while Scott remained All-Father.

He was good for a young man, none the less. From time to time he would send me a note saying he had liked something. He became almost fatherly. He even recommended a short holiday after I had been compelled to go to bed for a week with influenza. I took the chance and went to Llanfairfechan. A day after my arrival there, a pile of books came to me from the "M. G." with a note from C. P. S. As he was concerned about the hours hanging heavily on my hands, he thought

I might like to do some reviewing for the paper. He was not consciously mean; he just *gave* himself to the *Manchester Guardian* and expected his staff to give likewise. If his ideas about remuneration were severely economical the reason was not crude parsimony. He simply could not believe in making life easy for anybody. I think, too, that he looked far ahead and saw the coming of hard times for a newspaper of the "M. G.' s" uncompromising ideals. He would, I am certain, have gladly starved in the gutter on its behalf. So would I myself. And so have I—almost.

I had literally to dig gradual increases of salary out of the paper as the years went by. In the course of twenty-two years, my "emoluments" rose from £2 a week to £1,100 a year. I think I am the only "M. G." man who has ever been paid four figures annually for nothing but writing: I mean without having to combine writing with some administrative work in the office. Of course, when I achieved the thousand-a-year mark, I was a cricket correspondent as well as music critic.

In Scott's closing years I received an offer from the *Sunday Times*. Herbert Sidebotham had left the "M. G.," and after an interlude with Northcliffe, he settled down as "Scrutator" for the rest of his life. It was Sidebotham who brought about the invitation to join the staff of the *Sunday Times*. I laid the matter before Scott and he put his hand on my shoulder and said—as always in the circumstances, to anybody—"I have never stood in the way of any man's advancement." I had no intention, deep down, of leaving the "M. G."; I brought the offer to his notice to give him a sign that my value was rising in journalism at large. He retained me by an advance of a hundred a year.

A dear tyrant, the "M. G." I have never been able to break free from it. Others have made the wrench and have prospered in the accumulation of earthly goods. I doubt if they have ever afterwards known the happiness and the pride that comes from membership on the staff of the "M. G." Myself, I have, after much wrestling with beasts of Ephesus, remained on the "M. G."—once at the sacrifice of princely emoluments for a three years' contract with the *Evening Standard*. Michael Wardell pursued me relentlessly in 1935 or thereabouts. I am

ashamed to admit that by word of mouth I led him to think
that he had captured me. One day of imagined severance from
the "M. G." cured me; I thought I had decided to tear myself
away, and I wandered about the cricket field at Cheltenham
saying to myself, "This is my last season; my last few columns,
free to write anything, as much as I like." Then I went to
Salzburg for the music festival. That settled it; you had only
to tell any musician in Europe, any man of letters, artist—
anybody who was anybody, in fact, that you belonged to the
Manchester Guardian and at once they met you not as a press-
man, not as a journalist, but as a writer, free and civilised.

This crisis with the *Evening Standard* occurred after the
deaths of C. P. Scott and his son, Ted. Crozier, the new
editor, wrote a letter to me while I was at Salzburg. The paper
could not compete with the *Evening Standard*, but they would
add another £100 to my £1,000 a year. It was not the money
but one phrase of Crozier's that settled the issue, something to
the effect that on the *Guardian* I could give play to my "ideas
and ideals." He said the truth. And through him it was
really C. P. Scott that spoke; he was, in death as in life, in
spirit as in flesh, a tyrant *jure divino*.

    ·   ·   ·   ·   ·   ·

But reverting, as Shovelton would say, to my 'prentice
years on the "M. G."—though the glance forward into the
future of my status and income was designed, for sake of
ironic light and shade, and was not a mere digression. I have
looked at the files of the paper covering my first months on
the "Corridor." On the main literary page, I find to my
amazement (for I had forgotten it) a two-column review
over my initials, a day-of-publication review at that, of Sir
Percy Scott's *Reminiscences*. With much satisfaction I quote
the following passage—remember, it is by a young man
letting himself go under the very nose of the Jehovah of
editors:

"One gets the impression that Sir Percy Scott has passed
the major portion of his life beating the air before purblind
First Lords in a more or less vain endeavour to drive into

their skulls such facts as that a battleship will be all the better for having a gun on it. . . . The best idea of Sir Percy Scott's book will be obtained from a glance at the index under the category 'Admiralty.' Here are the references to what may be called the Sir Percy leitmotif. For instance: 'Admiralty, dilatory methods of VII-IX, 27, 41, 155, 269, 295, 308, 323; state of confusion in war-time, 200; blunders of, 276-8'; and so forth. As we read on we come nearer and nearer to the conclusion that the British Navy was an extraordinary illusion for many years—in fact, until Sir Percy Scott, Lord Fisher and Lord Jellicoe got their way. For years did the British Navy apparently impose on trusting foreigners when all the time they might have sailed up the Thames in perfect safety and done their worst.

"Sir Percy claims with proper pride that he was the pioneer of the system of director firing. His explanation of this is technical, and a layman cannot pretend to express an opinion on it. But the principle at bottom—which is that you are more likely to hit an object if you know where it is—must be acclaimed a sound one."

The austere *Manchester Guardian*!—and we young men were allowed to run about its columns like monkeys from tree to tree, throwing our nuts right and left. There was nothing we touched that we did not strive to adorn; not a paragraph appeared in the paper which did not contain evidence that a human being had written it. Even the anonymous reviews of Christmas books for boys and girls were done as though well worth somebody's while. If we could not (yet, at any rate) live on the heights with Montague, Monkhouse, James Bone, and Langford, very well then; we took our chances.

In a column article headed "Christmas Books for Boys and Girls," I unearth the following incredible passage from my pen. I am certain I could not (given the same unpromising material) compose the like of it nowadays:

"Judge Parry once said, if memory be trustworthy, that it is harder to write good stories for boys and girls than for grown-ups. Boys take their reading with such ruthless commonsense; they have no literary fads about them to be exploited by the writer who has nothing to say but who knows the tricks of the trade. The grown-up can be bluffed by flattery of his sense of style or of his so-called 'sense of psychological values.' He will see all sorts of hidden significances, fine shades, oblique revelations of scene and character in dialogue written this way—it is fashionable at the moment, in fact:

"'And so you——?'

"'Crudely speaking, yes. I might have.'

"'But that would have involved another?'

"Pearson looked at the right side of his shining briar.

"'Involved?' he said. 'If you like—yes, involved.'

"Blake's eyes glistened.

"'So that even if——'

"Pearson slightly inclined his head towards the window.

"'Obviously.'

"You cannot spin words like that with boys; they will have their authors up and doing, inventing, telling the tale from start to finish."

I quote these ebullitions to convey the yeastiness, the sap of apprentice days, under Scott and Montague.

Let the reader not jump to conclusions. It was not a case of undergraduate coxcombry. As we performed our somersaults, our tight-rope walking day by day, we were not allowed to forget that two and sometimes three ruthless ringmasters looked on, ready to bring us to order with a crack of the whip. Nothing essentially spurious ever got past Scott, Montague or Sidebotham. One night, I gave a leader to Sidebotham; he was in charge while Scott was in London seeing Lloyd George. Sidebotham, after reading a page or so, tore the copy into two exact halves and threw it in the wastepaper basket. He didn't compromise and stick it on the spike, where though pierced vitally, it might remain preserved. No; he destroyed it in my presence saying "Ha! ha! ha!" Then he rose from his chair even as shame was consuming me and turning to black hate; he gave me the smile of Bacchus, put a hand on my shoulder and said: "Come, my dear fellow; let's go and have a drink before closing-time." Not a word passed between us about the annihilated leader. Next day a leader on the same subject appeared written by himself, containing one or two ideas of mine, now presented and argued with modesty and wit. I shall never forget Sidebotham's "Ha! ha! ha!" that night; it was a laugh that went beyond onomatopœia, and approximated to parts of speech, which spoke volumes.

Montague gave me more and more rope. He let me loose in a Shakespeare Season of Sir Frank Benson. I am proud that in those days, when the London critics generally sneered at Benson, I felt his curious genius for the grotesque: he sometimes looked like Doré's Don Quixote, lean, gaunt—with a visage, not a mere face. About his production of *Hamlet* Montague gave me licence to write this notice:

"Sir Frank Benson's *Hamlet* is a dramatic rather than a philosophical study. Shakespeare would have liked it but not Coleridge. There are no metaphysics about Sir Frank. His attitude to the play would seem to be that if once you begin looking into the philosophy of it all, especially into the cloud-compelling stuff put there by the higher criticism, you will never be done. After all, *Hamlet* was written for the theatre, not for the study—though we frequently have to remind ourselves of the fact in this country. Even Charles Lamb thought *Hamlet* should never be acted.' What man is there,' asked Mrs. Curdle of Nicholas Nickleby, 'who can present before us all those changing and prismatic colours with which the character of Hamlet is invested?' Whereat Mr. Curdle responded: 'What man indeed? Hamlet? Pooh. Hamlet is gone, perfectly gone.' This was the satire of Dickens on Shakespeare criticism of the Gervinus-Coleridge school; and it will serve a useful purpose even at the present time. There are still learned folk who cannot see what lusty dramatic stuff *Hamlet* contains; the view is obscured by metaphysical fogs, 'the changing prismatic colours,' beaten up by exegetists. Yet, as Sir Frank Benson gave us to understand last night, Hamlet remains, as it was in the beginning, first and foremost a thing of the theatre. Shakespeare would probably go into fits at the schoolman's notions of *Hamlet*. 'Not an acting play?' we can imagine him saying, 'and I exploited every trick of the period—all the popular wheezes; a ghost; a mad scene; poison; a bout with rapiers; a play within a play; rivers of blood and a shambles to round-off everything.' The truth is that none of us nowadays can quite see the play as the Elizabethans saw it. Shakespeare no doubt dealt primarily with the old 'Hystorie of Hamlet,' attended to the tastes of audience, seldom going out of his way to dodge the conventions and fashions of the theatre as he found them. But his genius slopped over—to use the elegant term of Artemus Ward; there crept in his own questioning of life, death and immortality.

"All of which may be discussed to-day in terms not known or grasped by Elizabethan playgoers; and that is where our high priorities come in—but not pray God—into the theatre! So much does Sir Frank Benson see *Hamlet* from an actor's point of view that he does not hesitate to clear the way of the slightest obstacle to swift dramatic momentum. The famous' Wassail' speech, for example, which Hamlet indulges even while the visitation of the ghost is imminent, was shortened by several lines at this performance. The speech is, of course, dramatically irrelevant; it brings us up with a jerk even while we are riding to a climax. Shakespeare wrote it no doubt simply because in the theatre of his period the word and conceit were as important as the action; the groundlings looked for a set speech much as the audiences at Italian opera look for an aria. Ignoring historical influences on stage technique, Coleridge informs us that the inopportune discourse about breaking down the pales and forts of reason was an exercise on Hamlet's part to smother impatience by abstract reason.

"There was little abstract reasoning in the *Hamlet* of last night; it came to us as the finest acting play in the world, tense and vividly real. Sir Frank gives us as likeable a Hamlet as may be found on the English stage to-day, a passionate Hamlet as much a man of heart as of mind, with more of the grotesque rather than the classical, infinitely gentle at times—he is not harsh with Ophelia—yet mingling strength in proportion, though no longer does he carry the corpse of Polonius into the wings over his shoulder."

Nobody, surely, looked at a young man of the *Manchester Guardian* of those days without murmuring, "the wonder grew, That one small head should carry all he knew." What did Montague really think of this notice? Myself, I would have cut it with as close an imitation of Sidebotham's "Ha! ha! ha!" as I could manage. Doubtless the admirers of A. B. Walkley will appreciate the skill with which I utilised his views on Coleridge and the Wassail speech. Yet there was the root of the matter in the young man; the notice puts certain points of view about *Hamlet* as an acting play not common a quarter of a century ago. I wonder how many hours I spent mugging-up my material; and I forget whether I wrote the notice before or after the performance.

I reproduce these early works of mine for two reasons. I wish to convey an idea how the *Manchester Guardian* tested and trained a young man, but more to the point, because it pleases me to read them—as any man must be pleased as he looks back on the years in which he first spread his wings, and risked falls which a later prudence would not have countenanced. Such reproductions may not interest the reader; but after all, this is my autobiography, not his; he is under no obligation to read further in it; he was under none to begin. Interest in autobiography should begin at home, and though I hope to present my life and its setting attractively to others, my chief intent is to delight and engross myself. A modest or inhibited autobiography is written without entertainment to the writer and read with distrust by the reader. An autobiography should suggest that the writer is living his life again, day to day, or year to year. Later experience should have influence on the literary art only; it should not affect the scheme of things and betray that the writer is describing events from the point of view of the haven reached in the end after all—or not reached. An autobiography is not a biography; on every page the reader must be persuaded to think that what's to come is still unsure. At least, that is my idea of an autobiography; and I am trying to write one like it now.

.   .   .   .   .   .

In 1919 John Drinkwater's *Abraham Lincoln* was the play
of the year; it at last came to Manchester, everybody talking
about it. We on the "M. G." took it for granted that Achilles
would now come out of his tent; Montague surely would
deal with the masterpiece that had caused a stir in the English
theatre after four years of null-and-voidity.

On the Sunday evening before the Monday of the first night
in Manchester of *Abraham Lincoln*, Montague sent the press-
tickets for the production up to my room, with a note:
"C. E. M.—N. C. This play's had a long innings. Suppose
you take an over now—at Walkley's end." This was not just
a feather to put in my cap: it was a whole plume. But I knew
nothing about the play; and what was more, I was not
especially informed about the background of Lincoln: I knew
him mainly on the strength of a phrase about fooling some
of the people some of the time, etc., and so forth. My Schema
had not, obviously, been comprehensive enough. Here is the
notice I composed between eleven o'clock and midnight of
December 8th, 1919, after my usual day's work:

"A man who has been long in the wilderness is not
likely to ponder with the air of a connoisseur the drink he
may come across. Any old water will do. Playgoers had
been in the wilderness for a long time when Mr. Drinkwater's play arrived; we had traversed a Sahara of barren-
ness. Our tongues were hanging out. Naturally, *Abraham
Lincoln*, with its sincerity and flavour of literature, seemed
nectar to us. Again, there was the circumstance of the
moment in which we found it—the penultimate crisis of
the war, with America turning the scale and President
Wilson going forth holding aloft the torch and himself
awakening an echo of Lincoln. All of which framed Mr.
Drinkwater's play most aptly. Well, *Abraham Lincoln* has
been a long time coming to Manchester, and meanwhile
we are on the way back to a normal life in the theatre; our
palates are quite getting the old edge on; we can afford
now to turn over a new wine on our tongues. And the hour
which gave *Abraham Lincoln* its immense topical significance is gone; a good many of the captains and the
kings have departed. Nothing is left for us to-day but to

see the play as a dramatic fact, a thing of the theatre pure and simple.

"From this point of view we can understand better the difficulties which were in Mr. Drinkwater's way. The truth is that Lincoln was rather a stiff handful for a dramatist to tackle. Frankly, Lincoln does not give one the stuff of drama. He was perhaps a most imposing figure of a states-man—a Carlyle must have discerned trailing clouds of glory hanging about him, an occasion for another pæan on hero-worship. But the man was too sure of himself for the tragic muse; in all his vicissitudes God was with him he was sure. There was no equal struggle between the powers of good and evil for his soul; there were no ironic dis-sonances struck out by the internal life of his spirit and the outward show of his conduct. Even his death did not bring that sense of frustration without which we can have no tragedy; his end indeed, was a consummation; he might have chanted Nunc Dimittis with his last breath. He was not broken on the wheel of a flawed temperament, as Hamlet was or Michael Henchard. A great ideal urged him on and his faith and strength never really wavered. There was nothing in him of that awe of destiny which made Novalis say so darkly that character is fate. Lincoln stands to-day as a type of the conquering hero; young men are asked to study his life and take heart in the example of it. We do not contemplate Coriolanus that way, or for that matter any other dramatic figure. The gods were directing the storm on which Lincoln rode; they were accessories after the fact of his greatness. You cannot say of Lincoln, as you can say of every great tragic figure in life and literature:

"And the end men looked for cometh not,
And a path was there where no man sought;
So hath it fallen here. . . .

"Mr. Drinkwater seems hardly to have perceived the lack of dramatic stuff in his hero—clearly he did not intend simply to present Lincoln to our historical sense in a chronicle play; he himself has told us his purpose was the drama. Yet he took few of the liberties needed by obligations to dramatic significance. There is no suggestion, for instance, that we have here a Lincoln in whom the elements are mixed and turbulent (which of course might have been an historically false Lincoln but one dramatically potential); Mr. Drinkwater even reduces whatever obstacles Lincoln *had* to get over. There is, as a result, too little clash of character. We cannot realize the strength of Lincoln because nobody against him in the play is fit to tie his bootlaces. A chance was missed over Chase, who is left by Mr. Drink-water a mere stick. He might have been given a stature sufficient to provide some point of resistance to Lincoln; and from this an amount of conflict might have come. Chase was no man of straw; Lincoln respected his ability; also he saw the trouble that could easily have sprung from Chase's intrigues. Chase was sincere, too, in his belief that the country was going to the dogs because his advice was turned down. At any rate, only a little dramatic licence was necessary to make a fit protagonist out of Chase. As it is, Lincoln is left to enjoy a walk-over. Seward and Hook, even, are mainly quiescent. The picture of Lincoln, though, is beautifully drawn—in the St. Gaudens rather than the Barnard manner. Mr. Drinkwater does not ever write in the rough-hewn manner. He gives us a Lincoln with an affecting simplicity, strong in a gentlemanly way, tender in a womanly way, religious, patient, kindly. A Lincoln so to say, in a nice top-hat, a much more handsome hat than the one which, to the horror of Mrs. Lincoln, he actually did wear."

It is a notice heavy with the seriousness of immaturity, yet in the year 1919 it was not undistinguished; also it took an extremely unpopular view of the play. Montague did not disturb a comma of my "copy"; and next day another message was sent to me from behind the escarpment of shyness.

.   .   .   .

I have here brought the reader to my position on the *Manchester Guardian* as it was two years and nine months after I first walked trembling into the reporters' room; and

I have failed in artfulness if he is not now asking himself
two or three questions: "What about your cricket writing?
Where did that come in? And where's the music?" At the
end of nearly three years' work on one of the greatest newspapers in the world, I had arrived at the age of twenty-nine
and established myself as a reasonably competent all-round
journalist. Young men of the "M. G." were not, contrary to
a widespread belief, merely decorative. From Montague downwards, Scott insisted on technique from his staff resourceful
enough at a pinch to cope with any of the day's and the
night's challenges. Allan Monkhouse, known as the author
of *Men and Ghosts* to a select few, an artist in shades so fine
that compared to him Henry James was substantial, not to
say carnal, was in charge of the "Manchester Cotton" columns,
and he went on 'Change every afternoon to get the prices.
Herbert Sidebotham, a leader-writer born and Balliolised,
wrote the music criticism of the first performance in Manchester of *Der Rosenkavalier*. Scott did not believe in overdone specialism. The first leader-note he ever asked me to
write was about the sinking of some ship by a German sub-
marine in a neutral zone during 1917. At first I thought
Scott had sent the request for this leader to the wrong man,
and I went downstairs to see him. I explained that I knew
next to nothing about neutral zones or International law.
"We are shorthanded to-night," he said, "and there are plenty
of books and authorities in the office. You feel rightly about
this sinking, don't you? Very well then, my dear fellow;
express your feelings—and look up the facts for yourself!"

It is not surprising—is it then?—that I am tired of meeting
people who after first of all asking me if cricket was the subject that got me on the staff of the "M. G.," proceed to betray
bewilderment that also I should write on music. I have
already emphasised that as a subject for my pen cricket never
entered into my calculations in all the years when I was
trying to equip myself as a writer.

I became the cricket correspondent of the "M. G." by
sheer chance. In March, 1919, I suffered a breakdown, and
after I returned to my job, W. P. Crozier suggested one day
that I might recuperate myself by sitting in the air one or
two days at Old Trafford. First-class cricket was about to be

played again, experimentally with two-day matches after four years of silence. I might write reports on a match now and then, suggested Crozier. So I went one Monday morning to Old Trafford and described the first game there since 1914. It was understood that this open-air occupation would not interfere with my usual work on the paper; I returned to the Corridor each evening, as usual, after a day of cricket. So little did I dream of making cricket a part of my career as a writer that for long I contented myself with the barest descriptions, done in the conventional manner. Here is an extract from the first cricket report I ever wrote in my life; it appeared in the *Manchester Guardian* in June, 1919:

"Lancashire opened the new season at Old Trafford yesterday. It was a lovely day and a good crowd attended. It was indeed easy to feel the sentimental aspect of the occasion. One came into the enclosure from the dusty town, and there were for many an old cricket-lover strong tugs on the heartstrings as they saw again the soft green grass, splashed with spring sunshine, and the pavilion and the county flag streaming in the wind with the red rose on it.

"The excellent progress made in the match almost convinced one that the new-time conditions are already reacting favourably. Lancashire, batting first, completed an innings of 280, and dismissed Derbyshire for 136, causing them to go in again and lose two wickets for 33 (under the follow-on rule affecting a two-day first-class county match). The Lancashire batting was patchy. Makepeace and Hallows scored 43 for the first wicket . . . Tyldesley began shakily, settling down afterwards, and showing all his old mastery over the square-cut."

You will observe how conscientiously I observed the unities—if I may use so strong a term; how I entered into the freemasonry of the cricket-reporter of the period. "Lancashire, batting first, completed an innings of 280" . . . "Tyldesley began shakily, settling down afterwards" . . . "the excellent progress made. . . ." It sounds like a superior young man's parody of the "old-stagers" and of the Press Association. But it wasn't. I simply had no intention of writing on cricket for any length of time; this was a spare-time affair (for which I received no extra payment) and I fitted myself into the idioms and procedure of the sporting writers of 1919. I should have been the most flabbergasted individual in the world if anybody gifted in prophecy had told me as I sat at Old Trafford on that Monday in June 1919 that in another year or two I would be more or less famous up and down the land as a writer on cricket; and that the day was approaching when I would deal with Woolley of Kent in these words:

"His cricket is compounded of soft airs and flavours. And the very brevity of summer is in it. Woolley, so the statisticians tell us, often plays a long innings. But Time's a cheat, as the old song says. The brevity in Woolley's batting is a thing of pulse and spirit, not to be checked by clocks, but only to be apprehended by imagination. He is always about to lose his wicket; his runs are thin-spun. His bat is charmed, and most of us, being reasonable, do not believe in charms. There is a miracle happening on the cricket field whenever Woolley stays in two or three hours; an innings by him is almost too insubstantial for this world. His cricket has no bastions; it is poised precariously—at any rate, that is how the rational mind perceives it. But for that matter, all the loveliness of the world seems no more lasting than the dew on the grass, seems no more than the perfume and suppliance of a minute. Yet the miracle of renewal goes on, and all the east winds in the world may blow in vain. So with Woolley's cricket; the lease of it is in the hands of the special providence which looks after things that will not look after themselves . . . I can think of cricket by Woolley which has inexplicably found me murmuring to myself (that I might get the best out of it):

"Lovely are the curves of the white owl sweeping,
    Wavy in the dusk lit by one large star.

I admit, O reader, that an innings by Woolley has nothing to do with owls and dusk and starlight. I am trying to describe an experience of the fancy. I am talking of cadences, of dying-falls common to all the beauty of the world."

"And a path was there where no man sought"—it is certain that I never sought the path that led me to my writing on cricket, to my *Good Days* and *Days in the Sun*, one of which books was read by Arthur Schnabel who assured me he enjoyed it though understanding not the first thing of the game. I have been told by solemn-minded friends that I have wasted much of fancy and imagination on cricket, and that it is a pity I did not keep to the straight and narrow path of criticism of music and the allied and recognised arts, according to my original plan. I had no choice. In 1920, I was asked by the "M. G." to write on cricket every day, and to travel the country from Old Trafford to Lord's, from Sheffield to Canterbury. Here at any rate was a chance of a summer's rest from Manchester and office routine. Better still, I was given a substantial increase of salary; it was elevated to £5 weekly. And I could see England for the first time.

It was with very conscious art that I entered into my first and "yellow" period as a writer on cricket, seeing the players set against the blue sky and green grass. I overwrote, no doubt; but in the beginnings of anything you must take risks and explore your palette entirely. Then, later, with increase of experience and observation, the texture of your writing will strengthen even as it rejects excess and throws off the superfluous adjective. When first I wrote with serious intent on cricket, I got my images, my metaphors, before I went to a match. My first books, *Days in the Sun* and *A Cricketer's Book*, are obviously the "literary efforts" of one who is keeping his eye not so much on the ball as on his pen and style.

My later writings about the game were, as far as I could make them, based first on observation; only after I had looked at the object closely did I seek for the exact phrase; and even then it was humour and irony that guided the choice. I put aside the consciously picturesque note. None the less nearly all my critics persisted, whenever I produced another book on cricket, with their old labels about my "lyrical muse," my "rhapsodies in green," my "heroics."

Between 1920 and 1939, I wrote roughly 8,000 words a

week on cricket for the *Manchester Guardian* every summer
from early May to mid-August—nearly two million words
in twenty years. It is possible that towards the end I was apt
to repeat myself. From these two million words, I made my
books on cricket, seldom changing substantially a word in
articles often written in the confusion of crowds and press-
boxes. One or two of these books will, I think, last as long as
The Compleat Angler or The Hambledon Men. But never have
I regarded my cricket as more than a means to an end; that
end being always music and the savouring of life by a free
and civilised mind, as far as I could make mine free and
civilised.

To-day I look back with affection on all the days I have
lived in the fresh air and sunshine at both ends of the world;
and I have found both art and richness of nature on the cricket
field. As I say, I believe my books on the game will live. None
the less, it is as silly to describe me as a writer on cricket as
it is to speak of James Agate primarily as a writer on the drama
or, if I may use a stronger figure, to speak of Hazlitt as a
writer on Indian Jugglers and Fives. Nor am I properly
described as a music critic. I am, again like James Agate and
Hazlitt—and Bernard Darwin—before all else simply a writer,
with summer and cricket and the English scene one of my
themes; and music and what it means of genius and art, the
other. Cricket opened my door wide at last; and I could walk
henceforward in my proper direction—to music. It was the
idea of W. P. Crozier, until the other day the editor of the
Manchester Guardian.[1] He saw in cricket, before I myself so
much suspected it, an immediate career for my talents.

But—and I wish this to be the most important sentence
in the book—before Crozier discovered "Cricketer" for me,
the fates had convincingly revealed the future music critic of
the "M. G." to C. P. Scott, It all happened, even yet again, in
the chanciest way. Scott never went to concerts and was not
musical. By sheer vicissitude of international politics the
Russian singer Rosing entered Scott's life; they became
friends and Rosing stayed at The Firs with Scott while he
gave two concerts in Manchester. Langford wrote on the
first of these recitals, and though he appreciated the art of

[1] He has recently died—a great editor and a good man.

Rosing up to a point, he was much too deeply immersed in the style and musical form of German Lieder to see eye to eye with Rosing's and Moussorgsky's methods.

Scott sent me the tickets for Rosing's second concert. I felt awkward about it; for by now I had begun a friendship which for nine years was an enrichment of life. I don't think Langford took it very well at the time. Scott himself attended these Rosing recitals; his only appearances in a Manchester concert hall in living memory. Here is my notice of Rosing as it appeared in the *Manchester Guardian* of January 13th, 1920:

"Rosing's programme at the Gentlemen's Concert last night was, until he flooded it generously with encores at the end, arranged in contrasted groups, after his customary manner, the titles this time being' Christ,' 'The Seasons,' 'Love,' and 'Suffering.' And again we had a recital remarkable for the extraordinary range of the singer's style and the dramatic truth of everything he touched. Those of his critics present w ho, though they admit Rosing's interpretative genius yet deny him qualities of pure song, must have been considerably astonished at the amount of lyrical beauty he spilled over the music that craved for it. Duparc's 'Extase' was given with a tone of such fugitive loveliness that the song floated through the hall as lightly as petals from a flower. Brahms's 'Serenade,' given as an encore, had the most winning vivacity in the world; one has not heard it done with so light a touch and so sunny a grace since Gerhardt was here. And in Grieg's rather drawing-roomy 'Un Rêve' Rosing displayed a tenor voice of pure gold. There need no longer be the slightest doubt about it—Mr. Rosing can, whenever it suits his purpose, serve out the full measure of lyrical sweetness.

"He chooses, however, more often than not to follow the inclination of his temperament which, naturally enough, favours the realists of his own country. And here, of course, the airs and graces of the drawing-room, the embellishments of conventional vocalism, would be out of place. In the songs of Moussorgsky, for instance, Rosing is artist enough not to allow his singing to impose anything of mere decoration on the art-work; here his method becomes wholly *exposante*, to borrow Flaubert's term. Moussorgsky accepted more or less Dargomijsky's gospel, 'I want the note to be the direct representation of the word—I want truth and realism,' and Rosing embraces it just as courageously. He meets Moussorgsky half-way in a tone that does not try to gloss over the harshest veracity with the heart-easing power of a sweet accent; what is beautiful, we can imagine him telling us, is simply that which has character. As an interpreter of Russian song Rosing is, like Moussorgsky, Dostoievski and Gogol, definitely a Primitive, aiming at a realism of extreme simplicity, his outlook one of naked innocence. There is in his art something of the touch of the inspired amateur, a complete freedom from routine professionalism—the same touch we get in *Boris* and *The Brothers Karamazov*. In all the great Russian poets of realism the technical method is so simple, so close to nature, that we feel it is the instinct of the visionary and not the culture of academies which leads them to truth and to beauty. Only the less typical Russians, the cosmopolitans, are stylists in the Western sense of the word; the flavour of the *salon* itself is often in Turgeniev, and Rachmaninov might easily be squeezed in with the disciples of the German symphonists.

"So unabashed is Rosing's naturalism, in his characteristic moments, that one feels an inadequacy in the musical critic's stock vocabulary to discuss him fully. No other singer has so transcended the scope of mere specialised musicianship. He gives to song something of its original democratic appeal. But for the wonderful art of it all, we might imagine Rosing's song to be much as man must first have made it, to turn the day's pleasures and pains into communal music. Song with so much of common human nature in it as this is no more to be discussed exclusively in the language of the music schools than the poetry of Burns is to be discussed in the jargon of the prosodists. Its appeal is too universal for that. The truth is that Rosing's art has dramatic qualities to which his musical qualities may be said to be just accessory. In his happiest interpretations it is not only his voice that is in them: the whole

man is expressive. Last night Rosing sang the setting to
Nekrasov's 'The Wanderer,' and at the passage where we
hear the piteous lamentation of the starving peasant there
was a miracle for the psychologists on the platform.
Rosing's face was as though a light had been turned down
inside; at the cry 'Cold! Cold!' the cheeks, so it seemed,
became sunken; the body contracted as though intensely
chilled, the hands clenched, and, surely, the voice itself was
pinched. Like Chaliapin, Rosing is a great actor; his very
stance on the platform is significant—the entire body alive
with an eloquent animation, almost sculptural. All these
are factors in his art no less potent than his sensitive voice,
and the total effect is to establish an intimacy with his
audience which even an unfamiliar language cannot strain."

All the stops are out! You can feel the straining for effect.
Next day Scott told me that he was pleased with the notice
and he assured me that in the course of time the musical
criticism of the paper would be mine. He promised to give
me all the leisure he could spare for my, as he called them,
"studies." He even suggested that I might, at the paper's
expense, spend some time on the Continent acquiring
"experience and standards"; but this project for some reason
or other came to nothing. When I later visited Germany and
Vienna for music, it was at my own expense.

But I knew where I was, once and for all. With cricket as
a sound economic base, I plunged neck-high into music. For
three or four years I did little work for the paper in the winter
months. I had been nominated Langford's deputy, which
meant not more than a concert a week of secondary importance.
The whole of my days and half through the nights were spent
in music. I had vowed to myself never to write for the "M. G."
on music, as a responsible critic, until I felt I knew my subject
and had lived in it as deeply and intensely as any other man in
the country, not excluding even Langford and Newman. And
in May 1926, when Langford died and Scott asked me to take
on the job of principal music critic of the "M. G.," I told
him I would prefer to wait a year or two longer; not yet, I
said, was I quite ready; but he persuaded me out of this
opinion. He could not appoint another man "from the out-

side" simply as a stop-gap while I gave my music another touch of varnish, so to say.

So there you are. In 1917 I was being herded on the Manchester pavements by the insurance inspector, one of a rabble of down-and-outs; there seemed no future for me, no more than there seemed to be sun anywhere above in the Manchester sky. Seven years afterwards, I am "Cricketer" of the *Manchester Guardian*, declining offers from J. L. Garvin of the *Observer*. Grant Richards has long since discovered me and counted me amongst his many trophies as author-hunter. And ten years after that I am music critic under Scott and Montague; I wear a dress-suit at evenings when I attend Hallé Concerts. And young men look at me, even as I shyly looked once on a time at Langford and Newman. I am now a member of three clubs, including the Savage and the National Liberal in London. My salary is round about £750 a year—I have opened my first account at a bank, and I possess a cheque book all my own.

Part Two

MY SUMMERS

To
K.

I

CRICKET helped me in time to a balance at my bank; also it saved me, or should have saved me, as a human being. From boyhood onward the circumstances of my life had given me little time to do anything except educate myself. Even at Shrewsbury I did not learn to "play"; I was intent on burning with a gem-like flame, according to the custom amongst young men of the period. Walter Pater and his school had a good and a bad influence on us: he actually came near to making an æsthete out of an urchin born in Summer Place. Still, in the materialism of the end of the nineteenth century, it was refreshment and inspiration to read Pater, especially if you chanced to have been born in Manchester. Somerset Maugham has written of Pater's "heavily scented atmosphere" and "those hushed rooms in which it was indecorous to speak above a whisper." It was at any rate a change from "stink o' brass" and the blare of the political hustings and the haggling in the markets where it was wisdom to buy cheap and sell dear. Pater and Wilde came to us as much more than the oasis in the desert; we found enchantment in them, colour and intoxication. Culture in the one, plus sensibility; in the other we found wit without implicit social criticism, wit for the epigram's sake and nothing else.

But they both lured a young man of my nature, who had dwelt so much alone, into the belief that art and culture were things in themselves. Then came the intensive life and work in the Corridor of the "M. G."; there was little time for simple and objective enjoyment of everyday folk. I could not go even to a music-hall without searching for the right phrase or metaphor; Little Tich was a manifestation or not a manifestation (I forget how I decided the problem) of the Meredithian Comic Spirit. George Robey was Gothic or Rabelaisian or something equally recondite. I could not look at Sam Elton when he smashed tons of crockery but I must needs be put in mind of some theory of laughter—echoed from

Bergson. Cricket took me into a different element; I met unlettered people with no pretences, good craftsmen with bat and ball on the field of play; and for audience they had crowds that expressed themselves honestly. Many times I have left Lord's at the end of a summer's day of cricket and gone in the evening to Queen's Hall or Covent Garden, and as I have changed from one place to another, I have felt an acute lowering not only of standards of skill but of genuine English character; for taking them as a whole, concert and opera audiences in London do not ring true, with their absurd "fashions," their whoopings and screamings in the corridors at the intervals: "Marvellous, my dear!" "*Actually*, you know, I prefer Toscanini's Ninth!"

Though I had known Attewell and Wainwrigbt at Shrewsbury, I was not then in a position to see them as the equals in the eyes of God and nature with any literary lion in the world. Cricket in time proved my salvation from exclusiveness, and it should have cured me of intellectual snobbishness; but to confess the truth I remain to this day subject to recurrent fits of irritation whenever somebody praises my writings on cricket, and then adds as though by an afterthought, a word of recognition of my music criticism. Culture is a word with dubious associations but everybody knows what it really means. In England culture and the arts are so little normal to our lives that the effort even to get a hold on them tends to make for arrogance and exclusiveness. When I began to go to cricket matches for the *Manchester Guardian*, I kept for a long time apart from the crowds and the players. I wrote above the heads of the average reader who turns in his newspaper for cricket reports; I wrote above the head of the game itself. Hobbs was not enough for me as Hobbs. I had to see something æsthetic in him, or a symlnil of something, or as sculpture, with clouds of glory about him (instead of grit from the neighbouring gas-works). I concluded an article on Rhodes—the Yorkshire Rhodes, nothing to do with the Ægean, the Dorian Hexapolis and the Colossus at Chares —in this extraordinary way: . . . "a cricketer with a past so full of history's noises that, to those of us who have never known the game without its Rhodes, the sound is like 'the surge and thunder of the Odyssey.'" I wonder what Rhodes and all the other cricketers used to think of my apostrophes about them? I only know that one morning when I had condescended from the lyric strain to plain English which found fault with some bowling by Richard Tyldesley, the vast Lancashire lad, round and red of face, and inarticulate to the verge of eloquence—I only know that when he was shown my article, he remarked, without anger and as a man seriously contemplating a possibility: "Ah'd like to bowl at bugger soom da-ay."

For a while, as I say, I kept aloof from cricketers. I suspected they would bore me or indirectly burst the bubbles of the very literary fancies and conceits I entertained about them in my first and "greenery-yallery" period. Later I found that here was just where the joke came in. The famous cricketer, unlike the famous actor, vocalist, fiddler, pianist or "movie" star, is usually unaware of the fact that he presents a figure or personality at all on the field of play, except in terms of his value in runs or wickets; in other words, he is entirely practical and professional. When I read to Woo Hey the passage in my essay on him about the miracle that happened whenever he stayed in three hours, I think he resented in particular the sentence: "So with Woolley's cricket; the lease of it is in the hands of the special providence which looks after things that will not look after themselves." He said he had played many long innings, and I rather think he suspected I was casting doubt on the efficiency of his back-play.[1]

After I had come to know my cricketers intimately by watching them observantly while they were in action, and by revealing to them in bar and pavilion and railway train that I was not as austere as I looked or read, I began to write of the game in a way that does not just a little embarrass me to-day when I look back on it. My two different jobs brought me into touch with a wider range of humanity than I think can often have been thrown any one man's way. In summer I was for weeks in a world where nobody apparently ever read a book, or anything in a newspaper except the sporting pages. For days it was possible for me to talk with spectators

---

[1] The reader is at liberty, it he choose, to think that I have quoted this passege twice in this book much in the same way that Mr. Micawber, during his indictment of Uriah Heep. enjoyed one of his phrases so much that. under pretcnce of losing his place in his manuscript, he read it a second time.

and players and pressmen and never once hear an allusion to
the world at large, the world of ideas and policies and changes
in the destinies of nations. I do not think that the extensive
view which surveys mankind from China to Peru could
possibly be more comprehensive than the one given me by
my two professions: I had the chance to see life steadily and
in the whole from Lord's to Salzburg (or, more extreme still,
from Lord's to Kennington Oval); from Patsy Hendren to
Richard Strauss; from Lancashire and Yorkshire at Bramall
Lane to the Three Choirs Festival in Worcester Cathedral.

I began to grow two different personalities; for, after all,
one's personality is mainly the sum of the impressions received
from the external universe plus one's reflection on them.
At the end of each summer "Cricketer" of the *Manchester
Guardian* went into hibernation; and now and again, when
some article on the game was called for suddenly in the depth
of winter, I had very deliberately to wake him into action
and it took some time. I have distinctly felt one set of ideas
and feelings, in fact a different individual, gradually taking
shape and control of me as I have in an hour or two trans-
ferred myself physically and psychologically from Lord's to
Covent Garden. I have written of cricket in terms of music.
I have described Charles Macartney, the Australian batsman,
as the Figaro of cricket, not Mozart's but the drier-minded
one of Rossini. But I have never known "Cricketer" to invade
the preserves of "N. C.," music critic of the *Manchester Guardian*
—which is a curious point.

·   ·   ·   ·   ·   ·

I have met far more interesting characters amongst the
cricketers than amongst the musicians of England. Music
does not come by nature to English folk as a whole; and they
lose much of the ease of nature when they go in pursuit of it.
Amongst exponents of the recognised arts in England there
is only Sir Thomas Beecham whom I have found fit to compare in character and gusto of life, according to a personal
point of view, with A. C. Maclaren, on or off the field. No
living English musician, critic or performer of my acquaint-
ance is half the work of art to look at and to *experience* as

C. B. Fry. In himself he is a national gallery and a theatre and a forum. I would rather go into a pub with half a dozen North-country professional cricketers than into all the studios or pent-houses or Athenæum and Savile clubs in London. I have tried both, so I know.

The English character is, without doubt, the most humorous in the world; other nations and peoples beat us in thoughtful and passionate living. It is in unselfconscious action that the English spirit finds scope. The inhibited Englishman forgets himself when he is engaged in his various field sports; he is then elevated to the sublimely comic, and of course he knows nothing about it; for at last grace of nature touches him.

There are many things about cricket, apart from the skill and the score. There is, first of all, the leisure to do something else. Cricket, like music, has its slow movements, especially when my native county of Lancashire is batting. I married the good companion who is my wife during a Lancashire innings. The event occurred in June, 1921; I went as usual to Old Trafford, stayed for a while and saw Hallows and Makepeace come forth to bat. As usual they opened with care. Then I had to leave, had to take a taxi to Manchester, there to be joined in wedlock at a registry office. Then I—that is, we—returned to Old Trafford. While I had been away from the match and had committed the most responsible and irrevocable act in mortal man's life, Lancashire had increased their total by exactly seventeen—Makepeace 5, Hallows 11, and one leg-bye.

To go to a cricket match for nothing but cricket is as though a man were to go into an inn for nothing but drink. As I look back on my twenty years of days in the sun (sometimes it rained, I admit), I can scarcely believe that all the juicy characters I came to know on cricket fields have actually existed. I get them confused with the creations of the nation's comic writers. Emmott Robinson of Yorkshire; Rhodes and Hirst; Maurice Ley land and Parkin—they all come back to my mind endowed with the gusto of humorous genius: they are as satisfying to my sense of comedy as anybody in the range of our comic literature. I cannot flatter my creative powers by thinking that I have invented them myself; I have merely given a truthful account of them as I discovered them, as soon as I looked at or remembered them and forgot my adjectives and my "style."

There is Bill Worsley to begin with; he lives for me as completely and satisfyingly on the strength of a few immortal words as the young man in Dickens, who opened his mouth only once and murmured "Esker."

Worsley belonged to the hinterland of the county where existence is carried on near to the knuckle, where cobbled streets go up and down hill, where in the pitch-black of cold winter mornings mills 'sirens or "buzzers" awakened the dead, and the rattle of clogs was like the sound of a sort of Last Day or Resurrection. From one of the pits of Lancashire emerged this Bill Worsley, who kept wicket for the county in the great high noon of Maclaren's reign. He got his chance unexpectedly. The Lancashire Eleven was touring the West of England and the regular wicket-keeper received an injury to the hand which rendered him a casualty for the rest of the summer. A telegram was sent for reinforcements and was received by Bill Worsley on his back in a seam of a coal-mine. He was brought to the surface, where he blinked his eyes to get accustomed to the light of day. After he had slowly read the telegram he said, without emotion: "It's signed A. C. Maccle-aren"—he always pronounced it that way—"and it ses Ah've to pack oop and go to Edgbaston, Birmingham, and keep wickets for Lankysheer." He scratched his head and added: "Ah'm non so sure as Ah rightly knows where Edgbaston is." But his proud and admiring friends saw him to the train and bought the correct railway ticket, and Bill departed, with a farewell message as he leaned out of the carriage window: "Ah reckon Ah'll be back wi' thee all in a day or two. Look after mi whippets."

He duly arrived at the cricket ground of Edgbaston. Lancashire were about to play Warwickshire. Bill stripped and sat in a corner in the dressing-room. Nobody spoke to him and he, as he afterwards said, kept himself to "hisself." He was discerned by Walter Brearley, the fast bowler and an "amateur," meaning a "gentleman." Brearley, the kindest man and the friendliest in the world, hailed the newcomer. "You are Worsley, aren't you; wicket-keeper for us to-day?"

"Yes, sir," replied Bill.

"Come and have a drink," said Brearley: "We'll just have *one*, to baptize your first appearance for the county. This is your opportunity, Bill; just you keep a decent wicket and you can say good-bye to the pit, and have a grand life up and down the country. Come on, Bill—this way." Brearley led Bill to the bar in the members' enclosure. When they reached the counter, Brearley smote Bill on the back and said: "Now, Bill; what'll you have to celebrate this famous day in your life?"

"Well," responded Bill politely, "if you don't mind, Maister Brearley, Ah'll 'ave a Creem de month."

Brearley was rather taken aback. "A what?" he said. And Bill repeated with equal politeness: "A Creem de month, if you please, Maister Brearley."

Brearley concealed his astonishment and gave the order, including a can of beer for himself, which he picked up and drained at a draught. "There's luck to you, Bill," he gulped. Whereupon Bill drank his green fluid and said: "The same to you, Maister Brearley, and many of 'em."

Lancashire lost the toss, and Maclaren led his team into the field. When he reached the middle he as usual spent some time distributing his forces, waving men here and there, while Brearley measured his run and swung his arms and prepared to attack. The two opening Warwickshire batsmen came to the wicket, and Kinneir took his guard. All was ready. Then Maclaren at first-slip withdrew his attention from the bowler and the precise position to an inch of cover-point; he saw Bill Worsley "standing up," an inch or so from the stumps. "Worsley," he said, "get back a bit—Mr. Brearley happens to be pretty quick." "Just as you like, Maister Maccle-aren," said Bill, retreating exactly four inches.

"Farther back still," shouted Maclaren impatiently: "he's fast, I'm telling you."

"Just as you please, Maister Maccle-aren," reiterated Bill, retreating another four inches. To himself Maclaren said: "Well, if he wants his so-and-so head knocked off, very well."

The match began. Bill "stood up" to Brearley. Kinneir,

a left-hander and a most obstinate batsman on a good wicket, was in form. He scored ten in a quarter of an hour—rapid work for him. Then he moved gently over to the off-side and beautifully glanced at a fine angle to leg. Worsley also moved across, made a brilliant catch, and without a change of action or pause, sent the ball high into the air with a one-handed jerk behind his back.

"What the . . . what the . . ." expostulated Maclaren. But Brearley said, behind his hand, "Hush, Archie; you'll put him off! Marvellous catch!"

So Maclaren held his peace and the game was resumed. The next batsman was the formidable W. G. Quaife, most notorious of stone-wallers, almost beyond the powers of known science to get out on a hard wicket under six hours. He, too, began well and he, too, presently moved gently across his wickets and glanced exquisitely off his pads, fine to leg. And again did Worsley swoop on the ball, catch it, and with one comprehensive and encircling action jerk it sky-high behind his back.

This was too much for Maclaren. In spite of Brearley's muffled, "Shush, Archie; you'll only put him off. Marvellous catch!"—in spite of Brearley's kind admonitions, Maclaren approached Bill. "Well caught, Worsley," he said, "but damn it all, what's the idea of this behind-the-back foolery?"

"Well, Maister Maccle-aren," replied Bill, "we allus does it in t'Saturday afternoon league—a little bit o' 'fluence, tha knows, sir."

"You can't do it here," said Maclaren, "in front of all these people. Bless my soul. Now, Bill, get on with your job. You're doing splendidly. But no more bits o' 'fluence, if you don't mind."

As it happened, one or two Warwickshire batsmen took root, and Lancashire spent a long day in the field. But Bill acquitted himself well, though he did not get any more chances to make a catch. When they all came to the pavilion at close of play, it was discovered that Bill had been wearing primitive gloves. His hands were swollen and black. A pair of scissors was needed to cut his gloves away from his wounded hands.

Brearley's heart went out to Bill. He took him to the bar,

the same bar where at the beginning of the day they had drunk to Bill's first appearance for Lancashire.

"Come, Bill," said Brearley, "you've won your colours. You'll come with us on the whole tour now. No more pit for you, my lad. You've done 'gradely.' But for God's sake, get some proper gloves—and drop all that behind-the-back business. Can't do it at Lord's—Heaven help us. . . . Well, here's to you, Bill. Let's celebrate the occasion properly now. What'll you have?" And Bill replied, polite as ever: "Well, if you don't mind, Maister Brearley, Ah'll have a Creem de month."

Brearley was a gale of humanity in himself. After his career as a fast bowler for Lancashire was finished, he lived in London and, without compromising his Bolton accent and turbulence, became one of the chosen of the Long Room of the Pavilion at Lord's. Often I saw him gazing for a few minutes through the great windows at some fast bowler of these latter years. He could seldom bear to look for long; his eyes popped almost out of his head; the explosive red of his face heightened. "Ah could throw mi hat down the pitch quicker!" he would say. At Sheffield in a Lancashire and Yorkshire match, when he was tireless and bowled all day until his face resembled a boiled lobster, he experienced bad luck with appeals for leg-before-wicket. "Ah hit George Hirst bang on kneecap; and Ah'll swear to mi dying day he was in front—ball would a' knocked all three wickets down. But umpire gives it 'not out,' and then George hits mi over ropes and crowd, sarcastic-like, shouts 'Ow's that, Maister Brearley?' and next ball he hits me again over ropes, and crowd shouts 'Ow's that' again; so I knocks his middle-stump flying in two, and Ah runs down pitch and picks up broken halves of wicket and Ah brandishes 'em at crowd. And then Ah runs off field and comes back with six new stumps and gives 'em to umpire and says 'Here, take these, you'll need all bloody lot before Ah've done.' And he needed four on 'em, Ah can tell you."

I have spent whole days at Lord's and scarcely seen half a dozen consecutive overs bowled from noon to evening, yet my article of fifteen hundred words has appeared as usual next morning on the cricket page of the "M. G." "So many

things happen to you at Lord's," said J. M. Barrie to me after
he had spent some hours there. "And," he continued, "it's
astonishing the number of people you meet who know
you. Yesterday a perfect stranger in the Tavern, wearing
a cloth cap and a spotted handkerchief round his neck, put
down his can of beer and came up to me and said ''Ello
George!'"

It was through cricket I came to know Barrie. He was
crazy about cricket. After I had written to him complaining
of some changes from the original text in *Peter Pan*, he replied,
"I am elated to hear that you spent your sixpences on P. Pan
and that you know when bits of him fall off. I expect
the explanation is that the author is a little like Macartney
and tires of seeing himself always making the same
strokes . . ."

He not only admired Charles Macartney, most brilliant of
all Australian batsmen with the single exception of Victor
Trumper; he actually envied him. "He can do all that he
wants to do," was his significant tribute.

During 1926 I went to Lord's one morning with Barrie.
We sat at right angles to the wicket, a most unprofessional
place for me because I like to see the spin. But Barrie preferred the stand over the Tavern at Lord's near the dining-
room; I think he imagined he was taking me to a cricket
match as though I were one of his adopted grown-up children;
he asked me after we had sat in the sun an hour or so whether
I would like an ice-cream. Also he asked me what I thought
of J. W. Hearne as a bowler: "I mean do you call him—as
an expert—fast or slow?" J. W. Hearne was a slow leg-break
bowler, and I replied: "Slow of course; in fact, very slow."
Barrie meditated for a while, took another look at Hearne's
bowling and said: "For my part I should say he's pretty fast."
Here followed a pause for more meditation, then he added:
"You must come down to Stan way and watch me. I can
bowl so slow that if I don't like a ball I can run after it and
bring it back." He used this remark at a speech to the
Australian team later on; he never wasted a word. Seldom
could I get him to talk about anything except cricket.

I cannot recollect the name of any musician, artist or novelist who has played football of a serious standard of skill, with the exception of J. B. Priestley who, I believe, once appeared as a professional for Huddersfield or some other North of England team. Conan Doyle, Hesketh-Prichard ("Don Q"), E. W. Hornung, Alec Waugh, John Galsworthy, Clifford Bax, Arnold Bax—all of these various men of letters achieved at one time or other some measure of technique in good club cricket. Hesketh-Prichard was a really fine fast-bowler who played at Lord's for the Gentlemen against the Players. C. B. Fry, of course, was the Admirable Crichton of games; if he had put his mind to it, he might have won the highest honours in half a dozen lofty walks of English public life. He was responsible for Ranjitsinhji's *jubilee Book of Cricket*, and his own treatise on "Batsmanship" is the sort of book Aristotle might have written if he had ever heard of cricket and practised it. All in all, Fry is the most remarkable man I have ever come to know through cricket. He walked the field half Greek, half Malvolio. He taught himself to bat by logic and analysis. He worked out an anatomy of stroke-play, and transformed himself from a player of ordinary talents into the most prolific scorer of his period, apart from Ranjitsinhji. In 1934 when England were playing Australia at Leeds, I talked one evening with Fry in the lounge of the hotel. He became absorbed in a match between Sussex and Middlesex which had taken place some thirty years ago . . . (Imagine that Fry is telling this story, reclining in his chair, with an admonitory finger emphasising his points.) . . . "The game was anybody's," he told me. "When we went in again the wicket was good, and we scored pretty heavily. At close of play I was 97 not out. Then it rained in the night, and next morning the sun was shining. The wicket would become 'sticky' in an hour or so. It was, of course, our policy to get a few more quick runs and then declare. Well, I completed my century, hit two fours in an over; and then—bless me! if Albert Trott didn't clean bowl me with an off-break." . . . At this point Fry jumped from his seat and walked abstractedly in a circle, finger to mouth, saying, "I can't think what I was doing!" He went through the motions of a batsman playing an off-break, to the mild surprise of every other person sitting in the hotel lounge. "For the life of me," he repeated, "I can't think what I was doing!" He was speaking in 1934 of a match played at Lord's in 1903.

I have been told that if Fry had not "squandered" his talents on games and pursuits diverse and sometimes mutually exclusive, he might have distinguished himself in (1) politics, (2) the theatre, (3) law, (4) literature. For my part I think there are politicians and actors and K. C. s and authors enough; there has been only one C. B. Fry. And if it comes to political distinction, where is the other Englishman of our time who could have polled 20,000 votes at Brighton in those days after standing there as a candidate of the Liberal Party? I have heard only one man talk more to the dozen than Fry on all subjects and that was J. L. Garvin. Fry was a master of ellipsis and the rhetorical question. We voyaged to Australia together in 1936-1937; and every morning Fry held court amongst the deck-chairs on the *Orion*, as she ploughed patiently through the seas. He dressed differently every day; sometimes with topee and short leather trousers, as though about to trace the source of the Amazon; or in a scaled green sort of costume which made him look like a deep-sea monster; or in a bath towel worn like a toga. One day, to tease him, I said: "Good morning, Charles. No hemlock yet? Give us your ideas about the Iambic." In full spate came forth a swift survey of the origin and development of the Iambic, with quotations from all periods and writers, every sentence ending with "You see what I mean" or "However." A sort of intellectual Jack Bunsby; an original and fascinating man. Even Hitler heard of him and invited him to Berlin to consult him on the right way of physical training amongst die Jugend. It is a pity Fry does not speak German. Hitler might have died of a fit trying to get a word in. For Fry, I swear, talked all the way to Australia and all the way across Australia and all the way back home. At Melbourne on Armistice Day, the English journalists and the English cricket team were about to attend a reception; we were gathered in the lounge of the Windsor Hotel when the sirens announced the two-minutes' silence. We all stood side by side and Fry was next to me. Before all sound had subsided, I could not help whispering to Fry, "This'll irk you, Charles." He nearly died, but he checked his

retort. I think this was probably one of the most severely
disciplined acts of his career.

.   .   .   .   .   .

For twenty years I went to cricket matches north, south,
east and west, and I saw the blossom come upon orchards in
Gloucestershire, as we journeyed from Manchester to Bristol;
and I saw midsummer in full blaze at Canterbury; and I saw
midsummer dropping torrents of rain on the same lovely
place, the white tents dropsical: "Play abandoned for the
day." I saw the autumn leaves falling at Eastbourne. I have
shivered to the bone in the springtime blasts at the Parks at
Oxford. In a *Manchester Guardian* article I congratulated the
keenness and devotion of two spectators who at Leicester sat
all day, near the sight-screen, from eleven until half-past six,
in spite of an east wind like a knife. Then, as I was finishing
my notice, a thought struck me. "But," I added in a final
sentence, "perhaps they were only dead." I have seen English
summer days pass like a dream as the cricketers changed
places in the field over by over. Sometimes I have seen in
vision all the games going on throughout the land at the
same minute of high noon; Hobbs, easy and unhurriedly on
the way to another hundred under the gasometer at the Oval;
Tate and Gilligan at Hove skittling wickets while the tide
comes in; Hendren and Hearne batting for ever at Lord's
while the Tavern gets busier and busier; at Southampton,
Kennedy bowling for hours for Hampshire—Kennedy never
ceased bowling in those days; he could always have produced
a clinching alibi if ever circumstantial evidence had convicted
him of anything:
    "What were you doing on July 17th at four forty-five in
the afternoon?"
    "Why, bowling of course."
From Old Trafford to Dover, from Hull to Bristol, the
fields were active as fast bowlers heaved and thudded and
sweated over the earth, and batsmen drove and cut or got
their legs in front; and the men in the slips bent down, all
four of them together, as though moved by one string. On
every afternoon at half-past six I saw them, in my mind's

eye, all walking home to the pavilion, with a deeper tan on
their faces. And the newspapers came out with the cricket
scores and the visitor from Budapest, in London for the first
time, experienced a certain bewilderment when he saw an
Evening News poster: "Collapse of Surrey." In these twenty
seasons I saw also a change in cricket. It is not fanciful, I
think, to say that a national game is influenced by the spirit
and atmosphere of the period. In 1920 cricket retained much
of the gusto and free personal gesture of the years before the
war of 1914-1918. Then, as disillusion increased and the
nation's life contracted and the catchword "safety first"
became familiar and a sense of insecurity gathered, cricket
itself lost confidence and character. My own county of Lancashire provided a striking example of how a mere game can
express a transition in the social and industrial scene. When
Manchester was wealthy and the mills of Lancashire were
busy most days and nights, cricket at Old Trafford was
luxuriant with Maclaren, Spooner and Tyldesley squandering
runs opulently right and left. It was as soon as the county's
shoe began to pinch and mill after mill closed, that Lancashire
cricket obtained its reputation for suspicious thriftiness; care
and want batted visibly at both ends of the wicket. Not that
the players consciously expressed anything; of course they
didn't. But a cricketer, like anybody else, is what his period
and environment make of him, and he acts or plays accordingly.

The romantic flourish vanished as much from cricket as
from the theatre and the arts. I even reacted against the
romanticism in my own cricket writing. The lyric gush, the
"old flashing bat" and "rippling green grass" metaphors gave
way to, or became tinctured with, satire if not with open
irony. Hammond no longer inspired me into comparisons
between him and the Elgin marbles; I saw something middle-
class and respectable about his play, and was vastly amused
and relieved when occasionally he fell off his pedestal and
struck a ball with the oil-hole of his bat, or received a blow
from a fast ball on his toe. Bradman was the summing-up of
the Efficient Age which succeeded the Golden Age. Here was
brilliance safe and sure, streamlined and without impulse.
Victor Trumper was the flying bird; Bradman the aeroplane.
It was the same in music, by the way: the objective Toscanini

was preferred to the subjective Furtwängler. In an England XI of 1938, A. C. Maclaren would have looked as much an anachronism as Irving in a Noel Coward play.

But the humour of English character kept creeping in, even to Lancashire cricket. And I came to love the dour shrewd ways of these North-country "professors"; it was true to life at any rate, and not, like much of the cricket of the South of England, suburban and genteel. The Lancashire and Yorkshire match was every year like a play and pageant exhibiting the genius of the two counties. To watch it rightly you needed the clue; for years I myself had missed the point. There is slow play and slow play at cricket. There are batsmen who cannot score quickly because they can't, and there are batsmen who can score quickly but won't. In a representative Lancashire and Yorkshire match of 1924-1934, runs were severely discountenanced. No fours before lunch, on principle, was the unannounced policy; and as few as possible after. But fours or no fours, runs or no runs, the games touched greatness because of the North of England character that was exposed in every action, every movement, all day. Imagine the scene: Bramall Lane. Factory chimneys everywhere; a pall of smoke between earth and sun. A crowd mainly silent; tiard hats or caps and scarves on all sides. Makepeace is batting to Rhodes; old soldier against old soldier. Makepeace has only One purpose in life at the moment, and that is not to get out. And Rhodes pitches a cautious ball wide of the off-stump— pitches it there so that Makepeace cannot safely score off it; Makepeace, mind you, who is not going to put his bat any-where near a ball if he can help it.

Maiden overs occurred in profusion. Appeals for leg-before-wicket were the only signs of waking life for hours. Often I thought that one day during overs, while the field was changing positions, somebody would return the ball from the outfield and accidentally hit a batsman on the pads, and then eleven terrific "H'zats!" would be emitted by sheer force of habit. "Aye," said Roy Kilner, "it's a rum 'un is t'Yarksheer and Lankysheer match. T'two teams meets in t'dressin'-room on t'Bank Holiday; and then we never speaks agean for three lays—except to appeal." The ordeal of umpiring in a Lancashire and Yorkshire match during 1924-1930 was severe.

One day at Leeds, Yorkshire fell upon the Lancashire first
innings and three wickets—the best—were annihilated for
next to nothing. Two young novices nervously discovered
themselves together, holding the fourth Lancashire wicket,
while thirty thousand Yorkshire folk roared for their blood;
and the Yorkshire team crouched under their very noses, a
few yards from the block-hole. By some miracle worked
on high, the two young novices stayed in. Not only
that; they began to hit fours. One drive soared over the
ropes. George Macaulay, the Yorkshire medium-paced
bowler (a grand fellow off the field, and on it a tiger with
the temper of the jungle) glared down the wicket until his
eyes were pin-points of incredulity and frustration. And
Emmott Robinson, grey-haired in the service of Yorkshire
and whose trousers were always coming down, an old cam-
paigner who would any day have died rather than give "owt
away," kept muttering "Hey, dear, dear, dear; what's t'matter,
what's t'matter?" The two novices declined to get out; the
score mounted—forty for three, fifty for three, eighty for
three, one hundred for three. At that time the Yorkshire
captain was not a good cricketer though a very nice man—
an "amateur" of course; for even Yorkshire continued to
observe the custom that no first-class county team should be
captained by a professional; even Yorkshire carried a
"passenger" for the sake of traditional social distinctions.
But he was only a figurehead; the leadership was a joint
dictatorship; Rhodes and Robinson. This day the situation
got out of hand; the novices each made a century. One of
the umpires told me, after the scalding afternoon's play was
over: "Never again; no more 'standin'" in Yorkshire and
Lancashire matches for me. Why, this afternoon, when them
two lads were knockin' t'stuffin' out of t'Yorkshire bowlers,
the row and racket on t'field were awful. George Macaulay
were cussin' 'is 'ead off, and Emmott were mutterin' to 'isself,
and poor owd captain 'ad been sent out into t'outfield so's 'e
couldn't 'ear. At last I 'ad to call order; I said 'Now look
'ere, you chaps, how the 'ell do you expect me and me pal
'Arry to umpire in a bloody parrot 'ouse?'"

Roy Kilner, Yorkshire to the end of his days and for ever
after, once said that umpires were only "luxurious super-

fluities" in a Lancashire and Yorkshire match. "They gets in t'way. What we want in Yarksheer and Lankysheer matches is 'fair do's'—no umpires, and honest cheatin' all round, in conformity wi' the law."

The joke about Yorkshire cricket is that for Yorkshiremen it is no laughing matter. It is a possession of the clan and must on no account be put down, or interfered with by anybody not born in the county. When Hammond was an unknown young player, I went to look at him at Huddersfield one day when Gloucestershire were playing Yorkshire. I had been told he was more than promising. He came to the wicket and began well. I watched from behind the bowler's arm, through Zeiss glasses. Suddenly a ball from Emmott Robinson struck him on the pad, high up. Every Yorkshireman on the field of play, and many not on it, roared "Howzat!" Involuntarily I spoke aloud and said, "No, not out, not out"; through my glasses I had seen that the ball would have missed the wicket. Then I was conscious I was being watched; you know how you can somehow feel that somebody behind you is looking at you. I turned round and saw a typical Yorkshireman eyeing me from my boots upward to the crown of my head, his hand deep and aggressively thrust in his pocket. "And what's the matter with thee?" he asked.

No writer of novels could make a picture of Yorkshire life half as full of meaning as the one drawn every year in matches between Lancashire and Yorkshire. Cricket on the dole; nature herself on the dole. The very grass on the field of play told of the struggle for existence; it eventually achieved a triumphant greenness. "Tha can't be too careful." If it happened to be a fine day, well—"maybe it'll last and maybe it won't." And, if things are at a pretty pass all round, well —"they'll get worse before they get better." "Ah'm tekking nowt on trust." At Sheffield there is a refreshment-room situated deep in the earth under a concrete stand. I descended one afternoon for a cup of tea. A plump Yorkshire lass served me and I asked for a spoon. "It's there, Maister," she said.

"Where?" I asked.

She pointed with her bread-knife. "There," she said, "tied to t'counter, la-ad." So it was; a lead spoon tied to the premises with a piece of string.

Emmott Robinson was a grizzled, squat, bandy-legged Yorkshireman, all sagging and loose at the braces in private life, but on duty for Yorkshire he was liable at any minute to gather and concentrate his energy into sudden and vehement leaps and charges and scuffles. He had shrewd eyes, a hatchet face and grey hairs, most of them representing appeals that had gone against him for leg-before-wicket. I imagine that he was created one day by God scooping up the nearest acre of Yorkshire soil at hand, then breathing into it saying, "Now, lad, tha's called Emmott Robinson and tha can go on with new ball at t'pavilion end." Emmott cherished the new ball dearly; he would carry it between overs in person to the next bowler needing it after himself; and he would contain it in the two palms of his hands shaped like a sacred chalice. If some ignorant novice unnecessarily threw the new ball along the earth, Emmott gave him a look of wrath and pain. He was not a great cricketer in technique; but by passion and by taking thought he became so. But for me he will be remembered for the Yorkshire stuff in him. He had no use for the flashing bat school, "brighter cricket" and all such nonsense. He dismissed it with one good word: "Swash-buckle," he called it. Life had taught him to take no risks. On a cold winter evening a member of the Committee of the Yorkshire County Cricket Club was hurrying along a pavement in Bradford when out of the fog emerged Emmott, carrying a black portmanteau. "Hey, good afternoon, Mr. Houldsworth," he said. "Ah'm pleased to meet you."

"Good evening, Emmott. How are you?" Neither had seen the other since summer.

"Hey," said Emmott, "Ah'm a bit poorly, Mr. Houldsworth. Ah've got a pain." He indicated a place in his stomach. Mr. Houldsworth expressed anxiety. "Now listen, Emmott," he said, "you mustn't neglect it. Go to the hospital. Find out what it is. You needn't worry about expense, if any is incurred. The Committee will see to that."

Emmott pondered. "Well maybe you're right, Mr. Houldsworth. It's been 'urting me weeks now. Maybe Ah will try t'hospital. But . . ." He paused, then announced decisively, once and for all, "Ah'm 'aving no knife."

In time he was obliged to go into retirement from first-class cricket. It was sad to see him passively looking on if Yorkshire happened to get into trouble. The Yorkshire team without him was never the same again. After he had been absent from the side for a year or two, some mishap unexpectedly deprived Yorkshire of two men at the beginning of the second day of a Lancashire and Yorkshire match; and Emmott was requisitioned as one of the substitutes; there, once again, we saw him taking the field against the ancient enemy on an August Bank Holiday. He had not been in the field five minutes before he yapped out a violent appeal for leg-before-wicket. He was standing at backward-point and nobody appealed with him, not even the bowler, who was George Macaulay. The umpire who dismissed the appeal was the old Derbyshire cricketer, Arthur Morton; "Not out," he said derisively, and added, "An' look 'ere, Emmott; tha's not pla-ayin' in this match—so keep thi mouth shut."

Rhodes did not need Robinson's passion; he went to work in more devious ways. Nobody scarcely heard Rhodes appealing except the umpires. He had a throaty voice and the quiddity of him was expressed by the brass stud he wore in his cricket shirt. He lived in the Golden Age; he was the greatest slow bowler in the world when he was a youth. He saw Trumper, Maclaren, Ranji. But he kept his head, in spite of them. In conversation with him, I once had occasion to deplore that in modern years the square-cut was seldom to be seen, much to the loss of the game's brilliance. He unhesitatingly answered "Well, it never were a busine stroke . . ."

He played against Australia at Kennington Oval in 1902, and had to go in last when fifteen were wanted for victory by England. He and George Hirst got them; and the story goes that Hirst met Rhodes on his way to the wicket and said, "Wilfred, we'll get them in singles." It was the most unnecessary caution ever given a Yorkshireman, young or old. And it was at Kennington Oval that Rhodes ended his Test match career, in August, 1926; and he played a big share in winning the rubber for us. As he grew older, he naturally lost some of his spin. But, as he informed me more than once: "If batsman thinks ball's spinnin', then it is spinnin'."

Of Rhodes I wrote one of the best bits of prose of my life: it dates from my "second period":

"Flight was his secret, flight and the curving line, now higher, now lower, tempting, inimical; every ball like every other ball, yet somehow unlike; each over in collusion with the others, part of a plot. Every ball a decoy, a spy sent out to get the lie of the land; some balls simple, some complex, some easy, some difficult; and one of them—ah, which?—the master ball."

It is not known, and will now never be known, what Rhodes and Robinson in their hearts thought of Sutcliffe, who made his hair resplendent with brilliantine and wore immaculate flannels and on the whole comported with an elegance which in the Yorkshire XI was unique and apocryphal. He did not speak with the accent of Yorkshire but of Tedding ton. He would refer casually to the fact that he had yesterday "mootered" down from Pudsey to London. Witnesses could be called to testify that at Lord's Sutcliffe has held up fast bowlers in the middle of their approaches to the wicket and with a wave of his bat has removed some obstruction to his vision in the pavilion, probably a peer of the realm, who has bent double and crawled away into invisibility while members have gone red in the face at him and said, "Sit down, sir; sit down."

Sutcliffe rose to the highest place amongst batsmen of his period, and rose there as much by self-esteem as by technique. He simply refused to bow before the best ball in the world. I have seen him beaten by five consecutive balls in a Test match and at the end of the over he has crossed his legs, reclined on his bat, and surveyed the scene with the air of one not to be touched by vicissitudes that affect common folk. In a Lancashire and Yorkshire match he was fielding close to the wicket on the leg-side. The batsman hit a ball straight at him and it struck him a cracking blow on the ankle. For a second he was compelled to forget himself; for a moment he hopped about, in undignified pain. But when one or two of his colleagues, including Emmott Robinson, came towards him to see how badly he was hurt, he recovered poise and waved them from him as though saying: "Thank you, but we Sutcliffes do not have pain." The county capable of containing a Rhodes, a Robinson, and a Sutcliffe is, I should say,

capable of anything besides having as many acres as words
in the Bible.

The advent into cricket, and into the Yorkshire XI of all
places, of a Herbert Sutcliffe was a sign of the times; the old
order was not changing, it was going; the pole was fall'n;
young boys and girls level now with men; captains of cricket
were henceforth called "skipper" by all self-respecting professionals, never "Sir." Our Sutcliffes and Hammonds, with
their tailors obviously in Savile Row, have taken us far far
beyond echo of Billy Barnes and his rough horny-handed
company of paid cricketers of the 'eighties and 'nineties—
savages born too soon to benefit from Mr. Arnold Forster's
acts of Education. It was Billy Barnes who turned up late at
Lord's when Nottingham were playing Middlesex; he was
more than tipsy; but to prevent scandal—for he was a famous
man and beloved by the crowds—his captain sent him in as
usual, first wicket down. And Billy scored a hundred and
more in two hours, banging the ball everywhere, powerful,
safe, magnificent. Still, discipline is discipline; behaviour
must be seen to, so when the Nottinghamshire captain returned
to headquarters at Trent Bridge he felt it was his bounden
duty to report Barnes to his Committee, composed mainly of
Midland lords, squires and county notables. Barnes was
called before them and solemnly reprimanded. He had dis-
graced Nottinghamshire cricket—at Lord's, too. Billy listened
patiently, and when they had finished, he spoke:

"Well, your lordships, Ah can only say Ah'm sorry, reight
sorry, that Ah am. But, beggin' your lordships' pardons, it
strikes me as bein' like this, beggin' your lordships' pardons—
if Ah can go down to Lord's and get drunk and mek a century
'fore lunch, then Ah thinks it ud pay t'Notts Committee to
get mi drunk afore every match—beggin' your lordships'
pardon, of course."

The modern professional cricketer does not get drunk at
Lord's or often get a century there, or anywhere else, before
lunch.

.   .   .   .   .   .

Humour in Lancashire during recent years has been thinner than in Yorkshire. The difference in nature of the two counties may be likened to the difference in texture between cottons and woollens—and in the different economic conditions governing the two industries. There has been much "clemmin" in Lancashire; as a consequence the county's cricket has had as much grimness and parsimony as Yorkshire's, but much less than Yorkshire's saving relish and ability to expand at the right time and give us not only a Rhodes and a Robinson but a Sutcliffe and a Maurice Leyland.

I have known the arrival of the Lancashire cricketers to spread dismay at the summer festivals of England, say at Cheltenham, where retired colonels sat in their deck-chairs, and when they heard which side had won the toss said, very fierce, "Those Lancashire cads are batting." There was a memorable occasion, too, down at Hove, on the lovely field there. For the whole of the first day Lancashire stone-walled ruining the holidays for thousands. On the third day the position of the match was crucial; leading by four runs only, Lancashire were about to begin a second innings. The Lancashire professionals called a meeting to discuss policy—a secret session. The captain did not matter; he wasn't called in. After much serious probing of the situation, and of tactics and strategy, it was unanimously decided on the proposal of Frank Watson that affairs being what they were: "Well, la-ads, we'd better play steady."

For four summers and more I never deserted the Lancashire team; the county were champions then, even above Yorkshire, thanks mainly to the most beautiful of all fast bowlers of our time, the Australian McDonald. Everybody loathed us because, as Yorkshiremen declared, we let a "foreigner" play for us. Emmott Robinson would not even refer to McDonald as an Australian, but deliberately named him a "Ta-asmanian," pronouncing the word with a histrionic intonation which somehow suggested to us that in Robinson's opinion a Tasmanian was black and wore a ring through his nose.

Only here and there every season was I free to visit Lord's in those years. Interest in Lancashire cricket throughout my native county was so acute that once when I neglected the champions to write about England v. Australia, I suspected

that I would be accused by many of my readers of disloyalty-
In course of time my renown as a writer on cricket
enabled me to go to any match of my own choosing; and
on the whole I chose Lord's, and I have spent at Lord's
some of the happiest hours of my life. On the heart of
"Cricketer" the name of Lord's will be found graven; and
on the heart of Neville Cardus the names of Salzburg and
Vienna.

.   .   .   .   .   .

In 1922, I published my first book with Grant Richards
who at the time appeared in my eyes a bloom of clothes and
a brilliance of monocle. How *A Cricketer's Book* came into
being I will leave to Grant Richards's own words: [1]

"I have told how the manuscript of *Limehouse Nights*
remained for long on a shelf behind my desk. A like fate
awaited a later book, Neville Cardus's *A Cricketer's Book*.
He sent it to me in a dishevelled state in 1922. It was one
of those offers that do not immediately attract the publisher.
The packet was made up of newspaper-cuttings, and why, I
asked myself, should I be expected to interest myself in a
book which was to me made up of articles that had appeared
in a daily newspaper, even though that daily newspaper was
the *Manchester Guardian*? However, I had published P. F.
Warner's *Cricket Reminiscences*, and I knew that cricket had
some devotees who read books, even though their number
was not as great as one would expect; and anyhow, whatever came out of the *Guardian* stable was worth backing on
general principles. After a time, therefore, I brought myself
to a consideration of Neville Cardus's proposal; and although
I knew nothing about cricket, I said I would publish. However, I would have nothing to do with a cheap publication.
Cardus had thought of a shilling or a half a crown. I am
by no means sure he was not right. The price I set on
A Cricketer's Book was six shillings; thereafter I gave the
same price to *Days in the Sun* and *The Summer Game*.
    "Cricketers do not frequent bookshops, and neither
Cardus nor I made a fortune. Nevertheless I was proud of

[1] From *Author Hunting* by Grant Richards.

About a thousand copies were sold by Grant Richards of my firstling. But if it did not enrich him, I trust that it did not contribute towards any period of brief vicissitude. He was superb. As soon as he got on his feet again, he travelled to Manchester more than ever like Wilkins Micawber translated and seen under the conditions of eternity and Savile Row. It was then that he took me to lunch at the Midland Hotel in the finest French Restaurant extant. He implored me—that is the only word for it—to let him have another book by me on cricket. And again we ransacked the files. As a result, *The Summer Game* was compounded. He brought out an edition de luxe of it, at two guineas, each copy signed by the author. This I thought was the very ecstasy of quixotism. But he sold nearly all of them. Where they were sold and who bought them remains a mystery.

My early books, with all their rawnesses, obtained a public for me beyond the reach of the *Manchester Guardian*. Apparently a writer is obliged to publish a book before he can expect to be taken seriously by the bulk of the people; even one's daily and constant readers come to see fresh virtues in writings as soon as they appear between covers—virtues never discerned in the ephemeral columns of a newspaper. It is better, for a widespread reputation's sake, to publish a book that sells only 2,000 copies than to write brilliantly for years in any newspaper. That is, if it is a book out of the common run.

.   .   .   .   .   .

I have looked into an account I wrote of a journey from Manchester I went upon to write about cricket:

"Observe, happy man, from your bedroom window, at this moment as you prepare yourself for a journey to the South, observe the passers-by along the street opposite. They are going to work, going to the city, there to live stuffily in one dingy spot, while you—while you are going away for the beginning of a new cricket season. To-night these same poor souls will pass by your house again, back from the city, but you will not be there to see them return. By then you will be at the other end of England; perhaps you will have just been taken by the hotel porter to your room, just have unpacked, washed and gone out into the delicious streets, to delight yourself in them with the feeling of the miles you have covered that day. . . .

"At Wellington" (continues this diary of a pilgrimage), "or in some such place deep in the garden of our land, the journey is broken; there is a change here. The Manchester train goes out, leaving you exquisitely aware that you are now quite out of touch with Manchester. Your connection arrives—a train that obviously has never been in Manchester. The people on it have just as obviously never been in Manchester. Here, unmistakably, you are in a fresh hemisphere, entering on the last lap of your journey, through a drowsy landscape. And how peaceful is the closing hour of a day's railway travel; the mild agitations of the morning have spent themselves. The senses are tired at last of responding to new scenes, new sounds, new odours . . ."

Anybody reading that passage in cold blood might imagine that I had travelled on a magic carpet, to realms of gold, over minaret and hanging gardens. If I am not mistaken I had gone to Kidderminster to watch Worcester v. Lancashire. I confess that when I journeyed from England to Australia by air, on the most marvellous of magic carpets, one you could dine on, and have an excellent hock for lunch, I was not once inspired to such an Odyssey as the one described above, written in 1921. "Delicious streets" you will observe. Perhaps they were delicious, a quarter of a century ago. I saw them in time, whether streets of Kidderminster, Worcester, Canterbury, Leicester, Taunton, Tonbridge, Gloucester or Ashby de la Zouch—I saw them looking far from delicious, as the last rays from the summer evening sunshine fell like naphtha on pavements full of pimply youths in thirty-shilling suits and suede shoes, with their girl friends, nearly all bad of tooth, either going into or coming out of a Palais de Danse or Plaza. And the inns and hotels where I unpacked and washed in subsequent years: the same can for hot water, the same night commode with a tin clasp, the same wardrobe that came open suddenly after resistance, the same dressing-table with signs

on the top of it that some former guest had been careless with
his cigarettes, the same glass and water-bottle, and the same
sickly pink counterpane. And in the breakfast-room next
morning, the same cloistered dyspeptic gloom, and fried eggs
like baleful yellow eyes, and the same resigned waiters. It
was an England day by day losing character and all joy in
life generated by the individual. It was an England becoming
more and more unfriendly and shut up in itself and resigned.
Even at cricket matches in these country towns, I often felt
a sense of dejection. The local caterer supplied the lunches
for the crowds at a good profit, poor feeble stuff washed down
by bottled beer brought miles. The people sometimes hardly
seemed to possess strength to cheer boundary hits, when at
intervals they happened. The last time I sat on the rustic
benches of Taunton cricket field in summer, I watched two
Somersetshire professionals, both entirely of the town clerkly,
pushing and poking their bats at spiritless long-hops and half
volleys. And I imagined the ghost of Sammy Woods looking
on helpless to get at the bowling.

I came before long to dislike these miasmas of urban
monotony. There was at least character at Old Trafford and
Sheffield. But at last I made Lord's my headquarters, though
never a member of the M.C.C. and never free to go into the
pavilion during a Test match except by special dispensation.
Lord's conceded to the march of progress only on her own
terms, holding the balance between tradition and change. The
tulips were brought up to wear the M.C.C. colours. I always
felt that the M.C.C. did not in its heart of hearts approve of
a big crowd present at Lord's. When rain fell at Lord's,
putting an end to play for hours, the crowd was in God's
good time informed whether further cricket would take place
that day; a man was sent round the field propelling a con-
traption on wheels, like a velocipede, carrying a board on
which were chalked some tidings from the captains or the
umpires as to their intentions and the state of the wicket. I
have known Australians to visit Lord's for the first time and
loathe the feeling they received there of custom and prerogative.
But after a while I have known the same Australians thoroughly
assimilated, in love with the old order it stood for; they became
more royal than the King. They enjoyed seeing the patricians

in the Long Room at lunch, eating meat pies and drinking cans of beer—like patricians. Lord's was not, of course, all school-tie and patrician; it was a microcosm of London itself. There was the East End—near the Tavern—as well as the West End of the Long Room. When the promenade on the grass took place during lunch, Seven Dials was free to move with Belgrave Square; a Hendren is as symbolical of Lord's as ever the Hon. C. N. Bruce. Still, there is a limit to things; you can have J. W. Hearne at Lord's a sort of butler; you can have Patsy a head-groom or coachman; you can have big genial Jim Smith, out of the garden, so to say, or something to do with the buttery. But at Lord's you could not in decency have an Emmott Robinson permanently on the premises or any other embodiment of industry or trade. Cricket, I say, honours the *habitat*; the social historian w ill find in a study of it and its environment much that the blue-books omit.

A hundred times I have walked down the St. John's Wood Road on a quiet morning—that's the proper way to enjoy Lord's: choose a match of no importance, for preference one for which the fixture card promises a "band if possible." I have gone a hundred times into the Long Room out of the hot sun and never have I not felt that this is a good place to be in, and if the English simply *had* to make cricket a national institution and a passion and a pride, this was the way to do it, in a handsome hall and pavilion, a resting-place for the game's history, with its constitution to be found as much in Debrett as in "Wisden." I have looked through the great windows on the field of play and seen the cricketers in the heat, moving like creatures in another element, the scene as though suspended in time; the crowd a painted canvas; the blue sky and the green of the trees at the nursery end; the lordly ones slumbering on the white seats of the pavilion, or quietly talking. On the Friday morning when Hitler invaded Poland, I chanced to be in this same Long Room at Lord's watching through windows for the last time for years. Though no spectators were present, a match was being continued; there was no legal way of stopping it. Balloon barrages hung over Lord's. As I watched the ghostly movements of the players outside, a beautifully preserved member of Lord's, spats and rolled umbrella, stood near me inspecting the game. We did not speak of course; we had not been introduced. Suddenly two workmen entered the Long Room in green aprons and carrying a bag. They took down the bust of W. G. Grace, put it into the bag, and departed with it. The noble lord at my side watched their every movement; then he turned to me. "Did you see, sir?" he asked. I told him I had seen. "That means war," he said.

II

A boy looks upon his heroes at cricket with emotions terribly mixed. He believes they are as gods, yet at the same time he has no real confidence in them. He thinks they are going to get out nearly every ball. At least that is how I suffered on every day I sat in the sixpenny seats at Old Trafford and looked at Maclaren and Spooner and Tyldesley. An iron rail ran round the green circle of Old Trafford, and when I got a place on a front bench I would press my forehead against this iron rail and pray for heavenly aid for my heroes, as I saw them exposed to the barbarians from Yorkshire—George Hirst rolling up the sleeve on his great ham of a left arm, ready to swing it and hurl a new red ball at the wicket of Reggie Spooner, hurl it like a live coal; and Spooner seemed frail and his bat scarcely a solid, while all the other Yorkshire men swarmed round him. Then would I pretend to be looking on the ground for something while I closed my eyes and prayed that God would make George Hirst drop down dead before bowling the next ball. I loved Spooner so much that I dared not watch him make stroke. It is a curious thought—I probably *never* saw him at the moment which he actually played a ball.

Strangely indeed does a boy think that his favourite cricketers are the best in the world but still the most fallible and in need of his every devoted thought. I used to walk the Manchester streets careful not to tread on cracks between the pavements; or I would touch each lamp-post as I passed, and like Dr. Johnson I would go back if I feared I had missed one or not touched it with enough thought. But I was not propitiating the gods on my own behalf but on behalf of my darlings of cricket. The trials and suspense of my adoration of them! I cannot tell how the slender nervous and physical system that was mine ever survived the strain and wear and tear. No later crises of life—and I have known a few—have so sorely tried me.

Sometimes I got myself into difficult positions with God.

There was Victor Trumper for example, next to Maclaren and Spooner my most adored. He was an Australian and I was a patriotic English lad. I wanted him always to score a century, but I also wanted England to get him out first ball and win the match. Obviously, I realised, it would be unreasonable to expect God to do for me these two things at one and the same time; for even He could not make Trumper score a century and be defeated first ball; there were, I knew, limits to Divine Power, and I was reasonable enough not to embarrass God, so I reflected carefully about it, and presented my petition in the most accommodating terms I could think of; "Please God, let Victor Trumper score a century to-day for Australia against England—out of a total of 137 all out."

In 1904 Lancashire never once came near defeat until August, then at Leeds against the loathsome Yorkshiremen they were encompassed by peril—Maclaren and Spooner and Tyldesley and all. I could not go to Leeds, so how do you imagine I spent Bank Holiday, knowing that Lancashire were losing? I went into the city of Manchester, where I could be on the spot when the different editions of the newspapers came out with later and later details of the match. Outside the office of the *Manchester Evening News* I waited, while the hours stood still. I looked at the Town Hall clock and willed the fingers to move, screwing my eyes to see the slightest motion of them. I performed various acts to get the gods on my side and on Lancashire's side; I stood over a grid in a gutter and told myself that if I could spit through it without touching the bars Lancashire would after all be spared.

The city streets were more or less vacant, save for a few stragglers. Everybody was away, at the seaside or in the country. The August sunshine was full of dust and melancholy. Stray cats made themselves thinner and more pliable as they struggled to go through iron palings in deserted areas. Two o'clock and three o'clock and four o'clock; J. T. Tyldesley was still not out; Maclaren and Spooner had gone early. Four o'clock, five o'clock, to half-past six, close of play, then the coming of the news that paid for everything and lifted chains of staggering time from me and rendered me as happy as ever in my life—or as relieved—for Lancashire's day was saved by a century by Tyldesley—yes, even this horrible abysm of hours was bridged somehow for me. The day, after all, passed and spent itself, revealed its worst and its best, so imperceptibly that it seemed never for a second really to pass. And it was followed by to-morrow, and the day after, and all subsequent days, while as imperceptibly I passed with it and them, which is a thought that seems to me not accountable at all, as I write æons after, from a world far removed— a thought mysterious and pathetic.

.   .   .   .   .   .

I drank deep of these vintage cricket years. Trumper one day, Maclaren the same day; next day, Ranjitsinhji. When the Sussex team came North, the imagination of Manchester boys ran riot. You must bear in mind that forty years ago the England of the North was much farther from London than the crow flew or the railway travelled. To me, who had not yet put foot out of Manchester, Sussex was as though in another hemisphere. So that when the Sussex men loomed on our view in Lancashire, we beheld them like unto a cavalcade out of the warm South; and if it was not headed by Kumar Shri Ranjitsinhji on an elephant panoplied with gold and diademed with rubies, then a boy's fancy must not be counted more closely related to truth than obvious facts and appearance.

"Ranji" cast his magic over all his team; we saw them in the glow of his Eastern splendour. And C. B. Fry was his Grand Vizier, the subtle adviser to the Prince, the Machiavellian logician who evolved a comprehensive statecraft of batsmanship from "Ranji's," first and governing principle: "Play back or drive."

Fry is still a handsome man in his early seventies; when he was a young man he moved about the field like a Greek god. I once saw Walter Brearley, the fast bowler, hit Fry on the hand; and Fry walked almost to the fence on the square-leg boundary shaking his bruised finger, with not any loss of dignity at all, not to announce his agony to the world; he was simply absorbed, like a student of metaphysics, in the problem of pain.

my share in the production of these three books. Let me add that Neville Cardus, my friend, is a most difficult author to handle. In spite of the fact that the first proposal came from him—the result, I suppose, of some friend's urging [1]— he will not believe that his stuff is worth reprinting—and the getting of a second and third book out of him was as difficult as anything I have ever experienced. But what a writer! I went to Manchester once and ordered a luncheon in his honour. *Homard à l'Americaine* figured in it. He told me that he did not, generally, care for eating, but that he did care for lobster. I do not think he thought better of me for offering him such a meal. I like him none the less. An austere and sensitive figure."

I promise Grant Richards now—according to the calendar he has reached his seventy years but I don't believe it—that I shall prove to him, next time we meet in a reasonably sane and safe world, how an ascetic in time learned to eat and drink like a man. I chose him of all publishers and sent him my sheaves of cuttings from the "M. G." because since boyhood I had been attracted by his manifest love of books as things of the spirit and not commodities of trade. I wish I could have assisted in making the fortune he deserved.

The *Daily Telegraph* and the *Morning Post* each gave my first book a whole-column review on the day of publication. For a moment I entertained visions of a best-seller; and of course, like all authors, I urged Grant Richards to take more space in the papers to advertise me. I surreptitiously watched the progress of a pile of my book displayed for sale in the principal bookshop in Manchester. It seemed as solid and permanent as marble or any gilded monument. Time would never touch or decrease it, I thought. When next I visited London, I entered Hatchard's in Piccadilly, and by the subtle device of buying a book by another author I looked for a copy of mine. None to be seen. So I took courage and asked, "Have you a copy of *A Cricketer's Book* by—er—Neville Something or other," disguising my voice. No; they hadn't heard of it; besides, nobody bought cricket books except by P. F. Warner.

[1] This supposition was accurate.

In those days "Ranji" and Fry were tremendous. I often lay in bed at night and wondered how they ever got out. At a time when a batting average of fifty an innings was a sure proof of genius, Ranjitsinhji scored 3,000 runs in a season, average nearly 90. Then in 1901, the miraculous occurred; Fry scored six centuries in successive innings. He began with 106 against Hampshire, but we were not astonished at that; Fry was expected to score a century against Hampshire at any time. In the following match, and his next innings, Fry scored 209 against Yorkshire; the excitement began to boil and bubble.

It is hard nowadays, when every anonymous batsman can make a century, to realise the thrill that we experienced in that simple period of 1901, when our sense of wonder had not yet been blunted. The crescendo of Fry's six hundreds sent all schoolboys—and boys of every age—into fevers of amazement and admiration.

Imagine, then, "Ranji" and Fry in all their pomp in 1902 —they are, of course, chosen for England to meet Australia; nay, the English XI is built or gathered around "Ranji" and Fry (and Maclaren, of course). At Lord's England win the toss; Fry goes in to bat first with his captain, A. C. Maclaren. Ten minutes later we are dumbfounded; all over the land the incredible tidings flash on the humming telegraph wires. In every special edition of the newspapers the following statement is published, hot from Lord's—and never before or since has a piece of news from a cricket field created so immense a sensation, and never before or since has any one piece of cricket news achieved so certain an immortality:

ENGLAND BATTING. LATEST SCORE

ENGLEND O FOR 2 WICKETS

A. C. Maclaren, not out.................... 0
C. B. Fry, c Hill, b Hopkins.............. 0
K. S. Ranjitsinhji, b Hopkins............ 0

F. S. Jackson helped Maclaren to stop this outrageous decline and fall; at lunch England was 102 for two wickets. Then the weather broke, and it rained for the rest of the match, weeping for so much splendour cast down and humbled, by an unknown Australian of the name of—help us!—Hopkins.

.   .   .   .   .   .

Sometimes when I am writing these memories from long years spent in the open air watching cricket, my pen seems as though guided by an influence which is not a conscious part of me; do you remember the old-time "Ouija" board and "spirit writing"? The other day I began a fresh chapter of this book and found myself putting down on paper impressions I had not had in mind for years. Again I saw a boy walking down the Warwick Road, Old Trafford, Manchester, ages ago, when Old Trafford was surrounded by green fields. People went to cricket matches at Old Trafford in those days on a tram drawn by two horses. On the top of the tram, which we called "outside," the seats were not placed so that they looked to the front and towards the driver. There were two long benches, back to back, and when we sat on them, all in a row, we looked over the side of the tram. When two trams came to a standstill opposite one another, which they not infrequently did, we would find ourselves face to face with a row of perfect strangers only a yard away from us, suspended in mid-air, in conversational touch with us, yet for so brief a space of time that it would have been a vain thing even to try to make approaches.

Seldom did the boy that once was the present writer go to Old Trafford on a tram. You could buy a lot with a penny in those days: a bottle of "pop" and the stopper inside was a glass ball which we afterwards got out by breaking the neck —then we added it to our artillery of marbles, a glass "ally"! This "pop" was a highly carbonised form of liquid refreshment; and when we had slaked our thirst with it we would enter into competitions at belching, easy to begin with, but harder as they went on and the gas lost its effect. For a penny, with Queen Victoria's head on one side, a boy in those days could go far; with six of them he could watch Victor Trumper or A. C. Maclaren. But it was a terrible responsibility to walk miles to Old Trafford, where the skies are not always blue.

Outside the sixpenny entrance was a large board on which was painted the following sinister sign:

NO MONEY RETURNED

THE PUBLIC ENTERS AT ITS
OWN RISK OF THE WEATHER
By Order

The statement in itself was frightening enough. But it was rendered even more awful by that "By Order"; I never quite understood what it meant; it struck my young mind as almost Jehovahish.

In a world not yet gorged with sensation we believed in hero-worship and the Great Man. The influence of Carlyle was still on us. A. C. Maclaren, as I have told you, lighted a fire in me never to be put out. He had an aristocratic face; he walked the grass as though he lorded it; when he was setting his field he waved the players here and there with far-reaching gestures. You would see some nervous deep long-off dithering a few yards to the left, a few yards to the right, controlled by Maclaren's directing hands as they waved and made passes, until the man at deep long-off settled exactly into the place desired by the master mind. Maclaren would now take up his position in the slips; he would fastidiously pick his trousers at the knees and bend down, arms outstretched —not ravenously outstretched, not craving a catch, but waiting for one, as his due. When a snick sped to him from a fast bowler, Maclaren descended on it and the ball was thrown high in the air, with the same action which had scooped it up, an eighth of an inch from the turf—a great swift circling action, momentous and thrilling. Maclaren never looked to see where the ball went after he had thrown it high over his shoulder.

As I watched him my young eyes saw him robed in glory. Once a left-handed bowler named Hargreave played for Warwickshire, and with the ignorance of the heathen he came to Old Trafford, Maclaren's field of State, and there, in front of our very eyes, this same Warwickshire pleb clean-bowled Maclaren for o. I can at any time see it all happening; a warm afternoon; Lancashire had got rid of Warwickshire for a poor total. At about four o'clock the Lancashire innings began, Maclaren and Albert Ward. The captains always took the first ball. He asked for his guard from the umpire: "Two-leg, if you don't mind, George," like a lord of the manor benignly giving instructions on his estate (his autocracy was unfailingly gracious). He marked the spot on the crease with a bail which he picked up from the stumps, returning it to its socket in his own good time, while everybody waited. Next he surveyed the positions in the field with a Cæsarian eye. Now, at last, he was prepared to receive the attack; it was like a levée.

The rude inglorious Hargreave chewed a blade of grass while Maclaren attended to these ceremonies. He then slouched to his bowling place, ran a few steps and wheeled over his left arm casually, as though in the nets. Maclaren played forward —and you have not seen a cricketer play forward if you never saw Maclaren: a sumptuous thrust of the left leg, the bat swinging down, curved with rhythmic power. And he missed Hargreave's slow spinner which just, only just, removed the off bail. We watched in silence; we saw the great dethrone-ment. When Maclaren returned to the pavilion not a soul made a sound by word of mouth; but one or two members stood up as a sign of respect.

Yes, A. C. Maclaren taught me through the game of cricket the meaning of epic romance, style, generosity of gesture. When he batted, you could have said of him that

> for his bounty,
> There was no winter in't; an autumn 'twas
> That grew the more by reaping: his delights
> Were dolphin-like; they showed his back above
> The element they lived in; in his livery
> Walk'd crowns and crownets. . . .

To see Maclaren hook a fast ball—especially a fast ball of Ernest Jones—from the front of his face, was in those days an experience which thrilled me like heroic poetry; he didn't merely hook the ball, he dismissed it from his presence.

Once in a Test Match at Sydney, Maclaren won the toss and went in first with Tom Hayward. Arrived at the wicket,

Archie took guard in his customary lord-of-creation manner; a vast crowd waited while Maclaren stretched his shoulders, reviewed the fieldsmen in front of him, then looked round to the leg-side. Joe Darling had placed three men near Maclaren's legs in a close semi-circle. Maclaren addressed himself to Darling:

"Joe," he said, "what's the meaning of this?"

"What's the meaning of what, Archie?"

"Why," said Maclaren, indicating with a sweep of his bat the crouching leg-side fieldsmen, "why—what are these people doing here, Joe?"

"That's my field for you, Archie," replied Darling. Maclaren waved his bat at them again. "Joe," he said, "take them away."

"Take who away?" inquired Darling.

"You know what I mean, Joe," said Maclaren, "please take them away."

And Darling persisted: "But, Archie, I can set my field as I choose; get on with the game."

"Take them away, Joe," said Archie with undisturbed patience, "how do you expect me to make my celebrated hook-stroke if these damned silly people get in my way?"

Darling declined to change his field, so Ernest Jones bowled and the match at last began. Maclaren drove Jones twice or thrice for straight fours, then Darling removed a man from the leg-trap and sent him to the deep, behind the bowler. "Thank you, Joe," said Maclaren, "now we may proceed with the match like gentlemen."

He was incapable of a paltry gesture. Years after his day was done he came to his own Old Trafford; a Test Match was being played. During a deluge of rain I took shelter at the entrance of a tea shed and there I found Maclaren also sheltering with the crowd.

"Good lord, Archie," I said, "what are you doing here? Why aren't you in the Pavilion amongst the mighty?"

"Oh," he replied, "I'm quite all right. I didn't receive an invitation; probably it's miscarried. I'm writing about the match for the *News of the World*" At this moment a waitress emerged from the interior of the tea shed carrying a tray covered with a napkin. She was about to go through the rain to an adjoining enclosure for "lady" members; but Maclaren stopped her, and he took off his raincoat and laid it over her shoulders; then with a wave of his hand in the waitress's direction he said, "*Now*, my dear."

I saw the curtain come down on Maclaren's career. I was present at Eastbourne when Maclaren walked for the last time from an English cricket field, captain of the first team to defeat the victorious Armstrong and his men. The Australians won three Test matches one after the other in the wonderful summer of 1921; they had won five Test matches out of five during the winter of 1920-1921 in their own country. They came to England in the sunshine of our summer in 1921 and annihilated our players with cynical ease in the first three Test matches, after which they patronisingly allowed us to make drawn issues of the remaining two games, while they enjoyed themselves, as a cat with a mouse he has killed.

One morning in August a note came to me from Maclaren asking me to journey South to Eastbourne, where he told me a team of "amateurs" under his leadership (he was emerging from years of retirement for the occasion) were to tackle the Australians. His eleven would be composed of young cricketers mainly; the Ashtons, and Percy Chapman, then only a rosy-faced slim giant of a boy. "I think I know how to beat Armstrong's lot," added Maclaren in a postscript; "come and write about it for the *Guardian*." It so happened that on this August Saturday one or two important matches were beginning in London. Yorkshire were playing Surrey at Kennington Oval, a serious engagement fraught with consequence to the county championship; and at Ley ton my own county were playing Essex.

When I told my news editor that I proposed to miss these two events of consequence and that I wished to go to Eastbourne to describe the match between "Gentlemen of England v. The Australians" he would not at first hear of it. "Nonsense," he said, "it'll be all over in a day and nobody's interested. Your job is at the Oval with Yorkshire." But I persisted; I said I had a premonition that Maclaren would achieve something; anyhow the match would certainly be his last appearance in English cricket and therefore worth a column or two of my best rhetoric. Reluctantly the news editor agreed (it was W. P. Crozier) and I travelled to Eastbourne on the Friday, and next morning I found myself amongst the deck-chairs and the white tents, under a sky of sapphire. Not a single newspaper correspondent was present except myself, and the local reporters. Not one writer in London had thought it worth his while to come and see what sort of mincemeat Armstrong would make of Maclaren's innocents. And before the game was an hour old I felt a fool to be witness of it; I soon knew I was to become a week-end's laughing stock in the eyes of my editor and of my colleagues of the press at large. For at lunch Maclaren's team was all out for forty-three.

It was too late now to leave Eastbourne and catch an afternoon train to London; I had to stay through this farcical Saturday afternoon at the Saffrons while the Australians batted a picnic innings for just under 200 before half-past six. The match was, of course, as good as finished. I felt ashamed to write my customary *Guardian* article, and when on the Monday morning, I bought a copy of the paper I went hot and cold to see a long column about an anti-climax; my deputy was given pride of place for his account of Lancashire at Leyton. I went to the Saffrons again on the Monday morning, when the Australians took the field again with the intention of putting an end to the game before lunch. I had packed my bag and had sent it to the railway station; there was an express to London just before one o'clock; and I would be able to reach Kennington Oval in good time for the afternoon's cricket there. I went to the Saffrons once more on this Monday morning in August 1921, for sentimental reasons. Maclaren had gone in first on the Saturday evening, as a stop-gap; I wished to look on him as he faced, for the last time, an Australian fast bowler. He was bowled straightway by the lovely panther McDonald. As Maclaren came from the wicket, grey-haired and stooping, I slowly began to walk round the ground towards the exit gate; I was now definitely leaving for London. There was no need for haste; the train did not leave for an hour. I gently strolled over the grass, under the trees and their brown early autumn leaves, behind the little wooden benches that ringed the playing-field. As

I sauntered towards the exit gate I casually glanced over my shoulder at the game. I saw the veteran South African batsman, Aubrey Faulkner, and Hubert Ashton come together and heard their quiet strokes making echoes in the deserted place. By the time I had reached the exit gate I had seen enough. I retraced my steps a little; I sat on a bench facing the pavilion. I did not go to London that day. Or the next. I stayed on at Eastbourne. I saw Faulkner and Hubert Ashton make a great stand; I saw Aubrey Faulkner's last big innings. And next day I saw C. H. Gibson of Cambridge University skittle out the Australians; Maclaren won by 28 in a scene of heartbeats and shouts. The Australians would have given hairs from their heads to save themselves. Best of all, at the end, I saw Maclaren coming from the field, conqueror in the last great match of his career in England, his sweater hung about his shoulders and his grey head bared to the crowd as he raised his cap to acknowledge their acclamations.

At this incredible match, at this consummation of a great cricketer's life, the *Manchester Guardian* was the only notable newspaper represented. By my faith in Maclaren I achieved this, the only "scoop" of my career. . . .

I once waited (aged twelve) an hour outside Old Trafford after stumps had been drawn to see the cricketers, and at last Clem Hill came through the gates dressed in ordinary clothes, but I penetrated the disguise at once and I off-handedly informed a man next to me that it was Clem Hill. Nowadays, of course, small boys rush up to famous cricketers and demand autographs. One day (aged fourteen) I got into the district train outside Old Trafford after a Lancashire and Yorkshire match. To my awe, who should enter my compartment but A. C. Maclaren and Walter Brearley. I sat trembling as I gazed at these two gods come down for a while to walk the earth or, rather, to ride in an ordinary railway carriage. There was no other mortal being in the compartment except myself, and I held my breath. And Maclaren said to Brearley, "Well, Walter; you're a nice sort of bloody fast bowler!" and Agamemnon answered Ulysses thus: "And you're a bloody fine slip fielder you are, aren't you, Archie?"

My most precious memory of Maclaren is of the only

match in which I ever took part with him as one of the
players. He was captain of the other side and I was captain
of an improvised army called the *Manchester Guardian* XI.
The game occurred round about 1923 on the same sacred Old
Trafford field, where years before I had looked on Maclaren
so often. He was now, of course, an Old Master, retired from
the fray, but upright and authoritative. Heaven help me, if
on this same Old Trafford turf he did not come forth to bat,
with R. H. Spooner—the two heroes of my boyhood, here at
the wicket and myself opening the bowling. I prayed to
heaven: "Let me bowl him." An opportunity never dreamed!
If I could only get him caught somewhere. My first ball
broke back inches; Maclaren played forward (memories of
Hargreave!). And I missed his leg-stump by a hair's breadth.
The ball went for byes—three of them were run, then Maclaren, short of wind, said to me: "Well bowled, Cardus, that
was a good one. I never suspected you could bring them back
from the off. But so long as we know . . ." When I next sent
him another off-break, he calmly stepped back and his bat
swept it first bounce into the refreshment-room. So long as
he knew! He scored fifty not out that day and I think it was
his last innings of all. I am proud to relate that he hit me for
three sixes.

When I was a boy, Lancashire's first three batsmen, Nos. 1,
2 and 3, in the order of going in were A. C. Maclaren, R. H.
Spooner and Johnny Tyldesley. No team has ever opened an
innings with a more brilliant trio of stroke-players. Reggie
Spooner was the lyrical batsman—Herrick to the Gibbon
prose of a Maclaren innings. Tyldesley was Mercutio and
d'Artagnan rolled into one, if I may revert to my earlier
prose manner. He cut fast bowling square with the right arm
of a man in a smithy. I once saw a ball split into two pieces
after Tyldesley had cut it square. Or at least I thought I
saw it.

It does not always rain at Old Trafford. The ghost of a
happy small boy walks there, to this day. Old Trafford was
bombed by the Germans. I might have thought it was being
bombed, except that the possibility of bombs on cricket fields
had not yet occurred to us, when first I saw Gloucestershire
playing at Old Trafford round about 1899. Towards lunch-

time I left my seat to buy a bottle of ginger-beer before the crowd swarmed into the refreshment-room. I was placing my money on the counter, standing on tiptoe to reach, when suddenly there was a terrible noise and crash. Broken bottles and splinters of glass flew about everywhere, and I thought that the end of the world had come and that Professor Falb had been right after all. A man in the bar soothed my fears. "It's all reight," he said, in a strong and honest Lancashire speech, "it's all reight, sonny—it's only Jessop just coom in to bat."

After Ranjitsinhji and Victor Trumper, Jessop was the most incredible cricketer that ever lived. Nowadays when a slogger hits sixes, you will hear people call him "a regular Jessop." It is a libel. Jessop was not a crude slogger; he did not heave his bat about from a fast-footed position, rooted to the earth. A good bowler can get a slogger caught in next to no time by sending him an outswinger just a little short. Jessop scored thousands of runs at a great speed against some of the greatest bowlers in the history of cricket. Rapid scoring is not possible unless a batsman can cut. It is the presence of the cut that compels a bowler to avoid bowling that just-too-short-of-a-length ball which cannot be driven. Jessop had a flexible wrist, and his square-cutting was as terrible as his hooking. And so the bowler was obliged to pitch the ball up to Jessop's bat—and then he sprang upon it like a tiger. He was a small compact, sturdy man, with a square chin, and he walked to the wicket ferociously, then bent low over his bat. They called him the "Croucher". . .

the human catapult
Who wrecks the roofs of distant towns
When set in his assault.

At Kennington Oval in 1902, Jessop played the most wonderful innings in all the annals of Test matches. On a bad wicket England were trapped; they needed 263 to win. Three men were out for 10, and five for 48—the cream of English batsmanship; Maclaren, Palairet, J. T. Tyldesley, Hayward and Braund. Nothing apparently could be done against the Australian attack on the vicious turf. F. S. Jackson played a watchful game while the pitch was at its worst; but in the circumstances science was out of the question. For science demands some foundation of logic and order; and how was it possible for mortal batsman to apply known principles to bowling which on an insane wicket performed illogicalities of spin, and behaved like something in a Walt Disney film? Jessop came forth, and he at once took the game out of the prison of cause and effect; he plunged it into the realms of melodrama, where virtue is always triumphant. Before he came to the wicket on this lurid afternoon, the Australian team had been a ruthless machine—the unplayable ball and the clutching hand in the slips. In a short period this same Australian team was reduced to a rabble. Jessop scored 50 in 55 minutes; and then another 54 in ten minutes; that is, he made 104 in 65 minutes, in a Test match, on a bowler's pitch, after his team had lost five wickets for 48. Kennington Oval that day went crazy. People had been leaving the ground in thousands. Jessop caused delirium; perfect strangers embraced. The ball was a dangerous missile all over the ground and out of it. Fieldsmen went in danger of decapitation. The windows of Kennington were threatened, and the neighbouring streets were noisy with an excited mob who could hear, if they could not see, what was going on inside the Oval.

I watched my first Test match in this season of 1902. It was played at Manchester, and of course the weather was rainy. On a threatening morning, with clouds and sun struggling for mastery above Old Trafford, A. C. Maclaren won the toss for England. The wicket was wet and the outfield was heavy. Maclaren's strategy was directed at Victor Trumper. "Keep Victor quiet" were Maclaren's orders to his team as they went into action; "the pitch will be sticky after lunch, then we'll bowl 'em out as quick as they come in. If the Australians are only 80 or so at the interval, we've won the match, and the rubber. So keep Victor quiet, at all costs!" And the subtlest of England's cricket captains, the most imperial, concentrated all his craft in reducing Trumper to immobility. The field was set deep to save the fours; length bowlers as accurate as Rhodes, F. S. Jackson, Tate (father of

Maurice), pitched the ball where they imagined Victor would not be able to reach it.

The outcome of all this scheming, of all these canny protective devices, of all the plots and strategems to "keep Victor quiet," was that Victor scored a century before lunch. Years afterwards, a number of Maclaren's friends chaffed him about this extraordinary frustration of his generalship. We were engaged in a friendly dinner, after a good day's sport, and during coffee and liqueurs we harked back to the olden times. We challenged Maclaren: "Why, Archie, you must have slipped a bit when you allowed Trumper to win the 1902 rubber on a turf nearly waterlogged in the outfield. Did you place too many men deep, and allow Victor to pick up the runs through the gaps near the wicket?" Maclaren, who adored an argument, rose to the bait; he took lumps of sugar out of the basin and set them all over the table, saying "Gaps be damned! Good God, I knew my man—Victor had half a dozen strokes for the same kind of ball. I exploited the inner and outer ring—a man there, a man there, and another man covering *him*." (He banged the lumps of sugar down one by one, punctuating his luminous discourse.) "I told my bowlers to pitch on the short side to the off: I set my heart and brain on every detail of our policy. Well, in the third over of the morning, Victor hit two balls straight into the practice-ground, high over the screen, behind the bowler. I couldn't very well have had a man fielding in the bloody practice-ground, now could I?"

I was only twelve years old when I saw Trumper at Old Trafford on this deathless morning of July 24, 1902. His cricket burns always in my memory with the glow and fiery hazard of the actual occurrence, the wonderful and consuming ignition. He was the most gallant and handsome batsman of them all; he possessed a certain chivalrous manner, a generous and courtly poise. But his swift and apparent daring, the audacity of his prancing footwork, were governed by a technique of rare accuracy and range. Victor was no mere batsman of impulsive genius; he hit the ball with the middle of his bat's blade—even when he pulled from the middle stump round to square leg. In my memory's anthology of all the delights I have known, in many years devoted to the difficult

but entrancing art of changing raw experiences into the connoisseur's enjoyment of life, I gratefully place the cricket of
Victor Trumper.

.   .   .   .   .   .

With mixed feelings I saw the growth of my reputation as
a writer on cricket. A natural satisfaction contended against
revolt from the temporarily frustrated music critic in me I
know as "N. C.," whose place of abode in my consciousness
is located somewhere within the third frontal convolution of
the left hemisphere of the brain. "N. C." knew well enough
that in England a man who wins a reputation in one walk
or activity of life will need to work desperately hard to win
reputation in another. Even a dramatic critic is not as a rule
taken seriously whenever he turns his attention to music;
how could I reasonably hope then, to outlive some day my
national renown as "Cricketer" and be given the ear of serious
musicians? I emerged triumphant from the odds-against
battle in the long run; but vast armies of prejudice had to be
overcome. Without the support of the *Manchester Guardian*
and its good name for fine thinking, Hazlitt himself might
well have been discouraged and defeated in a country in which
all the arts are tainted with intellectual snobbishness.

I never dreamed that my writings on cricket would create
a cricket Intelligentsia; and I was as astonished as I was
delighted when Massingham of the *Nation* invited me in 1921
to contribute an "essay" on the game to his great journal. I
wrote for him the chapter called "The Cricketer as Artist,"
which is reprinted in *Days in the Sun*. Then, shortly afterwards,
Lord Birkenhead sent me a letter in his own hand asking me
for permission to allow him to include "Cricket Fields and
Cricketers," also from *Days in the Sun*, amongst his selection
of *A Hundred Best English Essays*, which he himself prefaced
by a short account of me, calling me "an enchanter." J. C.
Squire and Hugh Walpole and James Agate and J. B. Priestley
and J. L. Garvin and Edward Shanks—they all took me to
heart and gave me confidence at a time when I needed it.
Garvin almost embarrassed me in a review of *The Summer
Game* by beginning with this sentence:

"Amongst journalists Mr. Cardus—'Cricketer' of the *Manchester Guardian*—is a man of genius. Amongst writers of any kind there is none more conspicuously first in his own subject."

(Violent jealousy on the part of "N. C."!)

Then, in the same review Garvin described cricket in prose which turned me enviously green. For example:

"Before the stumps, the exposed hero or victim wields a club shaped with curious felicity, perhaps beloved like a Stradivarius; and eleven men are alert to take his life—one of them hurling a hard and crafty missile while ten others bend like leopards. And hearts may thump when the field is most silent, the action least, and the spirit deadly. The intelligent foreigner, puzzled to death (and bored to it) at Lord's, beseeches you what this means. It is the one thing about England you can never explain. A mystery-play, in another sense, it is alive with invisible elements. It grew like Topsy or the Constitution, or like the elms that seem as tall as steeples to small boys, as our witness remembers."

A. J. J. Ratcliff chose a cricket essay by me—my favourite —for an English prose text-book for schools; it was on Jolyon going to Lord's; a chapter which Galsworthy omitted strangely to write. At the end of this text-book was a set of examination papers; the student was asked to give examples of each author's rhythm, development and construction. I was most impressed by the questions posed about myself; I could not have coped with a single one of them. I have never known that gift, so necessary in a writer, according to Walter Pater:"the prescience which foretells the end in the beginning of the work of the intellect, the last sentence in the first of a prose-piece." I have seldom known where my pen was about to lead me in anything I have ever written. I have gone to work much as the artist in *Don Quixote* who, when he was asked what he was painting, said: "That is as it may turn out."

I wondered in these early days whether C. P. Scott looked at my writings on cricket after his first inspection of them. I seldom saw him now. I did not any longer occupy a room of my own in the office; I was here, there and everywhere for five months a year. I felt I was losing touch with the real heart of the paper, and I groaned when Beecham gave a matinée performance one summer day of *Pelléas and Mélisande*, and I was obliged to go to watch Lancashire at Old Trafford. It was no doubt through this temporary frustration of the other and real part of my personality that my cricket columns during 1920-1926 were many times used by me to get off my chest pent-up impressions of the arts and life in general. In July, 1922, I was goaded to send over the telegraph, to the sports sub-editors of the "M. G.," the following report of a day of cricket, on which A. P. F. Chapman and A. W. Carr played brilliantly. Without due warning I opened thus:

"The fun of the world is often enough realised only when it is over and done with. Most of us live in the past or the future, sighing for the good old days or straining eyes after to-morrow's vision. And history flies by and few of us see her thrilling colours; few of us even hear the beating of her wings. Did Paris fully savour the diet of happenings that went upon the Monday night of June 20, 1791, when Marie Antoinette fled from the Tuileries; when the Queen-lady, in a gipsy hat, rode through the night in the glass coach and lo! Fersen drove right northward? Did Paris let itself bask next morning in hot appreciation that now the world was living through the time of its life? Or did not old men go on declaring that things were hardly what they used to be, and young men go on yearning for the better years to come. . . . At Lord's to-day we heard now and again an old man crying out for another Maclaren, another Stoddart, even while Carr and Chapman flashed from their bats as stirring a beauty as ever . . ." etc., and so forth. Did Carlyle ever dream he would one day be pressed to lend his smoky eloquence to an extoller of English leisure, even idleness? His shade conceivably forgives me, for in the same article I dragged in Goethe neck and crop. . . .

One day Scott revealed that he had not altogether removed me from the kaleidoscope of his memory. I had returned from Old Trafford and written my column, had dined in my club and looked in at the office on my way home. A message waited for me on my desk; he wished to see me.

"Sit down, Cardus," he said. "I have been reading the proof of your cricket article. Now, as you know, the first rule on my paper is accuracy. You can be as fanciful with your prose as you like, but only from the basis of strict attention to the facts." He paused, and I waited for the thunderbolt.

"Now," he continued, "in your article to-day you write of a batsman playing with a straight bat, and you describe that his right elbow suggested an inverted V, and you compliment him in consequence. Now I agree that the inverted V metaphor is quite good. But surely you mean that it was the batsman's left not his right elbow that was so shaped?" To my horror he walked to the fireplace, picked up a long brass poker and went through the action of a right-handed batsman playing back with his left arm immaculately arched, to keep the bat straight. "I once played cricket myself when I was a boy—years and years ago, maybe, but I remember it all. When a batsman wishes to keep his bat straight, it is his left arm, not his right, that should suggest the inverted V. You must be careful, my dear fellow. Observation must always precede and control fancy and metaphor. Don't let it happen again, please."

Terror in my heart accumulated as he spoke; for he had walked into an awful hole, and I feared to expose his blunder to him. But for my own sake it had to be done. Swallowing apprehension, I said: "Yes, sir—but you see I was writing about Woolley; he's a left-hander—so well known that there's no need to allude to his left-handedness . . . and when a left-hander plays a straight bat it is his right arm that . . ."

He stopped me. I shall not forget it to my dying day. He said: "Cardus, I'm sorry. My mistake; my ignorance. I shall never again question one of my special writers on a point involving his own knowledge and observation." This was the most terrible of many experiences with C. P. S. in his room. I felt I had almost handed him the rope for his hanging or tripping—I had let him go on with his description of how he himself had once played forward; I had let him perform before me with a poker. I never afterwards dared to refer in conversation with him to this incident, not in our most friendly moments.

.   .   .   .   .   .

Early in 1926 I wrote to J. M. Barrie about a young actress I had seen in some provincial theatre playing Mary Rose; her name was Kathleen Kilfoyle and I thought she had come closer to the idea of the part than ever was within the more sophisticated scope of Fay Compton. When Barrie replied, he told me he had for years been reading me on cricket and would I come soon and spend a week-end with him at his flat in Robert Street, Adelphi Terrace. Another miracle. I had years ago pretended I was Sentimental Tommy; I had wondered whether Barrie would be my Pym. I had worshipped Peter Pan, or rather Captain Hook. All my earliest aspirations towards journalism had been kindled by reading Barrie's *When a Man's Single* and *My Lady Nicotine*; during the early nineteen-hundreds he symbolised a young man's most romantic notions about free-lance work in Fleet Street, pipe-smoking, and lodgings in London, and letters from editors commanding more and more articles.

In June, 1926, I accepted Barrie's invitation. It was at the end of a cricket tour and I arrived in London at nine o'clock on a chilly Friday evening, direct from Birmingham, where an England XI had been playing the Australians—a trial for the Test match due at Lord's in a few weeks. The Worcester-shire bowler Root had completely baffled the Australians with his leg-swerve on this Friday at Birmingham; and I had no sooner entered Barrie's flat and he had met me at the door than he asked, "What's this Root like? I've just seen the scores in the evening papers." I told him that I had written a most comprehensive account of Root's attack for to-morrow's *Manchester Guardian* and that I hoped he was too good a journalist to expect me to give away in advance my paper's "exclusiveness." He appreciated the point and next day he said, "I have read your description of Root; and now I not only know exactly how he bowls but I feel I could play him myself with confidence."

This week-end at Barrie's flat will make so strange a story that I must assure the reader that in telling it I have made no exaggeration and have carefully overhauled my memory. Maybe I suffered from delusions; I do not deny the possibility; the point is that if delusions did seize me they were so potent as to become inextricable from fact.

After Barrie had greeted me he showed me my bedroom and a shiver went down my spine when he told me, unnecessarily as I still think, that it had been "Michael's" room. (Michael Llewelyn-Davies had been drowned in 1922, almost four years to the day.) And now his manservant asked me for my keys. I had come South with only one suitcase, which contained the cast-off underclothes of the tour. There were other and even more intimate things in it. I had never stayed before at a house where a manservant in a brown brass-buttoned uniform asked you (in a tone of voice brooking no denial) for your keys.

This Thurston I have subsequently found out was a grand and sterling character. He spoke various languages, and would correct any loose statements about Ovid that he chanced to overhear while he was serving dinner. He had a ghostly face; he was from a Barrie play—so was Barrie, and the flat, and everything in it; the enormous cavern of a fireplace, the wooden settle and old tongs and bellows, and the sense the place gave you that the walls might be walked through if you had been given the secret. Barrie trudged the room smoking a pipe; on the desk lay another pipe already charged, ready for immediate service; he coughed as he trudged and smoked, a cruel cough that provoked a feeling of physical pain in my chest; and his splutterings and gaspings and talk struggled on one from the other. At last he came to sit facing me in front of the smouldering logs, and for a while the silence was broken by groans only to be heard in our two imaginations—the groans of men separated for ever by a chasm of shyness and uneasiness. Until midnight we lingered on. He offered me no refreshment. Thurston apparently went home to sleep each night. Or perhaps he merely dematerialised. Barrie knew I had dined on the train, but a nightcap would have been fortifying to me, I am sure; for already the spell of the flat high amongst the roofs of Adelphi was gripping me.

Next morning Thurston came into my bedroom with tea. He abruptly picked up my trousers and coat and disappeared with them. I had brought no other suit with me. For a frightful half-hour I imagined he was about to send them to the cleaners; and I could do nothing to prevent him. He brought them back neatly brushed, with my polished shoes. He showed me the bathroom, the most unkept I have ever known. The towels were damp and soiled; and round about the shelves were one or two shaving brushes congealed in ancient soap. A rusty razor blade on a window ledge was historical.

Barrie had his private bathroom; the unclean towels puzzled me. Was it the custom to bring your own towels when staying with distinguished people for a week-end? I dried myself as best I could, and now Thurston directed me to the breakfast-room, where he attended to me in complete silence, only once speaking to inform me that Sir James was staying in bed for a while but would be glad if I dined with him that evening. The formality of it all was perplexing. This was not my idea of the Barrie way of life. In after years it occurred to me that probably no other guest of my humble station in life had entered the flat for years and years and years.

I spent the day at Lord's and returned to Adelphi Terrace House at seven o'clock, where to my dismay a company of people was assembling. I forget all their names and titles, but the sight of E. V. Lucas consoled me, because of his large humanity. Nobody was dressed for dinner, which was thoughtful of Thurston; clearly he had revealed to Barrie that a dinner-jacket was not part of my miscellaneous luggage. I can remember nothing of the dinner-party save the occasional low chuckle of Lucas.

Next morning—Sunday—Thurston again served tea in my bedroom and took away my coat and trousers and waited on me, and watched me carefully at breakfast. He told me that Sir James had gone away until Monday; would I be in for dinner? I replied in as easy and affable a negative as I could muster and render audible. I spent the day in the parks and dined in Soho, and just before midnight I ascended the lift to the flat and let myself in with my latchkey and turned on the light. Not a sound. A cold collation had been laid for me on the table, with a bottle of hock and a silver box of cigarettes. I explored the bookcases, almost on tiptoe; there was a row of volumes of the Scottish philosophers—Hume, Mackintosh, Hamilton. I sat at Barrie's desk but got up immediately for fear I might be caught in the act. The great chimney corner, with no fire in it, glowered at me.

Thurston went through the usual ritual when I awoke after a middling night. The bathroom remained dishevelled. Having dressed I went into the breakfast-room, where at the table sat Margaret Ogilvie, to the life. She turned out not to be a figment of my now tottering brain, but Barrie's sister Maggie. How she came to be present, wearing a dressing-gown, was not explained. She was as gracious as could be, after the manner of all Barrie's women. She had "charm." She asked if I would call on her in her boudoir after dinner to-morrow evening and take part in a little musical "con-versazione"—for she loved music and would enjoy singing and playing to me. I did not dare inquire where the boudoir might chance to be situated or secreted.

After another day at Lord's I came back to the flat at dusk. Once more a cold collation and a bottle of hock waited for me. Once more the place was silent and, as far as I could tell without poking and peering and looking under tables and behind curtains, it was unpeopled. I poured me out a glass of wine then, as I drank, I heard the rumble of the lift and presently the door opened and a young man entered, in a dinner jacket. Without a sign of curiosity at my presence or at the absence of others, he remarked to me that it had been a lovely day. He sat on a couch, smoked a cigarette, and talked for a few minutes about the cricket at Lord's; he hadn't yet been able to look in at the match himself, but he had enjoyed my account of Saturday's play in the "M. G." I was liking him very much when he arose, and with an apology left the room and the flat. To this day I do not know who he was—probably young Simon out of *Mary Rose*.

Barrie was waiting for me next evening alone; we dined together and under the glow of a perfect Burgundy we thawed somewhat. He told me of his early days as a journalist and vowed he could never have made a footing in the London journalism of the present time—which was terribly true. He said that he had never been much interested in the theatre except as one who wrote for it. But it was difficult to keep him off cricket and he pooh-poohed my fears that perhaps I was wasting myself writing about it. He excused himself

from attendance at his sister's musical "conversazione" on
the grounds that he was unable to distinguish one note from
another. But he led me from the dining-room through another
room to the boudoir. I can only suppose it had been there all
the time; it was remotely Victorian in fragrance and appearance; and there was an upright piano with a fluted silk front.

Barrie handed me over to Maggie and escaped. She played
a composition of her own called "1914-1918" with a battle
section in the middle and a finale of bells and thanksgiving.
She next sang a number of Scotch songs in an expressive if
wan voice. When the music was over she asked me about my
early life and of my struggles. I looked young for my years
in those days and probably rather "lost." Next morning she
was at breakfast waiting for me. She told me that during
the night she had been in communication with my mother
"on the other side" and that my mother and she had loved
one another at once, and that my mother was proud of me
and that they, the two of them, would watch over and take
care of me. I was naturally ready to perspire with apprehension. Was I to be mothered or Wendy'd in this flat in the
tree—I mean chimney tops? The interruption here of Thurston
was a relief and a blessing, much as I felt drawn to the soft-
ness and kindliness of her nature. Thurston led me to Barrie
who wanted to say good-bye before I left; he was in bed in
a bandbox of a room, bare and uncomfortable—what little I
could see of it through thick tobacco smoke, for his pipe was
in full furnace as he lay there, frail in pyjamas, like a pigmy
with one of those big pantomime heads. He hoped I had
enjoyed my stay and would come again; the flat was open
to me at any time: I had only to give him short notice.

Thurston carried my suitcase down the lift cage. He got
me a taxi. In my highly emotional condition—feeling I had
emerged from another dimension, and only just emerged—I
forgot to tip him. I called on Barrie at the flat once or twice
after this experience; but never stayed the night. I prefer
my Barrie plays on the stage in front of me, where I can see
what they are doing; I don't like them taking place behind
my back in the night.

.   .   .   .   .   .

Amongst the friends I have found through cricket, Jack Squire comes nearly first. I have been in his company only three or four times, it is true; but I estimate friendship qualitatively not quantitatively. He is at one and the same time poet and human being; he has sensibility and humour; and it is not given to many of us to possess both. I count him amongst the few who have reconciled me to life in my worst moments. Only to look at him is satisfying and strengthening: a triumphantly ravaged face, quizzical yet kindly, with an air of nobility running to seed, to flower again immediately; worldliness and unworldliness in splendid contention—but all ready to cope with the best and the worst, late and soon (after some hard peering at things through and over his spectacles, which I think he dodges, as Nelson dodged his telescope, when it suits him).

My first meeting with Sir John was, I think, on the top floor of Lyons Corner House at Piccadilly Circus, where an annual dinner of some cricket club was being held. I was one of the guests and I arrived early. The room was deserted; by the side of the wall stood a long table covered with cocktails and gins-and-Italians, and cherries sticking up from them. It was like a field of poppies. I helped myself, to while away the time, and presently I was joined by Squire, and after we had made ourselves known to one another we proceeded to go down the poppy field as though with a scythe. I seem to recollect that during the dinner Sir John made a speech which startlingly digressed from the subject in hand—the toast to the So-and-So Cricket Club—and launched an attack on Jerry-Builders and Despoilers of the English Countryside. After the dinner ended he took me to the Savile Club where we remained until dawn discussing (rather heatedly) the sonnets of Shakespeare. He asked me why I didn't belong to this club, and I asked which club was it and he said, "Why the Savshe, of course"; and I said, "Savshe club?" and he repeated the same sound; and next day I applied for membership at the Savage Club.

I sat at Kennington Oval with him during a Test match; he was literary editor of the *Observer* at the time, and as we watched the game I suggested to him that J. L. Garvin ought to write about cricket for the paper. Without a moment's hesitation Squire said: "Yes, I can see the headlines already:

THE CRISIS IN CRICKET
PARTING OF THE WAYS
LEG-BEFORE-WICKET—AND AFTER

I have dreamed midsummer dreams of Squire's cricket matches, when he was captain of strangely diverse forces. Let me tell one of them now, before the vision fades:

One day in August, Sir John Squire came to me and said: "I want you to play for my team next Saturday at Taunton. Now this is not one of my comic matches—it's going to be a very serious affair. I want to win; we are playing the Somerset Stragglers—or some such name—I forget at the moment—but it's a team that lives in Somersetshire somewhere. And I want you to bowl for me—you can bowl, can't you?" I told him I hadn't bowled for three or four years. "Still," he said, "you *have* bowled some time or other in your life, haven't you? Well, that'll be a useful help in my team. I've got a good lot of players—listen." He pulled a piece of notepaper out of his pocket (with a heap of other scraps, probably the beginnings of poems or book-reviews). "Listen," he said, "I'll read you my team—very strong all round. First, there's Arnold Bax; now, as you know, he's a pretty good composer, and I believe he's just finished another symphony. Then there's his brother, Clifford—a first-rate man—did you see his play *The Rose and the Thorn* or whatever he called it? And Alec Waugh's coming with us; I believe he is working on another novel. C. R. W. Nevinson has promised to play for me too, and as you know he's one of the most challenging of our painters. Old Hugh Walpole is in my team also, and though his latest novel is hardly up to form still he's done some good stuff in his particular school, though personally I think his books are too long. However. Then I've asked William Murdoch—have you heard him play Brahms?—but of course you have; isn't it splendid? Well, there you are—there's the nucleus of a strongish team. We meet at Paddington, 4.30 Friday; and we're staying at the Old Castle Hotel."

We duly arrived at Taunton, and the great match began. Squire lost the toss, and we took the field in grim silence. Sir

John set his field elaborately, waving men here and there—
he had seen them doing it at Lord's. At last the struggle
began. I bowled severely, and now and then I achieved
straightness. We did well; wickets fell at convenient intervals.
After an hour of hot and arduous action, I thought I would
like to know the position of the game. In Somersetshire,
cricket score-boards are hard to discover; usually they are
erected under a spreading chestnut tree, and a boy fixes figures
painted on square bits of tin—just the total of the batting side,
the fall of the wickets, and the score of the last man out. I
couldn't find the score-board, so I spoke to Squire between
overs. "We're doing well, I think," said I.

"Remarkably well," he replied. "We've got 'em on the
run. Stick to it—keep your arm up."

"Yes, but," I said, "where's the score-board and what are
the exact facts of the situation?"

Squire peered through his spectacles all over the field.

"Of course there's a score-board. Anyhow, we'll find out
from the pavilion."

He called loudly to the pavilion: "How many have they
made? Is it five or six wickets down? Why don't you damn
well put the figures on the board? Hurry up!" But there
was no immediate response from the pavilion. We heard a
hubbub in the bar: "What's the score? Sir John wants to
know the score."

It transpired that in the excitement of the event no scorers
had been appointed at all. We had been hurling ourselves
about in the heat of the day quite unobserved. Everybody
not actually playing had been talking in the bar over a pint
of home-brewed. Nobody had added up the runs; not a soul
had taken careful account of the batsmen I had by the sweat
of my brow well and truly overthrown. We had been playing
heroically for more than an hour; Greek against Greek; no
quarter, with even Hugh Walpole reduced to silence. My
back ached from violent effort; we had—or at least I had—
captured a minimum of five wickets. And all the time we had
been utterly ignored and disregarded. The only spectator was
a cow—and he gave our activities but a momentary eye—when
a ball fell near him. Squire wanted to "compound" with the
captain of the opposing team over the unrecorded period of

play. "We took at least five of your wickets," he said. "Cardus claims six. Well, assuming an average rate of scoring at say fifty an hour, taking into consideration the long grass—let's agree that the state of the game is now twenty-five for five." But the Somerset captain insisted on an average of eighty runs an hour because, he declared, as none of his batsmen kept the ball down, the long grass in the outfield could not logically be dragged into the argument. After much heated debate, we had to begin all over again. Our attack naturally never recaptured the first rapture. Stiffness set into my joints, and after lunch even Hugh Walpole was asked to bowl, and after trying his right arm discovered that he could do better with his left. The result of the match escaped my dream.

It was, I believe, in one of Sir John's matches that two batsmen took root. His teams varied in talents and membership every match. At last one of the batsmen mishit a long-hop and "skied" the ball very high in mid-wicket. Of course, as usual, five or six fieldsmen advanced with outstretched arms to make the catch. With rare presence of mind and true leadership, Sir John cried out: "Thompson's catch! Leave it to Thompson!" Whereat each of the five or six fieldsmen retreated obediently—and the ball fell harmlessly to the earth. Thompson was not playing that week. Of no other man except Sir John could I—or would I—tell this, the best of all my cricket stories.

Towards the end of 1928 Squire wrote to me asking me to contribute a volume on cricket to the English Heritage Series, edited by himself and Viscount Lee of Fareham. The copy was not wanted for a year. I signed the contract and for forty weeks could not begin even the first sentence; then on a filthy November day in Manchester I received a telegram from Squire; by the end of the month my manuscript must without fail be in the hands of the printers. I wrote the little book in three weeks, mostly cold and foggy; I wrote it in Allan Monkhouse's room in the *Manchester Guardian* office, excepting the chapter called "Invasion," part of which came into being while I was travelling in a train as music critic from London to Birmingham for a performance of Mahler's *Das Lied von der Erde*. The closing sentence of *Cricket* held me up for several days; I could not for the life of me round it off. I

was in despair when one night, before going to bed, I picked
up by chance an old cast-off pocket-book; and looking in it
I found a quotation I had made years ago. It was a godsend;
my book finished like this:

> "In September 1739, Mary Turner, of East Hoathly,
> Sussex, wrote to her son a letter:' Last Monday youre
> Father was at Mr. Payns and plaid at Cricket and came home
> pleased anuf, for he struck the best Ball in the game and
> whished he had not anny thing else to do he wuld play
> Cricket all his life.' With that, our book can come to an
> end."

And I doubt if a book has ever come to a *prettier* end.

The last time I saw Squire was in the late summer of 1937
and I met him on a channel steamer from Boulogne to Dover;
he had been in Italy and I in Austria. We sat in the bar and
talked cricket. When we reached Dover, Squire said: "Now
you attend to the customs and I'll go and bag a seat in the
boat-train." I obeyed, but forgot to ask him for his keys.
The customs official had never heard of Sir John Squire, but
he was obliging. "I'll send a porter to the carriage and an
official, and the examination can take place there." So I ran
along the platform and when I saw Jack I shouted, "You've
forgotten to declare." Whereupon a perfectly strange girl
standing by—and a very pretty one—said to me: "Perhaps he
hasn't enough runs on the board yet."

.   .   .   .   .   .

You might well think that my life hereabout was as pleasant
as could be in an English summer. Each morning I would
arise and, if I were at home, go into the music-room where
there was a Bechstein, and the most musical gramophone in
the world; I would shave to any composer of my taste at the
moment; for I now possessed nearly every gramophone record
extant, none of which had cost me a penny, for I was reviewing
them every month for the "M. G." If I chanced to be in
London, I would sit and read on the terrace of the National
Liberal Club until it was time to go leisurely and like a gentle-

man to Lord's, or take the Underground to Kennington Oval.
Or maybe I would begin the day journeying South or West;
once I missed a connection and arrived so late at the match
that I decided to write my column not about cricket I had
not seen but about how I had that morning enjoyed breakfast
almost alone in a handsome restaurant-car while the train
glided through the Cotswolds and how I had lost sense
of time and place, and had arrived so late at the match
that I was obliged to write not about cricket I had not seen
but . . . and so on! The *Manchester Guardian* headed the
column:

STEADY BATTING BY LANCASHIRE

On the face of it, a tranquil and happy life. But there were
days when I was to be seen walking alone round and round
the edge of a cricket field, careworn of visage, with eyes glazed
with abstract thought. I occasionally found my daily task as
heavy as that of Sisyphus. I now wonder how I kept it up
morning after morning. Every journalist is haunted by the
spectre of Himself Repeated; it came before me often in
questionable shape. Not that I worried about my public; as
a rule, the majority of readers like a writer to go on saying
the same things over and over again. When my earlier and
"romantic" manner became acidulated here and there with
parody, I received letters of protest—for example when I
abruptly modulated (rather unsubtly too!) as follows:

"On Saturday Tonbridge was a pretty place in the sunshine; the soft light of summer, ladies on the lawns, blue
sky and clouds of fleece, the chirruping of birds and the
whirring of aeroplanes and the explosion of corks out of
bottles and good business at the bar—a perfect English
scene in this our land."

But I had to keep myself interested—that was the main
problem. I could not fall back on the score-board: I had
little sense of figures and never knew that Bloggs of Blankshire
had completed his century in five and a half hours. I could
not share the inspiration which was kindled in the bosoms of

my Press Box colleagues by patriotism and partisan interest; I was more than once "floored" for material when Hobbs and Sutcliffe batted all day instead of Bradman and McCabe.

Between 1926 and 1936 our cricket in the lump was as stereotyped as the council houses and flats and ribbon roads which more and more and month by month symbolised the post-war England. Whatever the occasion, England against Australia, or Eton against Harrow, the procedure was much the same—safety first; young boys were level now with men; the Eton and Harrow match was for years drearily drawn, each side afraid of a sportsman's gesture. "Alas," wrote J. L. Garvin, "that we should have lived to see the day when reporters may write innocently something like this: 'Every long-hop was infallibly punished; it was a master's innings.'" But what one reporter (who was not innocent, but myself) actually did write one day and, moreover, about a match played amongst the bunting and white tents of a cricket festival at Tonbridge, was this:

"In an hour Kent's total arrived at twenty, all told. Fagg in this time was guilty of four singles. I can imagine a contemporary cricketer going home after a day's play.

"'Well, Bill, and how have you gone on to-day?' he is asked by his wife as she gets his steak ready.

"'Oh, not so bad,' Bill replies; 'I batted nearly four hours.' Silence, and then from his wife:

"'Yes—but Bill, you're keeping something back. Did you score many runs?' Bill shuffles.

"'Well, I was in four hours and a half, if you want to know. And I only scored 62, I'll swear, God's truth.'

"'Ah, Bill—I knew you was hiding the truth. O, Bill, how could you?'"

.   .   .   .   .   .

For twenty years each cricket season was a ritual. Cricket matches are fitted to the same dates annually, so that for years ahead it was possible for me to know in what place I would be and what I would be doing almost at any given moment, morning, noon and night, during months of summer. I was

rolled round in earth's diurnal course,
with rocks, and stones, and trees.

On a certain Wednesday of the second week in May, I would
walk on to the Parks at Oxford, the greenest of cricket fields,
where you cannot put down a foot without treading on a
daisy, where grows every tree known to England and where
behind the red-bricked pavilion, in a wall, I discovered one
bitter spring day a robin sitting snugly in her nest. She
looked at me without a qualm.

On a certain Saturday in June I would pass over Trent
Bridge and enter the old ground and walk behind the
pavilion, where there were hens and apple-trees; then I would
go upstairs to the seats on top of the pavilion and sit near the
same oldest inhabitant, so old that every year he could not
look older by a day; and I would hear him (for he was deaf
and shouted hard) talking of Mordecai Sherwin. Down
below the white figures moved here and there on the same
turf once trodden by Arthur Shrewsbury. And the crowd was
the same, seen *sub specie aeternitatis*: different temporally and
individually maybe, different in dress and notions, but
rendered by the rhythmic iteration of countless cricket seasons
corporate and one with all other Nottinghamshire folk that
had sat there at this same hour of a June day, or in the future
would ever sit there.

On a certain Wednesday in August, I would walk to the
ground at Hove and watch Sussex and Lancashire, while the
breeze blew and Tate got excited and jerked up his hands each
ball he bowled, expecting a wicket every time; and I would
stand on the same spot of earth next year and the year after
that, watching the swerve and the spin. I saw Tate begin his
cricket when he was a lanky tawny youth. I saw him emerge
from competence and become famous from Brighton to
Adelaide, and there seemed no end to his life and energy, no
end to the fun of watching Sussex at Hove in August. And
I saw Tate come and go, with Duleepsinhji and Gilligan;
but at the end of all their days in the sun I was still there,
on a certain Wednesday in August, on the same spot of
earth at half-past eleven, watching the latest generations at
play.

The drowning man, they say, sees moments of his life in swift panorama. In a world nearly drowning at the moment I write these lines—a world which will be greatly changed even if it succeeds in coming up for the third time and is rescued—what do I, as a cricketer, see? Railway trains travelling across England, myself in restaurant-cars, in sumptuous cushioned privacy, gliding through the sunset after a scurry and a late and strenuous finish at Lord's; we are due now for the West, to play at Bristol to-morrow morning, and before we are through with our dinner, while we are taking coffee and liqueur, we shall have left London far behind and we shall look through the carriage window and see country fields in the twilight and catch glimpses of life mysteriously not connected with us—an old woman walking along a lane; a man knocking at a cottage door—then the train swings round a bend and they are gone, and we can never know what happened to them next. Trains criss-crossing at Crewe Junction; I am now going North to Leeds and Yorkshire. A week afterwards I come back at midnight to London, and next morning I take a taxi in Regent Street and say "Lord's," and the driver gives me a look that tells me he approves, and he takes his ease and rides me along the curve of Regent's Park, where we can see the boats on the lake and the children playing; and when we reach the main gates at Lord's there is time to look round before a fresh match begins, and see Patsy Hendren arriving, also the man with a straw hat—dating from Jerome K. Jerome and *Three Men in a Boat*—who spends all his life running here and there to watch cricket. If a game finishes at Lord's at noon, he drives his car to the next nearest ground, Kennington Oval, Gravesend, Brighton or Southend-on-Sea. The bookstall near the Tavern displays its sheaves and colours; if a big match is about to begin there are posters extolling the various gifted men of letters who will describe the event in the newspapers next day: "Reginald Thing's Brilliant Test Match Reports." "Bill Blank's Great Story." And so on, superlative on top of superlative. I saw a *Manchester Guardian* poster on view at the bookstall at Lord's, after the first day's play in a Test match. I had written two columns about it. The other papers' posters were even more than usually noisy about their "own" correspondents' powers of description.

THE LONG ROOM AT LORD'S
Photo: Sport and General

The *Manchester Guardian* poster announced, to the crowd gathering at Lord's for the second day of a Test match:

FALL OF THE
BULGARIAN
CABINET

One day I sat on a table outside the little café at Lord's, talking to the cricket correspondent of *The Times*. The sun was warming all the world. The ground was animated. The pavilion was filling with notabilities anxious to get a good seat. As I sat on the table dangling my legs and enjoying a pipe and a cup of coffee, I casually said to *The Times* cricket correspondent:

"Has it occurred to you that we are paid to do this?"

Paid to enjoy summer and cricket. I was also being paid to go after a day at Lord's to Covent Garden and hear Lehmann in *Rosenkavalier*.

"Yes," said *The Times* cricket correspondent, "it has occurred to me. And it's too good to be true, isn't it?"

"Yes," I replied, "it can't last."

A few weeks after this remarkable and philosophical conversation, Neville Chamberlain flew to Berchtesgaden to see Hitler.

Part Three

MY WINTERS—AND MUSIC

To
S. L.

ON A MAY DAY in 1927, Samuel Langford died in the old timbered house where he was born at Withington, a few miles from Manchester and not long ago a suburban, if not a rural place. For some time he had been failing but would not realise he was ill—probably could not: he lived entirely out of himself, with an interest in all things, an interest which was creative. I can use no other word. He was the greatest man I have ever known; and I have known men counted amongst the greatest by the world at large. Langford could have gone into the company of Goethe, of Coleridge, of Hazlitt, and of Shakespeare and all the Mermaid Tavern lot, been welcome there and at ease, giving and taking in the talk. Nobody who knew Langford will see anything of exaggeration in this claim on his behalf.

He began life scaring the crows from his father's field; his father was a market-gardener. Young Sam used a wooden rattle, and while he protected seeds and plants he read his first books. He learned his music in the little chapel round the corner. When Sam grew into a young man his father, with good North-country sense, decided he was not cut out for any profit-making occupation, so he was sent to Leipzig, where he spent most of his time in beer-gardens and at the Gewandhaus. His music-master was Carl Reinecke and from him (so Langford maintained to his dying day) he learned only one thing, but the "most important I was ever taught by another man; which was that it is the nature of song to go up and down—repeated notes are ineffectual in it." So if you hear or are playing a composition that contains many groups of repeated notes you will be well away from the scent if you treat it as "absolute" music.

In appearance Langford was a mixture of Socrates, Moussorgsky (as depicted by Repin) and Brahms. He was small and podgy, with shaggy whiskers and a dome of forehead. His small, narrow, pale-blue eyes were Bavarian-mild; but he was as English as an Elizabethan. He waddled over the earth, seldom lifting the soles of his boots from the ground.

His clothes fell about him loose as the skin of an elephant. He spoke in his throat like an Oxford don, and when he laughed—in a snigger and a sneeze and a whinny—his eyes disappeared. Without offence he suggested that as to toilet his concern did not go beyond the simplest and most pressing details.

I never heard him make a commonplace remark. It is a loss to literature that he did not meet his Boswell. His writings on music, though the most penetrating and, as prose, the richest in the language, reveal only the half of him. Conversation expressed the full man, and he never ceased and never talked for effect, or at you; he merely gave audibility to his thoughts during a polite recognition that you were present. No matter where he chanced to meet you he gave tongue to meditation, to wisdom and wit. Even along the busiest thoroughfare the flow of words—whole epigrams lost in his whiskers—would not halt. A vehicle might separate you as you both crossed the road; when you got into touch with him yards higher up you would find that his discourse had travelled a few paragraphs farther on during your temporary and enforced absence from his side. The course of his conversation was like his own movements along the pavement —ample, and unheedful of particular time or direction. In a free-fantasia he would discuss Bach, Land Values, W. G. Grace, Free-Will, "The smoothest of all poetic rhythms in which Dante turns his divine verse," The National Debt, which he argued should be thrown on to the back of nature who recognised no debts but one, Einstein, Mahler, Tod Sloan, Marriage, and Flowers. There was no change in the natural and humane texture of his ideas and expressions as he digressed from Ibsen to an affectionate and technical eulogy of a delphinium. With him the intellectual and the natural life were complementary. He had no patience with systems, and was ironic about education as it is generally understood in England. He believed that a man can absorb only what he needs, by imaginatively experiencing and living in a subject. C. P. Scott could never understand Langford's complex of intellectual austerity and physical unbuttonedness. Langford belonged to no class—upper, middle or lower. He was philosopher and poet and peasant. He despised the moral and

didactic point of view from which Scott and his school tended
to look at life and learning. He said of Montague's writings
that they'd be all the better for a "spade or two of dung out
of my garden." He was courteous in a curiously formal way;
he got it, I suppose, from the Leipzig of the late 1900's. His
approach to people of all sorts and conditions was simple and
friendly. But patience was needed with him. He had a touch
of sadism in his speech; I have seen men go out of his presence
biting their lips, hardly containing themselves. But I doubt
if he ever tried to score a point at the expense of anybody he
did not at bottom respect.

Some smack of Langford's nature, and some assemblance
of his mighty intellectual parts, have emerged I hope from
this description of him; for I wish the reader to understand
the searching comparison to which I was exposed when Scott
appointed me to the vacant post. Langford reigned supreme
in the music of the North of England during his twenty years
of office; every other day a column of literature appeared
from his pen in the *Manchester Guardian*, or rather from his
lead-pencil, for he could not cope with ink. Everybody knew
him; Richter himself was not a more familiar and symbolical
figure in Manchester amongst university professors and
crossing-sweepers and prelates and publicans. The cab-drivers
and carriers in the market and his close companions called
him "Sammy." His articles were cut out and pasted into
albums in the remote fastnesses of the North of England by
that now extinct school of workers and thinkers who tried to
build Jerusalem amongst the dark satanic mills and were
eventually betrayed. But Manchester University did not
bestow on him an honorary degree, though they offered the
laurel-wreath to many a lesser man. He omitted to publish a
book, was not civic-minded, and could never be trusted at a
garden-party. When, after his death, I edited a selection from
his contributions to the "M. G.," in a volume published by
the Oxford University Press, a book not many times surpassed
for understanding of music and life, written in prose not
inferior to any in all the critical productions of our time, it
sold not more than eight hundred copies and was soon hawked
in the bookshops' bargain-boxes. The North of England
public knew Langford was great and took him for granted;

the English public do not buy books on music unless they are obviously "helpful" towards "appreciation," or journalistically biographical. But I hoped when the book was published that it would bring his genius to the notice of other minds of quality dwelling in places where the *Manchester Guardian* was only a name. It has been suggested to me that had he written for a London newspaper he would have achieved a wide recognition. I doubt if any newspaper in the world other than the "M. G." would have printed a characteristic Langford concert notice. For example: imagine a column in *The Times* or the *Daily Telegraph* couched in these terms (a performance of the B Minor Mass of Bach is under review):

"In the 'Sanctus' we have the original prototype of how many Lisztian and other symphonic-poems in which the heroes are crowned with eternal garlands, in the most tedious ways. Bach's garlands of divine harmony are neither tedious nor obviously descriptive, and perhaps they escape the one thing because they are not the other. And of all ground-basses, surely the bass of this movement is the most original and the most sublime. . . . 'He planteth His footsteps in the sea,' says the Psalmist; but though such an expression carries us far, it is by no means adequate as a description of this divinely-moving bass part. The notes in their octave leaps are like vast pillars, not sunk into the deep but embracing in their height and depth an imagination of both heaven and earth; and if we add the sea, the combined images will not complete what one feels from the music. Such music, indeed, fulfils all those ideas in which music becomes a symbol of the universe. We see in its laws, as in a glass, the divine equipoise which is our ultimate conception of the universe. It is a modern idea that music cannot be poetic unless it is picturesque. When Bach sets his universe of music rolling, we do not ask what he is describing, but are transfixed by the power and sublimity of music itself. We ask for no other similitude or form; we feel ourselves in the presence of formal beauty in its essence. Such music transcends everything it tries to express, and we are carried up into it, not by the remembrance but by the forgetting of every other thing. All that passes is but a symbol, says the wise Goethe; and music, in one sense the most swiftly passing and intangible of all mortal things, is in another the essence of the imperishable. . . ."

Or, to take another example, a concert notice written "on the night," amongst thousands:

"Beethoven called the B Flat Quartet his 'Leitquartet'; and the judgment of the century that has passed since his death has confirmed the justice of his partiality for this composition. As the work of a deaf man these quartets assert triumphantly the imaginative nature of the musical art, and the heritage of this proof musicians may well prize in a world which is apt to associate music, not with the cleansing power of the imagination but with all the sensuous delights of the world. Literature, though it is born of daily talk, is known to lead men to the heights of austere and tragic thought. It is too easily forgotten that music has its natural home in the same place. One cannot speak justly of the short idyllic dance movements in these later quartets without regarding them as elysian in their very nature, and as removed by their ideality from every contamination of the world. And can we say less of those slow movements which are of such heavenly length that they hardly have the power to cease, and whose particles of sound are of such fineness that they are like the moist particles of the air on the loveliest of summer mornings? . . . If these beauties are born of human weakness and frailty, and rise from the hardness of a mere physical crisis—as the slow movement of thanksgiving from sickness in the closing quartet so touchingly depicts—then there is something to be said even for weakness and sickness as an inspiration for the arts. And when with that weakness goes such gigantic spiritual strength as the overtowering attempts of these quartets show, then we may regard with a solemn pride the human nature which is capable of such efforts in such extremes. It is something to belong to the same race of beings as Beethoven."

Newspaper criticism, so often and so rightly thought ignoble in its attitude to genius and in its own cynical smartness of phrase, was dignified and humanised as never before in our time by Langford. This was the man, this was the tradition I had to follow and not cheapen. John Barbirolli, when he was chosen to succeed unto Toscanini, was not confronted with a more solemn and more humbling ordeal. I knew that for a year at least, whether I wrote well or ill, there would be the unspoken thought everywhere: "This is not Langford; no; this is not 'S. L.'"

In his last few years he helped me, less by any precise instruction than by his company. For hours we sat in cafés in Manchester, deep under the earth on winter afternoons; his talk was a fire; not a crackling one but as a glowing hearth, steady and warm without obvious combustion. Once in June, after sunset, very late and still, he leaned over the gate of his garden and talked to me of Shakespeare's lyrics and of the fragility of loveliness in life. The air was full of the scent of his own flowers; and the wisdom of his speech, genial yet deep, seemed part of the beauty of the summer night.

He was not easy to work with. E. J. Phillips had to look after his copy, which he never read through after he had written it in a handwriting spiky and sprawling, rather like Shakespeare's. Sometimes he would go home and leave a pile of copy of which page sixteen was missing. W. P. Crozier decided to talk to him about his carelessness over his page sequences. "You must see to it, Langford," he instructed, "that your copy is properly numbered and in order and complete before you go home."

Langford listened like one most willing and cheerful to co-operate. Next night he in person took his article down to Crozier and with a smirk he said:

"There; I think you'll find that's all right."

Crozier scrutinised the sheaf of copy from top to bottom and said:

"Yes, Langford, but where's page one?"

Sammy had concentrated entirely on the middle and end, on the intricacies of 'teens and twenties; we at length found page one in his pocket, a huge bag of a pocket, with holes in it, where he carried newspapers, miniature scores, seed-catalogues, old half-eaten apples, and a broken remnant of what was once a lens in a reading-glass; Langford would not use spectacles and indeed his button of a nose could not have supported them.

He sent me one bitter winter night to Rochdale in Lancashire to write about a chamber concert. He came into the office after six o'clock in the evening, and at this short notice I had to set forth. He was himself attending a performance of *Meistersinger* conducted by Beecham. I had bought a ticket for it. I protested that he might have warned me yesterday of the concert at Rochdale. He had overlooked it, he said; so there was nothing else for it. I caught a train just in time, walked a mile over a bleak common in the face of a blizzard, and arrived at the hall only to find it in complete darkness. By aid of a flickering street lamp I discovered a poster announcing that the concert I had come to write about was not to be given to-night but next month. Wrathful and shivering and wet with sleet, I returned to Manchester; and Langford at last came in from the opera croaking the Quintet as he entered the room we shared.

"Good concert?" he asked. I told him there had been no concert, that he had sent me out into the wilds on a fearful night for nothing, wasting my *Meistersinger* ticket; that the chamber concert at Rochdale had not been arranged for this, a Tuesday night; that it wouldn't take place this month at all but next month, and not on a Tuesday but a Wednesday night. He listened amiably, then chuckled, "Well, anyhow, I got you in the right year, didn't I?" The curious fact was that he was a man who counted wit first of all of human qualities yet was never witty in his writings. I think that as soon as he entered the world of music, the whole man of him, he passed to a plane or dimension where he thought wit was not relevant. At a performance of *Parsifal* he shuffled and wriggled during the "Grail" scene. I was sitting next to him and I whispered, "You don't seem to be enjoying yourself." He replied, audibly enough: "Amfortas is the wisest man here to-night; he's brought his bed with him." But he would not have dreamed of using such a quip in his notice next day; he always referred to Ernest Newman as a comedian.

In November, 1926, the signs of the end were to be seen; he would not go to a doctor and nobody quite knew what was wrong with him. A cough shook him; but we thought that the gale of it merely touched the periphery of this loose mass of baggy humanity. It was his beloved *Meistersinger* that brought down his curtain. He came a little late to the performance; and he was so ill that he was put alone in a private box, where he wrote his notice during the intervals. I took it to the office for him and helped him to a taxi. Next day he could not move in his bed, for the first time in his sixty-four years. And the last of all his musical criticisms ended thus:

"When Handel, in his sublime moods, dissolved his hearers into ecstasies, he was said to bring all heaven before their eyes. Wagner, in *Meistersinger*, with a rarer and more all-embracing sublimity, finds it sufficient to reconcile man with man. When the tones of the quintet from *Meistersinger* melt and die upon the ear, that in essence is what they effect. The true hearer, in listening, is reconciled to his kind. And in this reconciliation is effected equally the opposite miracle of *Tristan*, the reconciliation with death. Music is an art of cadence, and however bravely, as in the overture of *Meistersinger*, the banner of tone may be opened out, the cadence and the fall of music must come, and the most humane and loving tones at last must fall upon the air. But that they may die as the sheer ripeness of a reconciled humour, from which every essence of sourness has been strained, and of which nothing but the purest love of one's human kind remains, is a lesson more thoroughly to be learned by hearing an ideal performance of the *Meistersinger* than by anything else the arts have given us."

That quotation contains my proof that Langford was a great man and a writer on music without parallel. Whoever can read it without a full heart and a better insight not only into *Meistersinger* but into the substance of music itself will, I hope, close this book at once. I do not think Langford would have troubled himself, even if he had lived to hear of it, about the contemporary reaction against Wagner and the discovery that the germ of Nazism came out of Wagner's music. Still, I am somehow glad that Langford did not live into the present age; that he died when he did die. His last column for the "M. G." was written in bed, the paper's article on the centenary of Beethoven's death. He wrote it on a Sunday morning and I went to his house to collect the copy, which was strewn over the counterpane; one or two pages had to be salvaged from between the sheets. He lay exhausted and his head was lain sideways on his pillow, so that he could see out of the little window, where a tree was putting forth the shoots of spring. The morning was fresh and sunny. He was dying in the bed in which he was born; the last he would see of the light of the world would come through the same latticed window.

He went into a doze and I talked softly to his wife. She was interested to know the name of a writer of certain back-page articles which at this time were appearing at intervals in the *Guardian* signed "W. G." "Who is 'W. G.'?" she asked me in a whisper. From the bed came a faint voice, spoken from far away out of the past: "'W. G.'?—why, W. G. Grace, of course." They were the last words I heard him say.

.   .   .   .   .   .

I was blessed in my two teachers—Langford the Platonist, Ernest Newman the Aristotelean: Spirit of Affirmation and Spirit of Denial. Langford taught me to feel and translate, while Newman taught me to observe and analyse. Faust and Mephistopheles!—without these two working in harness, so to say, no man can hope really to know art or life. Langford was like the priest administering the sacrament, the body and blood of Beethoven; Newman was the sceptic who while he aesthetically savoured the ritual was alert of palate enough to know always if the wine were good—*qua* wine. Newman never allowed me to take my eye from the object: the first task of criticism with him was (to quote Bayard Taylor's translation from *Faust*) to show:

> . . . no otherwise it could have been:
> The first was so, the second so,

Therefore the third and fourth are so;
Were not the first and second, then
The third and fourth had never been . . .

But Langford as constantly warned me that

He who would study organic existence,
First drives out the soul with rigid persistence;
Then the parts in his hand he may hold and class,
But the spiritual link is lost alas!

Newman remained outside the creative process, and Langford
was absorbed into it. To come into contact with these two
minds at the impressionable period of my life was worth more
to me than all the academies of music in the world. I first
met Newman when I was at Shrewsbury. By some stifling
of the shyness which was in those days my bane, I wrote to
Newman in the summer of 1916. He was then music critic
of the *Birmingham Post*. I was reading his books on Wolf and
Wagner with the fervour of a disciple; and I actually asked
him to come to Shrewsbury to spend an afternoon with me.
I was completely unknown to him at the time. To my delight
and—at bottom—my embarrassment, he accepted the invitation; he answered my letter promptly and said he would
reach Shrewsbury at 2.20 on the following Thursday.

For some reason which escapes me, I muddled the time of
his arrival. When I went to the railway station the platform
was empty. I asked a porter when the Birmingham train
would come in, and he told me it had "been and gorn." I
had of course arranged with Newman to meet the train, so
with a sick stomach I raced into the town. It was a hot day,
and it was unthinkable that he should go wandering to the
school looking for me. Besides, the discourtesy! I found him
strolling up and down outside the General Post Office, smoking
a cigar, dressed immaculately. In those days Newman had
not renounced the world, but was much a man of it; his very
walk, debonair and leisurely, told of the connoisseur in delect-
able experiences—told as much as his heavy lips, lidded
eyes, and the way he flavoured every word he uttered. Omnipo-
tence itself could not have produced a being more the opposite

of Langford, in every way, than Newman. When he removed his Homburg hat, revealing raven-black hair, a vision of Disraeli invaded the imagination.

I mumbled apologies about my blunder of missing his train, but he waved them into thin air and explained that whenever he lost anybody, or a rendezvous in any city went askew, he invariably proceeded to a General Post Office; it was his experience that a G.P.O. was a sort of Home for Lost or Strayed Appointments.

He told me he had lunched on the train, and he suggested a walk. We crossed the ferry and he admired the school grounds, though I was taken aback when he looked at the Speech Hall and asked if it was the Mortuary. I kicked myself for not having also seen the resemblance—a hideous brick affair at the back; and the back overlooking the playing-fields. We sauntered by the river, and he talked of Granados—a composer much in the air at the time—and of Elgar's new choral work: *For the Fallen.* He had not modulated yet to the science and austerity of his old age; he was not afraid of a personal, even an emotional reaction to music. In his quiet but telling way he inspired me. I took him into a café for tea; the thought did not occur to me to take him into a hotel and stand him a whisky and soda. He returned to Birmingham on the seven o'clock train. Why he went to the trouble and kindness to visit me at all will baffle me for ever; for he is not and never was the man to waste a moment of time, and certainly not given to sentimental interests in young aspiring music critics.

Years afterwards we developed a friendship strong enough to survive many a more or less acrimonious argument in the public prints. I attacked his belittlement of Furtwängler; and we laid into one another in the *Sunday Times* when he, as I thought, reviewed Langford's critical essays ungenerously— he described Langford as a sort of poetaster, or dilettante, who wrote "beautifully" about music but did not consider it *qua* music—and all the rest of it—Newman's "physiology," which in time became an obsession with him. But we never really sundered in our minds and our intellectual passions. He has, I suspect, seen in me too much of the same cultural soil that nurtured himself; we are both rationalists; and both of us

began as students of Hennequin and J. M. Robertson and the
"scientific method" of criticism, the method that seeks to
relate a genius to his environment, physical and mental. But
I have worn my rationalism with a difference; for it was
grafted in the beginning on a romantic nature. Newman
has described me in print as a "sensitised-plate" critic, implying that I react to a work wholly or mainly in terms of my
own feelings at the moment, with objective values disturbed
by the personal equation.

I tried to get the best out of both men, Langford and
Newman, much as the man in Dickens wrote his celebrated
essay on Chinese Metaphysics; he read the article in the
Encyclopaedia Britannica on China, then the one on Metaphysics
and combined the two. During his heyday, Newman was
not by any means objective and dispassionate in his reactions
to music and in his chastisements of performers. His change
to the calm aloof anatomist of recent years has been like the
conversion in old age of the rake who having led a riotous life
himself, well away from the straight and narrow path, warns
all and sundry against a similar licentiousness. In my youth
Newman was outrageously prejudiced; he applied his pet
theories right and left; he was impudently a *priori*. Thus
Wolf was a greater song-composer than Schubert mainly
because he possessed the finer literary sense and the nicer ear
for the accentuation, the prosody values, of the texts he set to
music. To this day Newman has been unable to hear a new
orchestral work except from the Wagner point of view of
transition; form in music for Newman simply must follow
the Wagnerian idea of a continuously developed tissue, the
next phrase the logical outcome of the one before; apparently
he finds it hard to understand that there are sorts of musical
minds, as subtle as Wagner's to say the least, which go to
work differently and can draw inspiration even yet from the
oldest and strictest A-B-A forms.

He once confessed that he wrote according to his lights—
or his liver. And he once told me that no emotion in the world
was more exhilarating to him than to enter a concert hall and
to feel that everybody on the platform, from conductor to the
player of the triangle, was hating the sight of him and fearing
him. I bow to nobody in my admiration of the Newman who

grew old and a little weary; he made an impressive sight in the Queen's Hall when his face became as disillusioned as the face of Bellini's Doge. Even then I doubted if he had expelled altogether the old Adam. Some of us have found it possible to enjoy both Toscanini and Furtwängler; but the German, with his nuance, was doomed to perdition by the venerable Newman almost before he convulsively let his baton attack a work. And it would appear that for Newman the septuagenerian, as for the Newman of his wild-oats period, there are no faults to be found in Hugo Wolf, and few virtues in the songs of Brahms. I hope he never succeeds in subduing his temperament utterly to the scientific method which when he was in his middle years he often put to strictly convenient uses.

I have read columns of Newman in the past with bated breath. The immense knowledge was there, but by the brilliant play of his temperament he was always uncompromisingly himself, a joy to read whether "right" or "wrong"; whatever these terms might mean in man's philosophy. He laid into pedantry with brick-bats. He dismissed a string quartet by some respected Royal Collegian in these terms—"this is not chamber music; it is lethal chamber music." He referred to another composition from the same worthy academical source in severe language, then graciously added: "But judging by the Opus number—265—it is presumably one of the composer's early works." He told us that Sir Hubert Parry was sickening for another oratorio. He compelled people not at all musical to turn to his column. He left Shaw and Runciman far behind in swashbuckling, and of course he held more of music in his little finger than the two heads of them put together. He was fearless. When he was critic on the *Manchester Guardian* he began a notice by informing us that it was "obvious" last night that Dr. Richter, conducting *Roméo* of Berlioz, had not known the score. Richter was then High Priest of English music and Newman was thirty-seven years old. He broke into lyrical periods about Gerhardt. "God," he told us, "may be able to create a better Lieder singer than Gerhardt, but so far He hasn't." He raved of Wolf as a lover of his mistress. He risked great falls. He asseverated that Strauss had taken the measure of Cervantes in his symphonic-poem and that in

future we should never be able to think of the book apart
from Strauss's music. He declared as emphatically that the
Sinfonia Domestica—one of the most musical of Strauss's
orchestral compositions—was the work of a man of talent
who once had been a man of genius; and next year Strauss
produced *Rosenkavalier*. He wrote of Mozart as of lesser
intellectual stature than Strauss: *Figaro* was the prattling
child, inspired maybe, but not capable of taking the measure
of the mind and sense of life of Beaumarchais. . . . He brought
to the difficult task of writing about music a lucid and athletic
prose; he was allusive and witty. He made criticism a gay
not to say profligate science. His first book, *Gluck and the
Opera*, was written when he was half-way through his twenties,
and it is a classic in the literature of music to this day; here
we have the historical and "documented" method applied by
a lively and personal mind. The first of Newman's several
studies of Wagner appeared in 1899; he has, I believe, dis-
owned it: he perhaps carried too far the theory that Wagner's
mind was entirely a musical one and that Wagner ran against
his own theory of music-drama, which was that music is the
means and drama the end. But this first study of Wagner is a
most remarkable book for any young man to have written
even in those earnest days of liberal education in England.
And it ends with one of the two best prose passages in all of
Newman's books: it should go into all the anthologies of
critical literature. Newman was not above "fine writing"
then; he who has come to scrutinize music much as a chemist
the contents of a test-tube, brought down the curtain on his
first study of Wagner thus:

". . . he was a brain of the rarest and subtlest composition,
put together cunningly by nature as no musician's brain
has been put together before or since. The muse of Poetry
seems to have dipped her wings into the lucid stream of
Music, disturbing it with suggestions of a world it had
never reflected before, deepening its beauty by closer associations with the actual world of men. This was the brain
of Wagner. There is none like him, none; it is almost
safe to say that there will be none like him to the end of
time."

There is a cadence for you!—why he doth it as like one of these harlotry players as ever I see—as like Cardus or any "sensitised-plate" literary man to the life!

Newman's quest of the absolute has been noble in his increasing years; we can feel the pathos of it. He looks back over the history of criticism and sees the futilities of much of it; the childish runnings here and there after new fashions, new toys. He is perhaps visited at midnight with spectral processions of his own mistakes; perhaps an echo from Browning comes to his ears: "What if all be error?" He is tired of what this man or that man thinks or feels about a genius. "Show me the mind of Bach at work; I am not interested in your adventures amongst the masterpieces. I am weary of what you tell me, apropos Beethoven, of yourself." Everybody must follow Newman up to a point in his distrust of writings on music that at bottom are non-musical, eked out with literary images that do not grapple with the organic life and structure of a work *qua* music. It is futile to describe a Sibelius symphony as though it were a Finnish landscape. Walter Pater set a bad example in criticism with his "She is older than the rocks," etc. Leonardo might well have protested "But what of my art?" Pater had some licence to be "literary" in his essays on painting; he knew what he was talking about. A relevant image can flash illumination into a composition; composers themselves invariably describe their works in "fine writing" peppered with metaphor.

But the approach must be along strict musical lines; I do not mean the lines of a programme analysis, all about first subjects and what the flute does with figure B in the recapitulation; nor do I mean the lines of a text-book on form. No two composers have regarded even sonata form in the same way. The approach must be of a mind which, because it has lived and thought and felt musically for years, can experience as though by instinct the chemistry of a composer's creative processes; and to the understanding of the language of music brings a poet's sympathy.

Experience has taught me (I speak here only for myself) that it is hard enough for the critic to express truth as he feels it within himself, without having at the same time to chase the antic will o' the wisp of objectivity: the Thing in Itself.

This is not to share the view that a critic needs only to communicate his gusto apropos one composer or another. The subtle bias of temperament from which none of us is immune —if we are artists in the slightest, and if we are not we should not concern ourselves at all with criticism—must be watched carefully. So that if it does lead a critic on the wrong track he will not be taken blindly along it. Let him remember Goethe's wise words to the effect that the master reveals himself by working within his limitations. And if he loves the arts, the critic will also revere them; and if he experiences them imaginatively, not by reason and theory alone, he will come to know and to sense an artist under just those laws and conditions by the observance of which the artist has been able to create at all. The whole study and culture of criticism, as I see it, is to gain entrance to vastly different worlds of the imagination, and to learn how to behave oneself while there; then to be gifted enough in expression to be able to give a vivacious account of what one has felt and thought while in those different worlds, whether one has "liked" them or not.

I take it that the difference between the trained critic's and the ordinary cultivated man's reactions to the arts is that the one has rationalised his likes and dislikes, and the other has not. But in the rationalising process—and this is where I differ from the later Newman—I believe as much in a logic of the heart as in a logic of the head. I gratefully recall some words on this point by De Quincey, in a passage warning us against paying too much attention to the understanding if it stands in opposition to any other faculty of the mind. "The mere understanding, however useful and indispensable, is the meanest faculty in the human mind, and the most to be distrusted; and yet the majority of people trust to nothing else, which may do for life but not for philosophical purposes." And certainly, we may add, not for the purposes of criticism of music; for music is an art which, as it is not made of words and everyday talk, does not address itself primarily to the understanding or strictly logical faculty. Music has to be experienced first by the ear of imagination; the critical process, the translating into definition and metaphor, cannot begin until the writer has been in the mind of the creative artist.

And he can win entrance only by sympathy. That was Langford's secret: he loved music as naturally as he loved flowers —which he also understood as floriculture, exactly as he understood music as science. He was the Hans Sachs of music, whoever (since Hanslick) has been the Beckmesser.

.   .   .   .   .   .

Writing on music in the *Manchester Guardian* has always taken the view that the music is the thing; the performers are mentioned only in so far as they absorb themselves and forget themselves in the general creative process. It is the absurdest convention of music criticism that it should pretend to estimate the technique of performance, a specialist's job. The music critic is not a teacher, not a voice producer, not an expert in what can be done with a piano, a fiddle, a trombone; his entire concern should be with his aesthetic reactions, and here he is (or should be) qualified by temperament and trained knowledge. I do not apologise for stating these elementary facts about the music critic's main job; they are to this day not generally understood amongst music purveyors.

I fell foul of Hamilton Harty almost as soon as I was given the reins of office and almost before Langford's ashes were cold; he wrote to C. P. Scott and asked if "this young man presumes to be a better conductor than myself." Scott replied that he hardly thought so but in any case he engaged me to write about concerts, not to conduct them: a simple but sufficient answer.

Another and major affair with Harty broke out suddenly, just as we were becoming twain. He made an approach to me shortly after Langford's death. I liked and admired him; he invited me to lunch with him at his club and he expressed the hope that we would work together for the good of music in Manchester. He did not, he assured me, object to criticism so long as it was constructive. A blessed phrase this; and usually it means that a criticism is regarded as "constructive," by the subject of it, if it is favourable. Harty shortly afterwards conducted the Ninth Symphony of Beethoven, and in the adagio—which is any conductor's severest trial—his tempo was extraordinarily dilatory. During the performance

I chanced to be sitting next to one of those curious individuals who "follow" music at concerts with a score; and at the end of each movement he marked down the length of time taken playing it, to a second. This man informed me that Sir Hamilton had beaten, in the adagio of the Ninth, the record held for thirty years by Hans Richter against all comers. Knowing that every conductor rightly dislikes an estimate of his tempo by a literal time-test, I mentioned in my notice next day that Harty had established a new record for slowness in the adagio of the Ninth Symphony, and I named the minutes and the seconds to a fraction. Harty send me a furious letter; he deplored that a music critic on a responsible journal should demean himself by attenting a Hallé Concert "accompanied by a stop-watch." Such mechanical aids, he added, might well be legitimate and helpful to a critic of Lancashire's batting at Old Trafford [this was a palpable hit]; but he submitted that Beethoven and himself deserved a judgment based on musical knowledge and feeling, not measured by "a mechanical time-test."

I deserved the irony. None the less, I had to retaliate. I replied to him thus:

"Dear Sir Hamilton,
"You are wrong; I would not insult you by applying to your conducting a test so crude. I do not attend your or anybody else's concerts supported by a stop-watch. But I must warn you, as man to man, that if you conduct the Ninth Symphony again in the near future I shall bring with me—less for critical purposes than for those of personal convenience—not a stop-watch but an alarm clock."

It was crude but it served. For several years to come Harty and I remained good friends, ready to join issue in private or public, at the slightest provocation.

Music criticism on the *Manchester Guardian* was, as you may have inferred, sufficiently austere during Langford's long reign. I hope I revered his tradition, and I hope I have never written of music except as one who is constantly bowing the head before the miracle of it. But there has usually been a journalist at my elbow, and I have never understood why in a column about music, even in the *Manchester Guardian*, a writer should not leaven the critical lump by a little flippancy here and there. In one of the first notices I wrote after I had succeeded unto Langford, I dealt with a singer in this heathenish strain:

> "Mr. Blank has a loud, not to say stentorian baritone. Also, he declaims his music with great emphasis. After he had expressed his devotion in Strauss's most hackneyed song, criticism could only lean back in its chair and wanly murmur 'But who deniges of it, Betsy?'..."

In a quarter of a century of criticism of music and drama and cricket I have gradually evolved a sound guiding principle —not to write about any event unless I have been there to see or hear it; at least it is as well to give the reader the impression that one has been, so to say, in the vicinity. It is not, I need hardly say, necessary for a music critic to remain at a concert from beginning to end; sometimes it is not fair and humane for him to do so, either to himself or the performers. But it is unwise to allude even indirectly to an event that one has not personally witnessed. Out of sheer kindness of heart I referred once to a performance I had not waited to hear. It was a concert for some charitable organisation, and I felt free to leave it at the interval. But during the second half, a well-known pianist was down to play the Ballade in A flat of Chopin, and as I did not wish my notice to ignore him altogether, I wrote that Mr. So-and-so played it in "his own aromatic manner," or some words to the same purpose. I was young fool enough to state that he played the piece named in the programme. Next day he wrote to the "M. G.," "venturing to point out" that I was so inexperienced and uninformed a critic of music that I apparently could not recognise the G minor Ballade of Chopin when I heard it. He had, behind my back, not kept to his original choice. I was in a predicament. The *Manchester Guardian* is always fair to reasonable criticism. The letter of the celebrated pianist was given a prominent place in the correspondence columns, and I was asked by the editor to add an explanatory footnote to it. I could do no better than this:

"I must accept Mr. So-and-so's statement that he played the Ballade in G minor. I can only explain my lapse by assuring Mr. So-and-so that from where I was sitting the music sounded like the Ballade in A flat."

On another occasion Samuel Langford withdrew from a concert before it was over, and missed a most notable occurrence. The first (or second—I forget which) flute of the orchestra fell down dead, or as near dead as mattered. But as Langford himself pointed out, as such a happening did not come under the heading of music criticism proper, he would not have referred to it in his notice even if he had stayed to see it.

· · · · · ·

The young swimmer in course of time finds in the advancing wave more of a challenge than a menace—at least so I have been told; for I myself have never tried to swim; as far as I know, I have the ordinary mortal's alacrity for sinking. But Swinburne declaims:

> As one that ere a June day rise
> Makes seaward for the dawn and tries
>   The water with delighted limbs,
>   That tastes the sweet dark sea, that swims
> Right eastward under strengthening skies,
>   And sees the gradual rippling rims
> Of waves whence day breaks blossom wise
>   Take fire ere light peer well above
>   And laughs from all his heart . . .

With something of the same exhilaration I threw myself every day into the seas of music and music criticism in the years following 1927, after a cautious trying of the water for a season. The *Manchester Guardian* gave me rope enough; they gave me almost as much space as I could fill; a column of "leaded minion" which meant that I could let myself go to the extent of 1,100 words about any concert or event worth while. No other daily newspaper in the world has day-by-day given to music the "M. G.'s" spacious attention. A new work was discussed comprehensively on the morning preceding its first performance; next day another column would review it again. No London concerts—or next to none—were advertised in the *Manchester Guardian*; none the less the paper allowed me to spend half my time there, and for every column devoted by *The Times* to music in London each week, the "M. G." and I contributed at least two.

On occasion C. P. Scott called me to heel. Here is one of his masterpieces of tactful admonishment and instruction:

January 24, 1930.

Dear Cardus:

You wrote a splendid notice of the Hallé last night, but alas! the sub-editor murmured. We were hard up for space as it happened, but apart from that, which is an accident, don't you think you ought to build for yourself a Procrustean bed? I am certain that you could make yourself quite at home in it. Nobody can put more stuff into a given space than you without any loss of clarity and grace. The particular bed I think we should set up is three-quarters of a column, stretchable on great occasions like last night to the full column, but never exceeding it. I claim your sympathy for the sub-editors, who in a given space have to satisfy the needs of half a dozen publics.

Yours ever,

C. P. Scott.

Could anything be more artful, more persuasive, more gracious—and more uncompromisingly final? The letter had the effect of keeping me within the column for at least six months. F. S. Attenborough, the chief of the sub-editors' room, who lived at high yet humorous pressure and was never still (so that it was impossible to engage him conversationally) blenched as he saw me coming up the stairs late at night, as he crossed the landing in his alpaca coat, flattening himself to the wall. "God!" he would say, "if it isn't Thursday!" (Thursday was Hallé Concert night.) And E. J. Phillips would "take" my notice, wait patiently for it, and deal with it like a scholar and a gentleman. No writer on music has known a better editor than "E. J." Probably he found my "copy" child's play in its legibility and general format after Langford's. The "M. G." did not commit the blue-pencil brutalities which transform the sub-editors' rooms of most newspapers into an abattoir. I have composed my column, returned home after midnight, and have been rung up from the office to this effect: We're terribly sorry, but to-night we are hard-pressed for space. Would you shorten your notice about ten lines or so and indicate where you'd like to cut it? . . . And over the telephone E. J. Phillips himself, proof in hand, would "blue-pencil" according to my reluctant directions.

Day by day I was free to explore music and my reactions to it; I was allowed to take risks and go my ways. And as soon as I had emerged from the shadows I decided at once, whatever else I achieved, I was going to enjoy myself. I looked at my colleagues: my critical brethren, as they sat in a row at the Wigmore Hall—the back row near the exit. I looked at them in their different seats of judgment at Queen's Hall. I seldom saw one of them showing evidence that he was enjoying himself. Now and again the flicker of Newman's cynical lips hinted that he was polishing some shaft to aim at some poor devil next Sunday; or at the best he was lost in a contemplation of the test-tubes of his own intellect. I hated the bulk of English music criticism for its dryness of nature and its parsimonious good-mannered use of the language. I remembered a saying of Sir George Grove years and years ago: "Isn't it strange how these critics can hear these great things" (the "Unfinished" symphony), "and I suppose enter into them and yet never show it by word in their wretched accounts."

If Lamb and Hazlitt had been able in their day to write about the theatre with imagination and gusto and knowledge; if in our own day Walkley and Montague and Agate could each in his own fashion make dramatic criticism suggestive, informing and stimulating to mind and imagination; if also they could bring to their daily work the variegated and personal prose of the essay-writer, why shouldn't a music critic go forth and do likewise?

There is, of course, a curious notion amongst English people (who are not musical except by effort or a miracle of nature) that music simply cannot be written about. Even Arthur Symons declared, in a depressed mood: "The reason why music is much more difficult to write about than any other art is because it is the one absolutely disembodied art, when it is heard, and no more than a proposition of Euclid when it is written." This is nonsense. A composition is not a fixed demonstration that means nothing but itself, addressed only to the logical mind. Music, like poetry, is a language through which men of genius reveal themselves. A sonata by Beethoven is no more like a proposition by Euclid than a sonnet by Shakespeare is. Maybe I should not dogmatise upon Euclid, for I know not the first thing about it (or should I say"him"?) but I know music, for I have lived in it and found it more real and less vague and more significant than the everyday life and speech of the common and concrete universe. In any case, nobody writes *about* music or anything else; he writes of himself as he feels and perceives himself under various impressions. I have my own ideas upon writing about music; but no fixed theory which I can recommend at large. Personally I have never written on music (or on any other subject) except for the purely selfish reason that I have liked it; and the impetus has come from delighted experience based on knowledge, plus some ability to write.

If there was any conscious plan at the back of my mind when I found myself firmly in the saddle it was to go to music not as other critics—that is, as though deprived of all their senses except that of hearing. There would be no fun for me to write of music as though from a vacuum, separated from warm tangible life. As I keep on saying, I do not find music "abstract," a series of propositions; an elusive Thing in Itself. Music is for me all the composers who have created it; a symphony is as much a part of Beethoven as the voice and mind and heart and humours of my best living mortal friend. I do not think of a work as a given form of music—sonata, or symphony, or étude, in such and such a key. When we listen to music, if we listen properly, we take part in a communion; we taste the body of genius, enter into the mind of the man.

I decided to set my notices against a background of actuality, to attempt a dramatic or psychological or picturesque interpretation of a concert, whenever the event moved me that way. I would use my scalpel with the rest of the anatomists

if the occasion called for it; it was as sharp, as well-set and
ground, as theirs. But first of all I would bring into play, if
I could, a sort of eye as well as ear for music. Arthur Symons
attempted to present an event to the eye as well as to the ear
of the musical imagination; but his knowledge of the art
was not deep enough. I now regarded myself as equipped almost
second to none amongst my contemporaries in music criticism,
culturally and from experience and by grace of an ability to
write more flexibly than any of them. It occurred to me that
if I were to try to get together an anthology of English
Criticism—chosen not only for the validity, real or apparent,
of the judgments expressed, but mainly as prose—I would be
able to draw profusely on dramatic and literary criticism;
and generously enough from art criticism. But where in all
the output of English music critics would I find a large-
minded way of writing, evocative and comprehensive, tran-
scending the immediate scene and concern of musicians only,
a prose which would be worth preserving for any reader of
culture and imagination and love of humane letters? In
Langford and Donald Tovey I would find many pages fit for
such an anthology, but where else? I determined to add to
them or perish in the attempt.

There were awful pitfalls to guard against—"mere writing
about" music leads to the intense inane. At first I naturally
floundered; and here is a warning example. (I was discussing
the "Eroica" symphony): "In the first movement—still a
marvel of symphonic expansion and unity in variety" (why
"still"?) "the main theme passes through some thirty or forty
changes, yet the music surges onward, suffering no let or
stay, till the imagination is filled with an awe like to that
felt by Shelley when he said 'Nought may endure but
Mutability.'"

In some way, because of a certain cadence, that piece of
fine writing seems to me almost the funniest ever written
about music; it is so blissfully unaware that it echoes the
Literary Lady "presented" by the Hominey in *Chuzzlewit*, who
declaimed: "Mind and matter glide swiftly into the vortex
of immensity. Howls the Sublime, and softly sleeps the calm
Ideal, in the whispering chambers of Imagination. To hear
it, sweet it is."

Ernest Newman called me a sensitised-plate critic (as we have seen), presumably meaning that I abandoned myself irrationally to impressions. This was an exaggeration and not fair to Newman himself. In my most unguarded moments I never excelled Newman's masterpiece of techni-colour refraction; his rhapsody in purple on the *Prometheus* of Scriabin:

"Listening to it solely as music only a congenitally unimaginative dullard, or a musician sodden in the futile teaching of the text-books and the conservatoires, could help feeling that here is music that comes as near as is at present possible to being the pure voice of nature and soul themselves . . . The wind that blows through the music is the veritable wind of the cosmos itself; the cries of desire and passion and ecstasy are a sort of quintessential sublima-tion of all the yearnings, not merely of humanity but of all nature animate and inanimate. . . ."

Here the panting reader will do well to rest for a while and renew his breath.

I was at first taken aback by Newman's denunciation of me; for I was just flapping my wings confidently for the first time; and after all, Newman was Newman. In London he was echoed by everybody except the young. But nature consoles; she taketh away and giveth. At almost the same time that E. N. was making good-humoured but effective sport with me, I received one day a note from Scott, enclosing a note to him from Montague, who, though now in his retirement in the Cotswolds, actually mentioned my writings on music in the "M. G." and in set terms approved them. One word of praise from Montague was worth more than all the riches of the world: I forgot at once the chastisements of my dear old schoolmaster Newman; they probably pained him more than they pained me.

.   .   .   .   .   .

In quest of more and more enjoyment I picked a bone with Sir Thomas Beecham during the Covent Garden Opera season of 1932. The sensitised-plate may occasionally distort the object as in itself it really is, but at least it cannot ignore or reject phenomena within its focus. Beecham produced *Rosenkavalier*, making one or two cuts which deprived important scenes of sense and character. In the *Manchester Guardian* I described these cuts as outrageous and unintelligent; apparently no other critic of a morning or an evening paper in London or elsewhere took notice of them; in any case it was not generally thought to be discreet to question the taste and authority of Sir Thomas.

He rose to the bait with his own maladroitness. He wrote not only to the *Manchester Guardian* but to the *Daily Telegraph* justifying the cuts in set terms; he stated that they had been sanctioned by Strauss himself. This was a "facer" to me, though instinctively I didn't believe it. I wrote to Strauss— but first of all I must, for the joy of reading it again, reproduce the relevant part of Sir Thomas's letter to the *Daily Telegraph*. It began with:

"For many years I have revered Mr. Neville Cardus as the classic authority upon our great national game, and respected him as a sound and eloquent writer on music" . . . (Everybody who has ever written to attack me in print on a musical point has been unable to resist pointing out that I am interested in cricket, to imply, of course, that I cannot possibly know anything about music: still, it was nice of Sir Thomas to say that I was sound and eloquent on a subject on which a great newspaper allowed me to write as I wished nearly all the year round) . . . "But," continued Sir Thomas, "I did not know that he may be included among our humourists. The picture which he has drawn of Dr. Richard Strauss as the helpless victim of vandalistic 'intendants and conductors'". . . (I had written nothing so general; I had merely drawn attention to two important cuts in a production of *Rosenkavalier*) . . . "is truly staggering to those of us who have been privileged to know this distinguished personage for many years."

Sir Thomas's main point was that "in the second week of December, 1912, I went to Berlin where I remained for ten days and discussed the production of *Der Rosenkavalier* at considerable length not only with Messrs. Furstner, but also with Dr. Strauss himself. On no occasion was the suggestion ever made that the work should be given in its entirety, or that the composer objected to the omissions we were proposing to make. Now, as I understand him, Mr. Neville Cardus is suggesting that the man who for over thirty years has occupied a position of pre-eminent authority in European music, and who at any moment could have insisted upon any conditions anywhere respecting the production of any of his works, is to be pitied as a powerless and protesting cipher, deeply wronged by the world of music."

Toujours de l'audace! The thought had never occurred to me that Sir Thomas's cuts in *Rosenkavalier* rendered Strauss a subject for pity, or reduced him to a powerless cipher. Sir Thomas's rhetoric, dictated after breakfast in his dressing-gown, I'll swear, was provoked by the fact that I had published Strauss's reply to my communication to him in which I asked him flatly if the two particular cuts in the 1932 production of *Rosenkavalier* had received his approval. Strauss assured me that he had not consented to the cuts and added that he was compelled helplessly to put up with cuts so long as the inviolability of works of art was not protected by law. He wrote to me with unexpected heat on the point.

Sir Thomas, we may be sure, was well aware throughout our little controversy, that my objection to the cuts in his *Rosenkavalier* production was a particular, not a general one. I was aware that cuts are supposed to be necessary in opera given in England, where long performances have to be adjusted to appetite and social usage. My point was that if opera must needs be shortened, the adjustments should be of a kind that do not detract from the essence of a character or spoil the sequence of a given musical period. To cut out, as Sir Thomas did, Ochs's "Da lieg' ich," is to ruin some of Strauss's best music and also to deprive us of the one opportunity we are given in the opera to feel some affection for the old villain, by seeing and hearing him caught off his guard. The second cut gave no excuse to the Marschallin for despising Ochs in her outburst "Da geht er hin."

I enlarge on this storm-in-a-teacup of years ago because I wish to present Sir Thomas in all his caprices and humours as I knew him; and to prepare artfully for the sequel. For several weeks Sir Thomas did not wish to see me; he left instructions to his man Smith in detail, that if I called at his flat he was not at home and that I should be carefully thrown down the stairs or into the area. But Sir Thomas and I have never been able even to pretend to a quarrel for long. We lunched one day that summer, and we winked at each other, like the Roman augurs. At about this time, Grant Richards, in harness with Geoffrey Toulmin, published a beautiful private edition of one of my cricket books, a hundred copies signed by the author: I sent a copy to the great man inscribed thus:

> To Sir Thomas Beecham
> from One Authority
> on Cuts
> to Another

It was Beecham who, during his seasons of opera in Manchester between 1914-1916, and by his conducting of the Hallé Orchestra in the same period of war, taught me that music was not entirely austere or serious. *That* point of view had been forced on me from the beginning: Manchester, as I say, was German in culture during my nonage. Beecham was the first to introduce poise, *savoir faire*, and even flippancy, into our concert halls. He is at bottom a connoisseur in attitudes and essences, patterns and flavours. He has always known, more than his fulsome thurifers of the London press, that his feeling for music, and consequently his conducting, have limitations. He seldom, if ever, essays the Ninth Symphony or the B minor Mass. He has no patience with a long stretch of Wagner. One night when I was at supper with him in Abbey Lodge, Lady Cunard called. She insisted that to-morrow night he should use a score for Götterdämmerung.

"You know very well that you don't know all the rhythmical changes."

With his incomparable blandness he replied: "There are no rhythmical changes in Götterdämmerung, my dear Emerald.

It goes on and on from half-past five till midnight like a damned old cart-horse."

In his most outrageous expressions of prejudice there is a grain of wild reason. He once drew upon him the disapproval of Elgar when he conducted a curtailed version of the A flat symphony. Before the beginning of the next rehearsal of the work Sir Thomas addressed the orchestra:

"Gentlemen, the composer of this immortal masterpiece has communicated to me that he wishes in future that we take the work in full and as written. That means, of course, we will play all the 'repeats.'" The irony of the remark will be appreciated by those who know how in the A flat symphony Elgar exploits the cyclic method of development. I have tried often to convert Beecham to Elgar. Apart from the "Enigma" Variations he has little patience with Elgar. He once dismissed the A flat symphony from one of our arguments by calling it "the musical equivalent of the architecture of St. Pancras Station." Neo-Gothic!

One Sunday morning, after a Leeds musical festival, he rang me up at my Manchester house; he was speaking from Harrogate. When "trunks" gave me notice of his call I expected something urgent. I did not know Sir Thomas then as intimately as I know him to-day; he is capable of a telephone conversation for pure conversation's sake from Seattle to Siam. He began this unexpected Sunday morning monologue by a review of the week's performances at Leeds. "Quite pleasant," he said, "very good bass voices, nothing like them in the world." He discussed some of the compositions played: Walton's *Belshazzar's Feast*, and Vaughan Williams. Then he reviewed all English music since Purcell, with the telephone operator interrupting every three minutes, and Sir Thomas saying "Please go away, my dear." For more than half an hour he spoke of English composers from Purcell to William Walton, but he did not once mention Elgar. At last I could stand it no longer. So I broke in: "But what about Elgar?" Sir Thomas replied, "What about him? Isn't he well?" He presently rang off, having filled in a moment of leisure in the day. He hates to be unoccupied; if he is not actually working, he must talk, or plan a libel action, or project a definitive edition of Beaumont and Fletcher.

If I could live my life over again I would not miss a single one of the many hours of talk with Beecham, especially those in his suite at the Midland Hotel in Manchester, following a Hallé Concert, after he had rid himself of those curious people who visit artists' rooms. Often have I finished my notice for the "M. G." and gone to my home several miles out of Manchester and got into bed; the telephone has rung and it has been Beecham asking me to come at once and have supper with him—time, I a. m.—and I have dressed again, called a taxi, returned to the city and passed through the now silent entrance hall of the Midland Hotel, and taken the automatic lift to his eyrie, where champagne was glistening, with oysters. There, in his dressing-gown, he would be host, fresh as though newly wakened, the evening's concert and the energies of conducting a formidable programme entirely forgotten; he would pour out the champagne as though it were the first bottle of his career; then we would begin to talk until dawn, and he would poise his cigar, and watch the curling smoke, and he would twist and twitch his nose, waiting for me to finish a sentence. By word of mouth we were polite and accommodating; but with our glances we spoke epigrams of innuendo. His range was without end, and once he sat down at his upright piano and in a guessing competition he beat me by playing and singing from memory some songs by E. T. A. Hoffmann.

The Beecham legend is, of course, only half-based on fact. He is not always the supercilious, unbending, not to say mincing little exhibitionist the concert platform knows, with his imperial beard and his waggery. Away from London, I have many times seen humour expel the measured egoism in him; he has unbuttoned, and roused the night-owl, if not with a catch, with a fearsome imitation of the latest Heldentenor at Covent Garden. During his tour of Australia, he one midnight howled and gurgled through Siegfried's Forging Songs until a rapping was heard on the other side of the wall of the room. Sir Thomas immediately stopped his noise *sforzando*. "Did I hear a knock?" he asked, and rising from the piano stool, with his arms clasped behind his dressing-gown, he walked processionally to the door, his face eager with inquiry. The rapping was repeated.

"Come," he said to me, "let us investigate."

He opened the door of his sitting-room and peered outwards.

"Ah, ha," he cried, "sayst thou so? Art thou there, true-penny?"

Then he knocked at next door, and I overheard the following dialogue:

An Australian Voice: "Shut that bloody row at this time of night. How do you expect anybody to go to sleep?"

Sir Thomas: "I don't expect it. This is not the time for sleep. To be up at midnight and to go to bed then is early, so that to go to bed after midnight is to go to bed betimes."

The Australian Voice (not at all mollified): "How do you expect a fellow to get any sleep in all that hell row? I've got to get up early and do a day's work."

Sir Thomas: "My dear fellow, *I* have to get up early and conduct the Brisbane Orchestra at a rehearsal, which is worse. Come, come, rouse ye. Thou art a scholar; let us therefore eat and drink."

And in a few minutes the tired business man was sitting in his pyjamas with us in Beecham's suite, filling himself with champagne, until Sir Thomas and I carried him back to his bed, and by now he was dead to all physical phenomena. Next day he departed from the hotel but left a note to Sir Thomas vowing he had never enjoyed himself so much in all his life, and regretting he had "passed out" so soon; as Sir Thomas said to me, showing me the letter, "The Australian is a heavy, but not a strong drinker."

So far from being the Malvolio of the public imagination, Beecham is really related to a more homely type. In spite of his love of chastising people with his tongue; in spite of a streak of cruelty and an impish maliciousness which he reserves mainly for his friends, he is at bottom good-natured and friendly. The Falstaff in him overwhelms the Whistler, as the sow her litter. He loves to get away from his legend, and to shout out, apropos of nothing at all: "You scullion! You rampallian! You fustilarian! I'll tickle your catastrophe." I think he is happy only working or in his dressing-gown; when he throws off his starched shirt and tails, he is just "Tommy" Beecham, likely to sit at the piano and play Chopin with style and modest technique, or to talk Dickens by the hour and quote chapters from him, or to discuss international law as an authority who has devoted himself to music and the arts in his spare time. He never utters the usual conversational commonplaces; and when he plays the fool the sources of his laughter are comedy of character, low or high, with the exaggeration of art. We got on well together because each was a good foil and audience. We agreed that men who do not like Dickens were not to be trusted; we agreed too that Dickens was not only the greatest revealer of English humorous character since Shakespeare, but also the greatest master of the Grotesque in our literature. I make this point of Beecham's love of Dickens because it serves as a quick way of illuminating a side of his nature not suspected by many.

Like all comedians he is serious and subject to loneliness of spirit. At times he can be caught off his guard: there is a lull in the banquet of talk and food and wine; then you will see his vision withdrawn; his blue eyes are momentarily lost and unhappy. And now you can understand why Beecham can conduct Delius incomparably.

He has never altogether forgotten he was born in Lancashire. It is certain that he has never realised himself, as man or as artist, more fully than during his sojourns in the North of England. At Covent Garden he seemed frequently frustrated; in the Beecham opera of Quay Street, Manchester, he was in his element, especially when he conducted Verdi's *Otello* with Frank Mullings as Othello, the greatest actor, next to Chaliapin, ever seen in opera in England, and a singer who, by imagination, transformed the defects of his voice into expressive assets. The Beecham opera of 1916, which would fill Manchester's largest theatre for three months at a stretch, eight performances weekly, was the best, in range and finish of style, ever known in England. Glyndebourne alone has equalled it, but the scope there was smaller. Beecham in Manchester produced nearly every masterpiece in all schools of opera: his *Figaro* was the most vivacious and yet the most pathos-shaded I can recall in a lifetime, with Agnes Nicholls the Countess Désirée Ellinger the Susanna, Frederick Ranalow the Figaro, and Frederick Austin the Count—and nobody else has passed across the closing scene of the opera with half of Austin's grace of bearing and suggestion of courtly cynicism

It was during an opera rehearsal at Manchester that Sir Thomas uttered one of his saltiest remarks. A singer—a good actor for parts such as Klingsor, but not exactly mellifluous as vocalist—was talking to Sir Thomas during a pause in the morning's work, while refreshments were taken. The singer chanced to mention his son at Oxford. "I didn't know you had a son," said Beecham.

"Oh, yes, Sir Thomas," replied Klingsor, "and I don't know what to do with him; he'll be leaving Oxford next year. He's not keen on anything in particular; doesn't fancy law or medicine, won't go into the City—doesn't seem to have any particular bent."

Beecham stroked his beard.

"Aren't you going to make a singer of him?"

"Oh, no, Sir Thomas. He hasn't got any voice at all."

"Ah, I see—a family failing."

It was not until 1931 that I met Beecham, much as he had loomed in my life for years. We came together at the Salzburg Festival of 1931, and as we now approach very rich comedy I must digress to introduce another character, small but important and juicy. I went to Salzburg in 1931, taking with me my friend James: that wasn't the whole of his name, but it will serve this story. As a small boy he was a victim of the "half-time" principle in the Lancashire cotton trade; he was wakened up in the dawn, sent into the mill, and after several hours' hard labour he was supposed to attend school in the afternoon. In the course of time he educated himself into a responsible secretarial position in Manchester; he lived to see his son win a scholarship for Balliol; he made himself into as enthusiastic a lover of books and the theatre and music as any I have had the good fortune to know and love; and he was for years a very fine non-professional actor; I count his performance of Clemenceau in Ludwig's *Versailles* one of the most impressive experiences in all my remembrances of the English stage.

James had never before been out of England until I took him to Salzburg in 1931. He was lean and cadaverous, unwieldy of limb and gait, with a kind of Jackdaw of Rheims bedragglement of hair for covering. He had spacious gestures, and was usually knocking objects of furniture over. In his decorous moments of life, when for instance he was reading the minutes of the last meeting, his English was excellent and his voice properly oracular; out of office and away from home the original Doric of Lancashire came out unalloyed and pungently. On our first night at the Salzburg opera we discovered that our seats were too near the stage. "Get 'em changed," said James, as we occupied our stalls and the orchestra gathered together. "Get 'em changed, can't sit here. Damned silly of 'em to invite you half-way 'cross Europe to write for the *Guardian* about opera and then give us pla-aces next brass!"

"All right," I said impatiently, "I'll attend to it in the morning. I can't do anything to-night."

The opera was *Rosenkavalier*. So perfectly did the orchestra play that, close as we were situated to the trombones, our ears were not afflicted. But during the interval James still complained bitterly and persisted with his "It's no good; you must get seats farther back to-morrow. Orchestra's all right but we want a bit o' perspective." Then the curtain rose on Act II, and lo and behold! Adele Kern as Sophie stood at the side of the stage, enchanting in ruff and panniered dress, as she clasped her hands and with eyes full of light of love, sang her rapturous "In dieser feierlichen Stunde." James leaned forward in his seat, transfixed by the beauteous vision. Almost unwillingly he tightly gripped my knee. Then he turned to me and noisily whispered, "Neville, lad; we're all right where we are!"

On one of Salzburg's mornings of rain which blotted out the mountains and filled the place with mists, I lunched with Sir Thomas for the first of many times; it was during this same lunch, which extended from one o'clock until late afternoon, that our conversation was interrupted by a waiter who brought to Sir Thomas a card. Beecham looked at it and said, "Count Esterhazy? Show him up." A large moon-faced man, in Tyrolean cape and leather short trousers, entered the room, came to our table, bowed low and said, "Sir Beecham?" He was one of the Salzburg Festspiele Intendants.

"Your pr-rograhm next week . . ." he began.

"Yes," collaborated Sir Thomas sweetly, "my programme?"

"The symphony of Mozart in C major," continued Ester-

hazy, then paused in obvious perplexity. (Beecham's programme included the C major symphony, K 200, which he
made familiar to London audiences.)

"Yes," said Sir Thomas, "you were saying the symphony
in C major of Mozart?"

"Well, Sir Beecham, we cannot tra-ace it."

It was the truth. Salzburg had apparently not yet discovered this little symphony.

Beecham turned to me. "How interesting," he said, "they
cannot trace it. I think it was composed in Salzburg about
half a mile from where we are now sitting—no, let us be on
the safe side and say three-quarters of a mile."

He satisfied the Count of the authenticity of the work;
and Esterhazy again bowed low and was about to leave us,
when "Sir Beecham" let go a parting thrust—unkind and
unprovoked, but irresistible.

"The remainder of my programme," he said, "contains,
as no doubt you will recollect, the second symphony of Brahms.
I think you will have no difficulty in tracing *that* masterpiece."

The following evening James and I sat in the Festival
theatre listening to the fifth symphony of Bruckner. A row
or two in front of us were Sir Thomas and Lady Cunard.
After the close of the three movements, each of them long and
exhaustive, there was a pause; and into a gallery at the back
of the orchestra walked a number of solemn musicians, armed
with tubas and trombones. Beecham turned round and gave
me an apprehensive look.

"Reinforcements!" I whispered back to him. He at once
rose from his seat in the dark, Lady Cunard with him. James
and I followed their example, and we all tiptoed through the
exits. In the foyer Sir Thomas approached me.

"What did you think of the Bruckner as far as you could
cope with it?" I asked.

Judicially he replied: "Ten times I sat up expectantly;
and ten times I recoiled."

A whole text-book on Bruckner could not express as much
as this relevant to Bruckner's methods, his strength and his
weakness.

"Come and have supper," he said. I told him I was enter-
taining a friend. "Bring him along," he added; and without

a glance at James, he took me by the arm and marched me
into the Salzburg streets, now dry and quiet in the moonlight.
We walked to the restaurant of the Mirabell Gardens. I looked
over my shoulder and saw a sight I shall never forget: Lady
Cunard had taken James's arm with one hand, while with
the other she gripped her evening gown while she hobbled
in her evening shoes over the cobbles. James was profuse and
gallant.

Arrived in the Mirabell Gardens, Sir Thomas ordered a
sumptuous repast, with champagne unstinted. James had not
usually found life as regaling as this; the bubbles quickly went
to his head, and soon he was leaning across the table, slapping
Beecham on the shoulder saying, "No, Tommy, that's where
you're wrong." Beecham's nose twitched violently, and the
eyes of Lady Cunard goggled; but they rapidly summed-up
the great occasion and the man.

And now we entered a violent argument about opera in
England. "You critics," said Beecham, "are always belittling
English opera. Do you forget my efforts?" I assured him
that I for one had not forgotten; but, to draw him out, I
emphatically stated that opera in England is acquired, not
natural, while in Central Europe it is as instinctive and
natural to the average man as cricket or golf to the English.

Beecham pooh-poohed. "I could give opera to-morrow
quite as good as they produce it here in Salzburg." And now
I spread my bait. "Yes," I argued, "that's all very well, Sir
Thomas. *Tou* could produce opera in England, no doubt.
But listen. If all the singers, musicians, conductors, stage
technicians working at Salzburg to-day were to be somehow
killed in an earthquake or drowned in a cloudburst, the opera
would still go on—they'd bring a fresh lot over from Munich,
or somewhere else, in a jiffy."

"Well," sniffed Sir Thomas, "and what of it?"

"Why," I said, "if we were giving opera in England and
only *you*—you alone—happened to die suddenly, why the
festival would automatically and irreparably come to an end
at once and for ever!"

"Nons—" roared Sir Thomas, then stopped. He was
about to pronounce the word "nonsense," but didn't. He
twitched his nose, stroked his beard, then said, quietly and

accommodatingly, "You are quite right; you are quite right." It was simply not in him to say otherwise.

A few minutes later he embarked on his theory of music.

"You critics are always writing about the meaning of music, the ethic, the *Weltanschauung* of the composer, and God knows what. The whole point of music is that it should sound well. Never mind what it signifies. Music should have wings and float and give delight. Take, for instance, the opening of the C major symphony of Schubert. . . ."

In a corner of the restaurant a little string orchestra was playing music—no tin-can stuff, but soft waltzes; and a number of elegant personages were dancing. "God!" ejaculated Beecham, "stop that noise!" He called for the *maître d'hôtel*. "How can I demonstrate to my learned friend here, the beauties of Schubert's music if that damned strumming goes on perpetually? Please have it silenced."

What is more, it quickly was silenced, and round our table gathered all the elegant personages, many of them adorned with decorations, crosses and stars and sashes. And they produced menu cards on which Sir Thomas could write his autograph; then they handed them on to us for ours. When I lie close to death the vision will return of James, enormous cigar in his mouth, leaning negligently back in his chair, writing with a flourish the autograph of James Ramsbottom, saying: "Don't mention it, your Excellency; don't mention it, pleasure's mine."

During a rehearsal of his concert at Salzburg with the Vienna Philharmonic Orchestra, Sir Thomas demonstrated his appreciation of the character of James. The hall was occupied by several of Europe's most distinguished musicians who sat close to the platform absorbed in Sir Thomas's methods. Amongst them were Strauss, Clemens Kraus, Walter, Weingartner, to name only a few. In the back seats, concealed as we thought in the darkness, sat myself and James. At the end of a dazzling finale of the Mozart symphony Sir Thomas whipped round, and directing his gaze over the heads of the notabilities to our places at the back, he shouted: "That all right, Mr. Ramsbottom? Any suggestions?" And James, without a quaver returned, "On quick side, a bit."

It was after his concert, given on a beautiful Sunday

morning in the Mozarteum, and while Sir Thomas was sitting in the artists' room, crumpled in his morning coat and striped trousers, that a man plunged through the door in a tremendous state of exaltation; he was English of the kind that enjoys raving disproportionately about all things foreign.

"What playing, Sir Thomas!" he burbled, "what strings! Did you ever hear such phrasing! And the woodwind!" Beecham eyed him patiently before asking, with much gravity of mien and voice, "But have you ever heard the Bournemouth Orchestra?" The Englishman collapsed like a pricked balloon and he disappeared and was seen no more.

To this day a number of heavily-degree'd English musicians affect to distrust the foundations of Sir Thomas's culture and knowledge. They refer to him, indirectly rather than directly, as an inspired amateur. This school of thought hinted much the same of Delius; and for long it declined to recognise Elgar who, poor soul, was more or less self-educated. Beecham at least had been to Oxford, while Delius was known to have lived many years in Germany and studied music there. Here we have the three most original spirits known in English music since Purcell, if we leave out Sullivan, whose pre-occupation with comic opera, to the neglect of oratorio and symphony, was naturally deplorable and deplored. Beecham as a fact is the most studious and most musically absorbed man I know. In all the years of my friendship with him I have come upon him, surprised and discovered him, at all hours of the day and night, in his own flat or in hotels, on railway trains, or ocean-going liners. Always has he been reading a score or a book worth w hile. He once said to me: "My chief merit is one I never get any credit for—patient and persistent industry." He is at all hours of the day an austere recluse, never out of his dressing-gown until late afternoon, unless engaged at a rehearsal. His most flippant waggery springs from a serious point of view; as I say, he never talks trivialities. His best sayings are not known to the world—only his obvious "cracks." I prefer his wit when you can see it rising uncalled to his mind, and his main object is bald statement of fact. Thus—one morning I ran into him near Langham Place and he told me he was travelling to Stockholm that day to listen to a new tenor and see about some stage-setting likely to be useful at Covent Garden. Three days later he rang me up from Abbey Lodge asking me to lunch.

"I thought you were in Stockholm," I said, "you said the other day you were going there."

"So I did," responded the voice, "and I have been to Stockholm. I had no intention of settling there."

A star danced when he was born, no doubt; also a star shot and fell to the earth. There is mischief perpetually in him, and it grimaces even when he himself is perhaps not consciously calling it forth. That is why, I suppose, some sudden caprice will spoil an interpretation of Beecham now and then; some "playboy" trick of acceleration or crescendo. It is said that Toscanini once called Beecham the English Pagliacci; there is a grain of truth in it. Nobody would describe Beecham's conducting as intellectually and emotionally profound. To do full justice to him we must look at him not only from a musical but an *extra*-musical angle. There is something histrionic about him, as man and as artist. Only by some imaginative mimicry could Beecham present, for example, Sibelius as vividly as he does; for I doubt if in his heart he counts the music of Sibelius as part of a genuine musical style. One night at a Hallé concert, during the interval, Professor Samuel Alexander came to me carrying his cumbrous aid to hearing, rather like a camera. "I suppose he is a great conductor," he said, with reference to Sir Thomas. I assured him that such was the case. "As a mere layman in music," proceeded the greatest living metaphysician of those years, "I am not competent to judge, so I'll take your word for it. But. . ." and here his eyes twinkled, "I am in my own way something of a philosopher. And a philosopher's material is supposed to consist in part of some slight knowledge of human nature." A pause, then: "Speaking strictly as a philosopher of course" (he jerked his thumb over his shoulder indicating the rostrum on the platform), "the man's a charlatan" —the voice rising to a high chuckle of glee on "charlatan." I am certain he intended it as a compliment.

It is an abuse of language to apply the word genius to a man not creative of enduring work, though there may be something material, savouring of cash values, to estimate the activity of the human spirit in terms of what it permanently bequeaths to us. Genius may surely be regarded as a thing *sui generis*, a flame that burns not to warm or illumine the world, but simply because in the general clash of vital forces a spark has been struck, or spontaneous combustion has occurred.

If we describe Beecham as a man of talent we speak a half-truth. Better to risk the word genius and go more than half-way—for half-way to the truth is not even across the frontier. I cannot account for him except in terms of genius; other conductors surpass him in knowledge and understanding of music, in technique and experience, but few of them can leave behind so strongly an impression of a unique influence. I suggest that we must for convenience's sake call a man a genius if we cannot explain how he has come to be what he is unless aided by some personal force hard to define. Toscanini, to a large extent, can be accounted for without reference to the inexplicable and indefinable; he would have been great even without his genius. Not so Beecham. For Sir Thomas takes risks which the rational mind would not sanction; from the basis of knowledge he trusts daringly to improvisation. He comes to his interpretations often "on the night" by a swift act of comprehension. He goes into music as a swimmer into a sea; you might say he conducts almost by ear—which is no belittlement, at any rate, Samuel Butler wrote: "Life is like music; it must be composed by ear, feeling and instinct, not by rule. Nevertheless one had better know the rules for they sometimes guide in doubtful cases—though not often."

No living conductor shares Beecham's range; he will give vivid readings of more different styles of music than anybody else. Versatility is not, of course, a certain sign of creative or interpretative genius; as Oscar Wilde remarked, only the auctioneer should appreciate all schools of art. Beecham, as I say, keeps away from the austerities of Bach and Beethoven. He is too shrewd to allow cosmopolitanism to diffuse itself into dilettantism. If he misses the tragic intensity of *Tristan*, the girth and amplitude of the comedy of *Meistersinger* and the gradual epic sweep of *The Ring*, he brings compensations; he mediterraneanises Wagner, to use Nietzsche's term. He concentrates on the melody in Wagner and lends to the score as a whole a fineness of style that is fascinating even if it does reduce the stature and lighten the harmony and the rhythm— and rhythm was not Wagner's strong point, for the simple reason that often he was preoccupied with slow-moving harmonic transition. In *The Ring* performances at Covent Garden between 1930 and the outbreak of war, Beecham persuaded people violently in reaction against Wagner to listen to the London Philharmonic Orchestra playing the Wagnerian "melos"—the unending flow of melody unburdened by heaviness of accent. When an objection was made by a critic to Beecham's tempi in Wagner, that they were too quick, Beecham produced metronomic evidence to prove he had conducted each music-drama in *The Ring* at much the same pace as Richter's. Beecham artfully did not point out that an illusion of quicker movement can be created by the conductor who lightens the harmony. A fat man and a thin man walking side by side down the street do not proceed at the same tempo; the fat man is moving faster than the thin man. Beecham reduced something of Wagner's harmonic weights; hence the illusion of quicker tempi.

German musicians did not admire Beecham's Mozart; they said it was too elegant, too superficially melodious, short of fundamental harmony, a Mozart of mincing gait, a courtier of his period. During recent years the Germans discovered a "dæmonic" Mozart; psychological (and of course metaphysical) exegesis rooted out of his music evidences of complexes, sexual frustration, and all the rest of it. As a consequence, performances of Mozart in Germany became intolerably tasteless and unmusical. The German musical æsthetic at no time helped towards the right approach to an understanding of the most impeccable of composers in style and poise. And with the advent in the nineteenth century of Kultur in German music the spirit of Mozart departed. Who, for example, but a German could have committed the enormities of the cadenzas supplied by Hindemith to the modest, youthful so-called "Adelaide" violin concerto of Mozart?

No German composer has been able in my lifetime to conduct Mozart felicitously. I was unfortunate enough not to hear Strauss's interpretations. Richter's Mozart was four-

square, prosaic, slow-moving, unsmiling and bourgeois.
Besides, Richter was not a German. Beecham's distaste for the
Teuton musical aesthetic was an asset when he conducted
Figaro; as I have already written, I have heard no *Figaro* of
finer and lighter texture than Beecham's, none that came
closer to the comedic spirit which observes the way of the
civilised world and doesn't protest too much, and receives
the ironies with pressed lips. On a certain visit to Berlin, Sir
Thomas accepted an invitation to attend a performance at
the State Opera of *Figaro*. Half-way through it was observed
that he was sleeping peacefully in his box. They politely, but
with obvious sorrow, reprimanded him afterwards. "But,
Sir Thomas," they said, "we have been led to understand that
Mozart was your favourite composer."

"Only when I conduct him myself," Beecham replied, quite
agreeably and modestly.

But it is not enough to discuss Beecham only as a conductor. His influence on English musical life for years was as
powerful and refreshing as that of Bernard Shaw in the theatre
of the 'nineties. He opened doors and windows; he expelled
a dusty and dowdy parochialism. He introduced colour and
vivacity to English music. To many a young man of those
days the Beecham opera opened ears for the first time to the
delights of music—pagan, I regret to say. Even into what
once was known as the provinces of England Beecham penetrated, civilising the hinterland, setting the local "Watch
Committees" by the ears with a sensuous exoticism of stage
production never before witnessed in these places of non-
conformist darkness, all in association with the art which to
most of the natives had been known so far only in the form of
mortifying oratorio. This is not to belittle the spade-work
done earlier by travelling companies directed by Carl Rosa
and Charles Manners and Joseph O'Mara. But these pioneers
needed to pay their way and keep more or less to a "popular"
repertory, with what the bill-posters described as an "Aug-
mented orchestra" on special occasions, drums and extra brass
in private boxes. It was Joseph O'Mara who, after a profitable
season in Glasgow with *Faust* and *The Bohemian Girl* and
Maritana, decided in a full spate of idealism to produce *Tristan*.
"I'll spend some money on the orchestra," he said. The trouble

was to find adequate brass. A euphonium and a competent performer upon it were discovered in a public bar, and it was decided that he would "do." The score was accommodated to him; and at the first rehearsal the conductor confidently began the Prelude to *Tristan*. The euphonium failed to emit a vestige of sound at the point where it had been agreed that he should announce the death motif. The conductor began again, and once more the euphonium player remained silent, in spite of a most unambiguous "lead." The conductor stopped the orchestra and turned to the private box. "Why didn't you play?" he asked. And the man with the euphonium asked in a pronounced Scottish accent, "But mon, are we still in the six-eight?"

The old touring companies actually made opera a popular entertainment for the masses. I saw (rather than heard) *Der Freischütz* for the first time in Pitt Hardacre's Comedy Theatre. Charles Manners and his troupe packed the theatre (gallery, sixpence) with an English version of *Meistersinger*, and a very good singer named Lewys James was the Sachs. Every autumn the Theatre Royal in Manchester was crowded each night and on Saturday afternoons for the Carl Rosa Opera Company; and *Tannhäuser* and *Lohengrin* were "box-office certainties." E. C. Hedmondt, in spite of a voice that held the top notes only by strenuous physical convulsion, was an intense demon-possessed Tannhäuser until the third act, when he achieved a most tragic sense of discharge of evil and of all manly self-reliance. Arthur Winckworth was one of the best Wolframs I ever heard. The conductor was the father of Eugene Goossens, a wonderful man of rare conscience and thoroughness. These opera companies provided the general public with the evening's recreation which nowadays is the monopoly of the films. There was little musical atmosphere about it all, no doubt, and the productions were palpably "stock"—a segment of Venusberg would turn up to-morrow night in Seville, while the noses of the high priests in *Aïda* were never sufficiently Coptic. The point is that there *were* opportunities, in the provinces of England of those days, to get acquainted with opera if you happened to be poor to the verge of poverty.

Beecham was responsible for a revolution. The irony is that he so raised the standards of production and performance that the touring companies were driven away from the large cities. Then, when he relinquished his work in opera outside London, the touring companies had lost their grip. Having experienced the best, the crowd would take nothing inferior. That is why Sir Hamilton Harty made one of his prettiest remarks when he was asked why he did not conduct opera during the declining years of the ill-starred and gallant British National Opera Company. "There is now no hope for British opera in the provinces," he said. "It is dying of T.B."

Beecham did for opera in England what can be done on the Continent of Europe only by large government subsidies. It was a bold experiment and I think it would have conquered and established solid and lasting foundations if Beecham had not been obliged to immerse his genius in the complications of the Covent Garden estate. But for what he actually gave to us, during the halcyon years of 1912-1920, we must remain grateful, for he opened the eyes of the blind and made the deaf hear. If Toscanini or Bruno Walter or Furtwängler had never lived at all, the condition of music in Europe and the course of musical history in the cities of the Continent would to-day be much the same, developed from a long and organised princely or State patronage. Without Beecham, the most lustrous page in English music for centuries would not have been written at all. He was in those days a great impresario, as well as a man of culture and a musician. Best of all, from the greater heights of human nature and the art of living, he was a sort of civilised *édition de luxe* of Arnold Bennett's "Card"; he identified himself in a shabby community of cash values with the great cause of cheering us all up.

.   .   .   .   .   .

Until I had lived twenty years I had, as I have written, not travelled more than a few miles beyond my birth-place. After the Shrewsbury chapter came to an end I returned to the confinements of Manchester for another ten years, except for a rare journey, not far distant, in the capacity of a reporter, during the few months when I worked in Haslam

Mills's room. So broadly speaking I did not, in thirty years, see any but a provincial world. But I never was much interested in the solid and concrete external universe. Later in life I surprisingly found myself crossing the Equator; one afternoon I walked alone through the streets of Colombo, streaming with heat, but I was entirely bored in half an hour. I returned to the ship. We were on the way to Australia, and for the rest of the day's call at Colombo I had the *Orion* almost to myself until midnight. That was the only time I went ashore on my first voyage half-way round the world. It was much the same when I journeyed by air from England to Australia years afterwards; the white fields of clouds over which we flew, in a solitude of eternity, this was an experience for the spirit; but the terrestrial phenomena of the trip occupied my attention only by means of a sequence of reflex actions. I was no more impressionable than a camera when I stood by the Sea of Galilee; and if Christ Himself had appeared before us, walking the water, I should have allowed the crowd to rush ahead in front to do the gaping.

I was a born introvert, I suppose. In Manchester for nearly thirty years I walked the same circuit, thousands of times, from boyhood, down the Oxford Road, but not there, not there. One day I bought a copy of the *Stage*, a thrilling chronicler of the theatre then, and I read of Irving's production at the Lyceum of *Faust* In a flash I was transformed to London. I could not have been more than fourteen, and I had not yet been anywhere near London, but no London known to me afterwards was so real and so true; for this London was built for me out of what I had lived through in the columns of the *Saturday Review* when Max Beerbohm wrote for it; and from G. R. Sims's column every Sunday in the *Referee*—"Mustard and Cress," composed in a room looking on Regent's Park "opposite the Ducks."

If I did not attend first nights of Shaw plays at the Court Theatre, then I must have read A. B. Walkley in vain. I heard the chatter and animation at matinées of *Peter Pan* at Christmas-time, and I shared strange, not to say esoteric, charms of poung life as I walked in the slime of the Manchester streets, and dreamed. I shall recapture for long a moment of vision when I first read Alfred Noyes's lines about—

> . . . a barrel-organ playing somewhere in a London street,
>   as the sun sinks low.
> Though the music's only Verdi, the melody is sweet.

I was walking in some faded avenue, a cul-de-sac in a Manchester suburb, near a forlorn park; before me stretched a
vista of houses that had once known prosperity, with gardens
that had weeds in them and the air of a fallen day. The soft
melancholy of a city on an autumn evening nearly laid me
low, as I read the jingle of Noyes; and I was as completely
transported to some quiet purlieu of the Kensington of the
period as any I subsequently came to know in later years by
the accident of physical presence.

Stendhal said that for him a landscape needed to possess
some history or human interest. For me a place must have a
genius in the air, a sort of distillation of years, a pathos of
perspective, a mist of distance. In a word, it must have ghosts
of lost wandering life, now forgotten by the extrovert and
contemporary world. Historical and archaeological interest is
prosaic for me; I do not particularly wish to see the house
in which the greatest poet was born; but to walk from
Grinzing down to Vienna on a September evening, as twilight
deepens and the lights of the city begin to twinkle, and to
feel the sense of the past, almost to hear the vanished beauty
and song whispering in rustle of leaf or wind, and in some
hurrying footfalls on the roadside; to feel an awareness to
all the hearts that have beaten here, the hopes and the strivings
in these old houses, huddled in deserted gardens; birth and
marriage and death; the comings-home at the day's end, the
glow of candlelight and wine and fellowship that surely
seemed perennial and everlasting; the security of life at the
crest, and now not only dead but lost to a world that must
for ever be up and doing—this for me, is to live and to "go
places." Every great city is a palimpsest not of facts and
events but of atmosphere and feeling, shaped by the irony of
transition. That means I cannot enter into an unexplored
land, a new land, where nature has not acquired an aesthetic
and a pathos. Mountains and grand canyons and plains and
mighty rivers are only so much geography in my eyes; mere
contour-maps built on a large scale. A sunset in the Indian

Ocean once bowled me over because it was like the closing scene of *Götterdämmerung*. I suppose I am a far-gone case of the Ruskinian "pathetic" fallacy; the external universe must appeal to me as a theatre or as a series of dissolving views, with the lantern turned inwards to my own soul.

.   .   .   .   .   .

I do not know whether this book so far has presented the writer as a man of a tolerably happy temperament; I have not put down a single word consciously to "present" myself. I have told my story in a soliloquy, or rather memory has dictated it, and I have been nothing more than an amanuensis. Happiness, as the world seems to want or to know it, is a strange idea to me. There are few material circumstances that have the power to satisfy more than a part of me; usually there is a spectator watching from the back of my mind, a little bored. Only when I am entirely alone, enjoying a book or music, is he quiet. So I see to it each day that I spend six hours in solitude. I have not met half a dozen people in my life who have been able to absorb more than a small part of me, the passive critic as well as the active romantic. The spectator at the back of my head—I can put my finger on him—can cause in my general state of being a feeling of discomfort that is almost as unpleasant as toothache. The feeling is at its most painful when I sense that I am talking to a nature of different texture from mine. And it is not a matter of opposed or dissimilar ideas. It is a pure emotional reaction, affective. A scientific mind normally repels me, but I have been happy with at least one kindred spirit amongst scientists, because I have tasted a texture of temperament behind all the science, warming and approachable. Any extrovert is for me the last word in tedium; and the tedium of externality is life's most searching trial. The objective everyday universe is only so much material for my sensibility or imagination to play upon; and sheer "play" it must be at times, as much as a more austere occupation. Humour is a necessary salt, and without a corrective of cynicism all seems foolishness and callow.

I cannot make mere acquaintances either in life or the arts.

If I do not feel some manifestation of love I cannot enter that world where awareness of self dwindles. My belief is that happiness comes only when the ego is absorbed into a state of being that transcends primary self. The paradox, as I feel it—and I am no psychologist, though once on a time I studied those experts not at the time discredited, up to William James, I think—is that by becoming entranced out of a sense of personal identity one achieves a more integrated and more responsive ego. An aesthetic love goes through a sort of Hegelian process of negation and affirmation of self, arriving at a Becoming—an enlargement and intensification of the I, so that the condition of bliss, if and when it arrives at all, is the sum-total of Neville Cardus as obsessed or possessed by the book he is reading, or the music he is listening to, or the man or the woman under whose spell he has fallen. At such moments the critic "N. C." is out of work. All of which is probably a hashed platitude of metaphysics, with more than a flavour of Schopenhauer; but it is the truth. I who have been called egoist a thousand times cannot understand the pleasures of egoists—those, for example, who seek satisfaction in a work of art mainly because they, so to say, "agree with it," and find in it a projection of their own personal tastes, which is much as though a man loved a woman for her opinions or for her pedigree. I used to despise the patriots at cricket matches who applauded bad strokes by English players if they happened to get runs when runs were badly wanted. Egoism, like patriotism, is a good thing only if it can lose itself in love that goes beyond self and finds a greater, because less restricted self.

I am not making a plea for austerity. My point is that a glass of wine is best drunk with one's thoughts on the bouquet, the ritual of drinking rather than on thirst or a personal craving for liquor. I could not love myself so much did I not love the sources of pleasure more.

A plain case of the "sensitised plate"! When Newman applied the term to me as a writer on music I took it, as Smee put it, "as a sort of compliment, Cap'n." But I think he made too little of the fact that the plate was indeed sensitised. Even in those early days I had grown some extremely fine and responsive antennae or cat's whiskers, developed after much adjustment and squeezing through narrow apertures and scarcely-opened doors. I could at once become absorbed into music; I ceased to feel that I was listening to it from the outside; I was drawn into the composer's mind almost to the point of taking part in the creative process. In a word, I surrendered myself to music as a lover to his mistress; hence the disapproval of me by the scientific school of criticism, less scientific really than moral and didactic at bottom.

It was and it still is my belief, that interpretative criticism cannot begin until the art-work has been lived through. The critic must of course rationalise his "impressions," "erect them"—as Remy de Gourmont says—"into laws." But the impressions must be experienced first. It is not possible (at any rate it is not possible for me) to enter different worlds of the imagination if one's reason holds suspiciously back. There must be a preliminary "suspension of disbelief"; and disbelief often means prejudice. The true critic must collaborate in the creative act; in short, he must be as much a man of imagination as of knowledge and judgment. I cannot think of three English music critics who seem to me to have imagination at all. When I was young (and every critic is young until he is forty) I was prepared to take chances with whatever critical credo I had so far worked out. I have since received confirmation of my early intuitions: reason and the rationally formed credo can deliver no opinion until the imagination has been seduced by the creative act. Even a bad composition must be understood, penetrated and even suffered, first-hand. The material of criticism, the evidence so to say, is the recollection in comparative sanity of what happened to one while under the spell. The critical credo is proved embracing or narrow by trial and error; the critical antennae are developed while groping in the actual territory of the creative artist.

This, at any rate, has been my own way of polishing my touchstone, and like any other technique of criticism, it remains of no value to anybody except myself. If I have at times strayed and lost myself, I have at least the consolation of knowing that I have "been there"; I have really journeyed in the realms of gold because I was willing to surrender to the hypnosis. I have been a good medium.

In all this I am only saying in another way, "in anderen

bischen Worten," as Gretchen puts it, that the critic should be a poet. Indirectly I am also saying—and perhaps not so indirectly—that I am myself a poet as well as a critic. It is not a boast; a man is not responsible for natural gifts, and can take no credit for having been born with them.

     ·   ·   ·   ·   ·   ·

In 1929 I met Delius when he was in London for the Festival of his own music conducted by Beecham. He invited me to call at the Langham Hotel one Sunday afternoon; and his attendant carried him into the sitting-room of his suite and flopped him down on a couch, where he fell about like a rag doll until he was arranged into a semblance of human shape. There was nothing pitiable in him, nothing inviting sympathy in this wreck of a physique. He was wrapped in a monk-like gown, and his face was strong and disdainful, every line on it graven by intrepid living. He spoke with some scorn of English music in the main. "Paper music," he said with a North-country accent there yet, "should never be *heard*. Written by musicians self-conscious . . . afraid of their feelin's." Next he turned his attention to *The Times* critic, H. C. Colles I think it was. "Says I am obsessed by the chord of the some-thin' or other. Do you know about chords? I used to, but I've forgotten."

Then he told me I had rather missed the point, in one of my articles, of one of his own works. "But," he added, "if you got my meaning wrong, you *understood* my language." "Thanks," I said. "I know your country; I've been there."

"You're young for the job on the *Manchester Guardian*," he said. (I was thirty-nine years old but looked younger, with what James Agate called a "Traddles-like countenance.") "Don't read yourself daft. Trust to y'r emotions."

I might have quoted, but I was discreet enough to keep it to myself:

> Grau, theurer Freund, ist alle Theorie,
> Und Grün des Lebens goldener Baum.

The theory should, at any rate, come after personal experience and much humble surrender. Most music critics get no further into a work than a little beyond the technical or "stylistic" frontier; they are too dependent on their "theories" to loosen grip on them for a minute; without theories, they might come to nothing. My own errors, countless and sometimes reprehensible, have never arisen from arrogance, but rather from the blindness which intermittently comes with love. But love can also make one clear-sighted. In time I reached the conclusion that the "sensitised plate" was no more unreliable than the scientific microscope; what is more it produces an impression of some vibration and colour, even if a little distorted by the chemistry of temperament.

I write down these reflections as an indication of the direction taken by my mind and way of life as I matured. The struggle to get out of the rut, the excitement of becoming one of C. P. Scott's "young men" at the age of twenty-six—a little late, perhaps too late; the difficulties of combining two different occupations and of outgrowing "Cricketer": these preoccupations exhausted for years most of my driving force. Then, at last, it was possible for me to rest on my oars a little; now I was at liberty any day confidently to sign a column of writing on music in the *Manchester Guardian* knowing "it was good." I had time to take stock. The ambition of youth had been realised. And soon, sadly soon, it was shown to be not the bright star that had led me on through the years of encircling gloom. It was a long way to have travelled, so far that ironically it enabled me to catch a glimpse of a finer prospect. Here I was, forty years old, with no serious book written and better known amongst thousands of readers, even "M. G." readers, for my contributions to the literature of a game. The joke was that I now hated sport more than ever, and that cricket itself appealed less and less to me each year, the more I saw of it now, in its competitive and technical aspects.

But more than any other factor in a growing feeling of futility was the sense that in England I was, as a musician and a writer, losing touch with my colleagues and the general atmosphere. During the years immediately following 1919 I gave myself up entirely to consolidating my cultural gains; in other words I more and more devoted myself to the masters who had helped me. I paid my debts by re-reading and re-living

them. More and more I isolated myself from the contemporary
scene: during winter months I often saw nobody at all,
except for an hour at lunch in my Manchester club. Steeped
as I was in the material of my own art and calling, the days
went by or through me; I would spend a week preparing to
write a notice of a Hallé Concert, exploring the music to be
played and the living background which inspired it. It was
during this period that I fell so utterly under the spell of
Goethe's *Faust* that I was able to quote from memory the
whole of the Prologue in Heaven in German.

As I grew older, at the noon of a man's years—the thirties
—I discovered that the further I read into the old writers the
more they became significant and potential of truly progressive thought and imaginative experience. Then, one day,
I woke up and came to the surface of my own period. It was
like revisiting the glimpses of the moon. I felt solitary amongst
much alien corn. A new generation had arisen and it was
unhappy and hot and bothered. More remarkable still, the
period—in London at any rate—was dithering with self-
consciousness. Post-war This and post-war That! Indignation
and frustration—not on the part of the poor devils who had
actively suffered and, because they had been alive in the false
dawn of the 1900's, could taste the full bitterness of the disillusionment. No; the "pessimism," the gnashing of teeth,
and the debunking of "hollow gods" of tradition was under-
taken by intellectuals who had been infants in 1914, mostly
born comfortably enough, and of no abnormal sensibility or
thinness of skin. This younger generation was not content
to knock at the door of the established premises; they "gate-
crashed" with intent to total demolition. It might have been
good fun for them if only they had been constitutionally
capable of enjoying any sort of fun. But self-pity made them
rather unamusing. This was the real sentimental age in
England's cultural records. The Victorians had slobbered
indulgent pity upon objects outside their own complacent
selves; Dickens had wept over Little Jo (but also had laughed
himself black in the face over Little Swills). Tennyson had
shed his idle tears for the grace of a day that is done. The
sentimentalists of the 1920's slobbered about themselves; they
were misfits in a world shattered. Not by their fault, of course;

SAMUEL LANGFORD

that is the point. They were denied remorse that has something of poetic heroism in it. No art, no humour, no
creative impulse worth while, can come from the egoism of
self-pity which so easily breeds the assertiveness of the
inferiority complex. With all reasonable admiration for
writers of the 1920's, they never grew out of their talented
adolescence.

I turned to their books and their music and their poems
after my immersion in say, Dickens, Thackeray, Meredith,
Wagner and Strauss—to name old masters most vulnerable to
the scorn of the "new synthesis"—and I could find neither
wisdom nor humour. The trouble was that even those who
swore by the contemporary "movement" didn't seem happy
in it; and by happy I mean alive and absorbed out of themselves into a higher and more active and comprehensive
reality.

.   .   .   .   .   .

It is perhaps necessary here to point out that young men
of thirty years ago did not read books and listen to music
and attend theatres and art galleries to "integrate their personalities," or to seek out some "higher synthesis." Most of
us had no conscious aesthetic at all; we never dreamed of
relating our enjoyment to any a priori psychology. Maybe
we inherited something of the Victorian earnestness, though
free now from moral bias. Montague and Walkley and Newman and James Huneker and Arthur Symons had stimulated
in us a more vivacious and less austere approach. Now and
again, I admit, we would indulge a certain didacticism; I
remember a period when I made marginal comments in books
with a pencil, such as "Very good," or "True," or "I agree."
For the most part we were content to run around the bonfire
of the arts, happy if we could pick out a flaming brand here
and there and hold it up as our own.

The arts were for us sources of excitement and delight. If
an author could exercise a spell we were ready to surrender,
like children drawn to the chimney corner; we were entirely
oblivious that such-and-such a writer was "bourgeois," or an
"escapist." As I gave myself to Thackeray and Vanity Fair,

and lost my own identity in the departed world of the book, I failed altogether to realise that "socially the background of the novel is perfect" but the "characters castrated"; and that Thackeray's "flunkeyman" was heightened by the "taboo on sex." I confess that until the other day when I read a brilliant essay by V. S. Pritchett on Thackeray these shortcomings or characteristics in him remained unrevealed to me. Likewise, when Gulliver entranced me late at night in bed (and I read surreptitiously with a shaded candle; for reading in bed was not generally approved in those days) I missed a most important point, which according to Mr. Pritchett is that Lilliput is "the clinic we have come to live in" (perhaps it hadn't yet become *that*, thirty years ago); "it is the world of irresponsible intellect and irresponsible science which prepared the way for the present war." But, since Mr. Pritchett goes on to point out that the Dean himself "did not foresee this," no doubt the shortsightedness and insensibility of a young man of the first decade of the twentieth century will be understood and pardoned.

The post-war "Intellectual" impinged on me with the advent of a number of blithe spirits into the "Corridor" or editorial side of the *Manchester Guardian*, straight from the universities. They spoke in high voices confidently intoned, and invariably they began an address to you by saying "Tell me." They did not show to the elders of the newspaper the deference due to pedigree. When I was a young man on the "M. G." and I had to go and see Scott in his room, or Montague, I would, so to say, practise for half an hour, get ready for it, clear my voice, take hold of the handle of the door of the great man's room and then not turn it but pass on, pretending to myself that there was something I wanted to see Wallace about first—or Crozier. But the sons of the braver new world walked into Scott's lair with no qualms and even emerged without the rose-pink of intense relief, concentration, and collapse on their cheeks such as would be seen on the face of dear Old Attenborough, Chief of the Sub-Editors, who always wore an alpaca coat and was so polite that he would flatten himself against the wall of the Corridor if anybody was passing by him. Old Shovelton once answered the telephone in the reporters' room; he was sitting down at the time. "Who is it?" asked Shovel ton. "Mr. Scott," replied the voice. And Shovelton stood up at once. There were only two recorded instances of an "M. G." man entering, or coming out of, Scott's room without some slight agitation of nerves. One of them, an old hand from Yorkshire, was called in by the All-Father to account for a slip in Latin contained in a report of a Degree-day at Manchester University. Scott "dressed him down" mercilessly. "You should know by now," he admonished, "that the rule of the paper is that no copy containing classical allusions in the original language is allowed to go up to the compositors' room until it has first been passed by somebody in the 'Corridor.'"

The old reporter listened respectfully, waited until Scott had finished, then said "Mea culpa," and retired.

The other occasion was when Scott somehow locked himself in the lavatory. He did not use the one available for the "Corridor" in general; he had his own sanctum. One night the sound of very fierce knocks was heard emanating from inside the door. The news spread terribly round the entire office. The question was who should go to Scott's assistance with the master key. Nobody was willing to be a witness to Scott in a position of no power and no dignity. So "Wigan Jim" was asked to come forward. "Wigan Jim" was a long, lean, gawky handy-man, who carried copy and proofs to and from the composing-room; he had an Italian look about him, though born in Wigan, and always reminded me of Cecco, one of Captain Hook's gang. "Wigan Jim" was given the key, and as he approached the scene of the rescue, he was heard to call out in a pleasant voice: "It's all right; won't be a minute; comin' sir." And after he had opened the door it is credibly reported that he asked Scott, with some flight note of admonition: "And 'ow did yer come to get yersel' shut up in there?"

But young 1920 kept its hands in its pockets wherever it went, even on the "M. G." under Scott, and not even a last-minute commission to write the long-leader was regarded either as a disturbance or a compliment. This was a new breed altogether, the sign of another direction or orientation in culture and manners of the country. The discovery had been made of the possibility of careers for the educated classes in journalism and literature and music and the theatre. Once on a time the young men from the universities looked to the Army, the Church, Politics, and the Civil Service and School-mastering. Frank Swinnerton (also a *Manchester Guardian* man) sums it all up in his *Georgian Literary Scene*: "Now there is Literature as well. Hence the pedagoguishness. Talent and taste cannot be taught, but aesthetic rules can be taught, and if you call any æsthetic dogma a' principle' it can be used ever after as something indubitable and made a foundation for artistic practice."

It was even so in our music. Since the B.B.C. increased the demand for music in Great Britain, composition has also been changed into an accredited profession, and not only that, but musical criticism as well. This was—let us call it—the Aseptic School; the only difference between them and the Victorians was that while the Victorians had suffered from moral inhibitions, theirs were emotional inhibitions. The reaction against Wagner and rhetoric in general was understandable, but to react from Wagner to folk-song and concertantes for six flutes, blow-pipe and tabor was like a spinster's giggling rush for cover. An acidulated antiquarianism set in: spinets and donnishness. Musicology instead of a humane feeling for music. Taste was better than ever no doubt (that was the trouble); the actual technique of composition became more selective and sophisticated, and the same signs were to be found in novel-writing and literary criticism. But it was all a product of education and middle-class breeding; there was no hint that these people, these dilettantes, ever felt deeply or were impelled riskily by imagination. We could anticipate their direction day to day, their preferences and their prejudices; they would be as consistent as sterility.

At this point in our island story the B.B.C. ventured upon a Festival of English Music, the most comprehensive and pro-longed in my experience; and I had already suffered much on behalf of organised efforts to put the British composer on the world map. Often I am disturbed at nights with a pro-cession of departed shades passing before me like the ghosts in *Richard III*—Stanford, Parry, Havergal Brian, Bantock, Holbrooke (perhaps the most gifted of the lot), Bridge, Boughton, Harrison, Ireland. Sometimes one of these forlorn

shades points a wan and reproachful finger, and addressing
me professionally, says:

> Let me sit heavy on thy soul to-morrow!
> Think, how thou stab'dst me in my prime of youth
> At Worcester.

There were usually consolations, though, at the Three
Choirs Festivals. For one thing, they took place in the West
of England mellowness of late summer, and there was Elgar
there to lend the touch of genius; and Shaw was one of the
Cathedral stewards, so little the rebel in music now that he
would sit through the *Elijah* of Mendelssohn, either engrossed
or fast asleep. But an English festival of music in the depth
of a London winter, the Queen's Hall opaque with a fog that
might easily have been an emanation from the music! The
sensitised plate lost his patience over this enterprise and the
Manchester Guardian did not alter or modify a single sentence
of the following:

> "The B.B.C.'s Festival of British Music continues to
> keep people out of Queen's Hall in thousands. The public
> of London are endorsing wholeheartedly the Continental
> opinion that we have no composers really worth while. . . .
> We have a heap of dexterous writers of music who, as far as
> experiments in style and technique go, are quite as interesting
> as any of the contemporary composers of Germany, Italy,
> Austria and France. But most of them lack passion and
> love of full life; most of them in fact compose like maiden
> ladies. Curious that England, which produced Shakespeare
> and Keats and Swinburne and Byron and George Meredith,
> has not given us one composer whose music is equal to a
> really warm ballad to a mistress's eyebrow. We compose,
> as a people, as though from acquired culture and not after
> the manner born."

A decade has passed since the above paragraph was written;
as far as I am concerned it remains true, in spite of Benjamin
Britten. William Walton has since written a symphony. As
proof that I was not, as *Manchester Guardian* men in bulk are

said to be, a friend of every country but his own, I must record here that I welcomed with arms not less open than those of my colleagues the advent of an English composition not debilitated and merely "cultured." Already in 1931 I had praised *Belshazzar's Feast* in enthusiastic language: "It is certain," I wrote, after the first stupendous performance at Leeds under Malcolm Sargent, "that nowhere on the Continent of Europe at the present time would one be likely to hear a composition of more convincing power than Walton's *Belshazzar's Feast*."

To my sorrow and no doubt to my loss, the Walton symphony has not retained for me its power; the vitality I feel has too quickly hardened into a formula of insistent rhythm and harmonic emphasis, with an obvious disinclination to be easeful, quiet and simple. But at least Walton composes like a man with something to say, even if he is in labour while saying it. The output of his contemporaries is destined before we are much older to go the way of the mightily conceived tone-poems and choral odes and music dramas of Holbrooke, Bantock, Holst and the rest. If only our Brittens and Tippets and Berkeleys could think of a single melody that would take possession of the memory, one chord that would once and for all pierce the musical consciousness. If only they could hurl us, whether we were ready to be hurled or not, into a new work—as Strauss hurled his contemporaries into *Rosenkavalier* at one swift attack of the horns, or as Elgar hurled us into the violin concerto. Even the admirers of our present-day "white hopes" don't pretend they are ever "hurled"; rather, they are persuaded by taste and fashion to give their cultured ears to the various "Diversions" and "Sinfonias" and "Sinfoniettas" and the rest. By the side of Kodaly's *Psalmus Hungaricus* even the *Belshazzar* of Walton is the Old Testament in musical technicolour. I can think of few examples of convincing English music composed in the last dozen years or so. And among them is Rubbra's setting of Donne's *Hymne to God the Father*, which was sung in the Wigmore Hall round about 1938 by the Fleet Street Choir. My impression of this work was one of beautiful and personal choral writing that penetrated to the subtle essence of Donne and his poignant mingling of passion and austerity.

There is a fine sensibility moving darkly in the symphonies of Arnold Bax, but he tends to let his texture become congested; he over-scores because, I think, he does not always as a composer seize quickly enough the conception that visits him as a poet. We cannot as a musical people even produce a number of songs that sing their way to the heart. Here again we find the produce of education: good taste and a far nicer sense of literary values than Schubert ever possessed. There are precious few English songs that seem to have sprung inevitably and raptly into being, and the best of them are in the *Wenlock Edge* cycle of Vaughan Williams, whose Fifth Symphony is a beautiful testament of our greatest composer since Elgar.

. . . . . .

It was in this same curious period of London's musical history that a new public invaded the concert-halls. In the past the audiences attending serious concerts had been either musical or had been attracted for reasons of high society. Men of letters seldom interested themselves in music until, during the 1920's, the new Dilettantism began to make itself felt rather ridiculously in Queen's Hall and in the columns of music criticism of certain weekly reviews. Schnabel was lord of all pianists, and Toscanini was All Highest amongst conductors. Nobody admired Schnabel in Beethoven more than myself: I wrote columns about him in the *Manchester Guardian*; from one of which I quote now, in spite of a suspicion that as I do so I am inclined towards blushing. (Schnabel played the B flat major concerto of Mozart and the C minor concerto of Beethoven, with the Hallé Orchestra conducted by Hamilton Harty on February 8th, 1934):

"The concerto was composed in the last year of Mozart's life on this earth; Schnabel's playing had shadows on it. The melody went through many inflections, yet so sensitively and subtly controlled were they that not once did they suggest anything so prosaic as changes of tone-colour externally applied. The transitions were from within; the heartbeats, so to say, of the music's life. With Schnabel we begin at a concert and end at a communion. This is not a rhetorical statement. For what is a beautiful performance of music by Beethoven and Mozart if it is not an act that brings before us the essential substance of the minds of the men who composed it? Mozart and Beethoven as mortals died the common death ages ago, but what it was that perished in them then was of merely temporal account. Their music was not a matter of craftsmanship, but a thing thrown off from them and given independent existence in time and space. It was the only stuff of life in them that mattered. And so when we hear interpretation of last evening's actuality we are not listening to the music of Mozart and Beethoven; we are (as far as we are not clods) with Mozart and Beethoven. It is a solemn thought, and Schnabel is responsible for it.

"He corrects the familiar view of Mozart as a sort of dancing-master, a man of eternal bowings and scrapings, a "period"creature, nicely scented. Schnabel's Mozart has masculinity, his sweetness comes out of strength; his music is a"third of his life," not a chapter in the evolution of music. On the other hand, Schnabel's Mozart is not a subject for the psycho-analysts of our day; there is no obvious "daemonin" Schnabel's Mozart. The conception is true to a reading of the score—seen in the light of loving study of the composer's style, the loving study of a lifetime."

The general view is that Schnabel is not a Mozart player at all, that he lacks purity and delicacy of tone, the Mozartian poise; but I am content to let my impression of 1934 remain. I am congenitally incapable of following a fashion; I do not believe that anything fine in music or in anything else can be understood or truly felt by the crowd. There must be an enigma in all the arts, a sanctum into which only a few may enter who are prepared to live apart from the world. I am an intellectual snob—if the term means that I am not willing to share grace that has fallen on me only after much devotion and hard work as a novitiate. The right to appreciate a great work of art is as rare and must be as dearly bought as the right to depreciate. Often I have reached an opinion after

much wrestling, after many setbacks to personal inclination—
for even the sensitised plate has its responsibility to objective
conscience of sorts—then I have written my notice in the
"M. G.," many times taking hours over it, with the last train
or bus missed, and the night outside dark and wintry; and
I have walked home head down to the blizzard and have
wondered whether I should not return to the office, or telephone to suggest a modification of a phrase a little overdone
or of a judgment not yet quite clearly rationalised. And next
day I have been greeted by somebody whose main job in life
is in another and more lucrative direction, somebody without
opportunity or desire to give more than a few minutes'
thought to the problems discussed in my notice, and he has
announced complete agreement with my article, or rather, he
has announced a complete sharing of riches found by me
only by long, diligent, faithful and patient seeking.

It was out of irony against the Fashionable Intelligence
that I wrote my notorious Horowitz notice—the one in
which I described him as "the greatest pianist alive or dead."
This phrase was taken from its context (not at all to my dis-
pleasure) in an "M. G." article, was reprinted in various
languages on the covers of gramophone records, and distributed all over the world. It was, I believe, translated into
Japanese with some gain to forcibility. The notice was written
after a Horowitz recital in Queen's Hall, given at the height
of the Schnabel "boom." Before I heard Horowitz I read one
or two articles which described him as the greatest living
pianist, an obviously silly claim to make of anybody. I went
to Queen's Hall in May, 1931, very much on my guard, but
the technical brilliance of Horowitz bowled me out middle-
stump. This is how I wrote of him:

"During the last few months a number of musicians
have given me to understand that the greatest pianist alive
is Horowitz. I heard him on Friday for the first time, and
as I came away from the concert I realised that the half had
not been told me. I am ready to believe he is the greatest
pianist alive or dead. His technique and style are comprehensive, masterful and sensitive—I hope the reader will
perceive that I am choosing my words with moderation . . ."

To this day, and to an address in another hemisphere, I receive solemn letters asking me if I ever heard Liszt, Rubinstein, Tausig, von Bülow, d'Albert, Busoni, etc. As Mr. Darling says in *Peter Pan*, ". . . it's a lot of use trying to be funny in this house." Not that I think I was far wrong about Horowitz as a player of the piano, as an artist of the keyboard. I remember the movement of his hands that night in quick passages; it was impossible to distinguish one from another; they reminded me of the propeller of an aeroplane. In motion you cannot see the tails of it; they are lost in a circling invisibility. Then, when the aeroplane is coming to a descent and a resting-place, the form and parts of the propeller suddenly take outline. So did it seem to my vision at this concert of Horowitz; you could see his hands becoming separable and individual to the naked eye, as soon as the music changed to a slower tempo.

.   .   .   .   .   .

I have told of my change of opinion about the Walton symphony. The sensitised plate was bound to get out of focus here and there. Then, of course, I was still provincial—outside the "movements." No reconsideration of verdict and point of view exposed London's most celebrated critics to the charge of inconsistency. The public doesn't trust the writer who discovers from later experience another aspect to his conception of the truth. In my *naïveté* I thought I might admire (for example) Toscanini *and* Furtwängler. I was innocent enough at times to praise both, and at other times to question each. But the fact is that Toscanini stood for the objective score, "music *qua* music," while Furtwängler was just another sensitised plate. Newman set the general attitude to these two conductors; praise and nothing but praise for Toscanini, and, *pari passu*, blame for Furtwängler. It was much the same with W. J. Turner on Schnabel; so with Capell on Beecham, Cecil Gray on Sibelius. Consistency, at all costs, not to the logic of one's own æsthetic reactions but to one's dialectical commitments. Before a day's events in the welter of London's music, I often amused myself making forecasts of the latest opinions and information. Ernest would ride for Sibelius whatever the weights; there was not the slightest chance that he would wear the Furtwängler colours, and if he accepted a mount in the Brahms stable he would look for some shortness of symphonic wind somewhere. Wolf was of course a winner before the flag fell, whether the horse were Ganymed or Verborgenheit. Edwin Evans apparently was engaged by the Stravinsky stable for life. . . .

Constant Lambert and Borodin, the Sitwells and Rossini. It was Lombard Street to a china orange that this new Intelligentsia would praise Berlioz at the expense of Wagner. Colles of *The Times* would have needed a surgical operation to render him aware of a single fatuity in Parry; and Francis Toye swallowed Verdi whole, from *Oberto* to the *Quattro Pezzi Sacri*. It was a sort of party-politics of criticism; or like a great Assize in which the various composers and artists (having been warned in advance that they'd better be careful) looked around the court to see who was representing them. The critics kept to their particular briefs—let the other side produce the evidence against. I remained obstinately out of the swim. I could not understand why one and the same mind and set of sensibilities should not enjoy Toscanini and Furtwängler and find in each conductor different qualities and different limitations. I certainly could not understand why admiration of Toscanini's noble interpretation of the Ninth symphony of Beethoven should presuppose acceptance of his ungenial and rigid hammering-out of the Seventh symphony. I could bow the head at Furtwängler's intensely tragic *Tristan und Isolde* and decline to extol his hyper-sensitive, almost neurotic handling of *Meistersinger*, I could listen to a song of Brahms without asking why he hadn't treated the poetic accents or stresses as faithfully as Wolf would have done. In short, whatever the errors of judgment I committed, they were not predictable. Sensitised plates do not register impressions before the event or the object is there to be photographed. I do not forget that Oscar Wilde warned us that only the auctioneer should appreciate all schools of art; I am not arguing in favour of Eclecticism. Each of us is bound to remain more or less cut off from some of the good things of life and of art by reason of natural and irrepressible antipathies. Just as no one system of moral values is adequate as a measure of social conduct, no one set of aesthetic values can be of much use as we go through our experiences in the arts.

It was an asset in these years to remain at a remove from London, to be able to savour the best of it and keep away from "tendencies." There was too much confident chatter about the processes of creative imagination; London (it was the same in all the other cities, no doubt, but I am writing an auto-biography, not the history of the world) was becoming a more and more difficult place for an artist to find what Goethe called the "undisturbed, innocent somnambulatory state." All talents were exposed to the social crowd and to the glass of fashion. "He who does not keep aloof from all this," said Goethe to Eckermann, "and isolate himself by main force, is lost."

.   .   .   .   .   .

One of my heart's desires when I was a boy was to wear a fur coat and walk along a railway platform smoking a cigar, with a porter following me laden with my luggage. In the course of time this dream was more or less consummated, though, to say the truth, I have never possessed a fur coat, and I do not like cigars in public places. As I have already related, my first considerable journey occurred in May 1912, when I took my tin box and my two pairs of spectacles to Shrewsbury and began a brief but not inglorious career as a professional cricketer. Since then I have been increasingly undomiciled. When I wrote on cricket and music for the *Manchester Guardian* my life was extremely peripatetic. In the insurance office of the Flemings I would occasionally (when the brothers were away on holidays and the head clerk had taken a day's leave) pin a note on the door announcing that I would be back in ten minutes, and then I would go into the Reference Library for an hour. The time came on the *Manchester Guardian* when I was perpetually leaving messages with the chiefs of staff: "Back next month."

A man's history is often to be traced in his addresses. When I worked anonymously in Powell's draughty back-room on the "M. G.," opening on the staircase, I could be run to earth easily. Then I found Allan Monkhouse's comfortable office on the first floor, so it became necessary to seek me out in two places. Next when I was made cricket correspondent, the procedure involved looking in Powell's room, or upstairs on the first floor, or to say: "He's probably at Old Trafford." In 1920, when I was sent over England in the summer with the Lancashire XI, the area to be covered by investigation and inquiry was first in Powell's room, and if I wasn't there, upstairs in Monkhouse's room, then to wait until I returned from Old Trafford, Lord's or Northampton. James Bone, our London editor, at last began to protest gently to me of my elusiveness, especially after I had been appointed music critic; for now the induction was obliged to cast a wider net still. "Not in Powell's room? Not upstairs? Not at Old Trafford, the Oval or Southampton? Well—try the Hallé Concerts, the Leeds Festival, or Queen's Hall." In 1930, I was at liberty to go abroad to cover concerts, and next, in 1936, I decided to accompany (just for fun) an English cricket team to Australia. It was at this point that Bone arrived at the limits of his patience. "Neither in Powell's room nor Monkhouse's; not at Old Trafford, not at Lord's, not at the Worcester Festival, Glyndebourne or Salzburg. *In Melbourne?*—why, the man doesn't even keep to one hemisphere. . . ."

Not until the spring of 1919, when I was twenty-nine, did I go to London; and it was only for a day. At this time I had got into a cul-de-sac on the "M. G.'s" corridor; at every turn stood a heavy obstacle to a young man's advancement in every department—Montague here, Sidebotham there, Langford stark in my path, Ivor Brown bulky to the right, each a dismaying pillar, a male caryatid, as though permanently and immovably fixed to the very building. One day during a black period I read an advertisement in the "Printers, Pressmen" column of the *Daily News*. A new weekly "literary" journal was about to be published in London and an assistant-editor was wanted. I made an eloquent application on "M. G." notepaper; and I was asked to journey for an interview at the office of George Newnes in Southampton Street.

I departed on the 7.20 train to Euston, in a packed third-class compartment, and at Crewe (where in another existence I had spied upon the porters invading the luggage van where my tin box reposed on its way to Shrewsbury) I bought a bun and a cup of coffee. When I emerged from Euston at noon I found my way to Trafalgar Square, and was disappointed at the smallness of the Nelson column; and for a while I walked amongst the pigeons wondering how they escaped being trodden upon. At half-past two I climbed two or three floors in Newnes's publishing offices; I was too uncertain of myself to go up with a crowd in the lift. On an angle of the stairway I saw a green poster of *Tit-Bits* offering its readers £5 a week for life. Then I came upon the room of my destination, and I was taken to an inner office, where Wilfred Whitten sat at a desk. He told me of the new "project": a paper for readers not "high-brow," but eager to know their way about amongst the masterpieces. The journal was to be called *John o' London's Weekly*; my job would be to help Whitten as sub-editor, with occasional book reviews and articles thrown in, salary five hundred a year and a three-years' agreement. At the time my pittance on the "M. G." was two pounds ten a week.

The temptation was very strong; and I was asked to sign the contract straight away, as it was necessary to get the first issue out within the next month. I liked the look of Whitten's mild face and spectacles; I liked his gentle voice. He was joined by an enormous man with a cigar; I forget his name but he represented business, brass-tacks, and put a fountain pen in my hand and pointed to the dotted line of the contract. When I played for time, he moved the cigar from one end of his mouth to the other and told me not to be silly; this was a great opportunity and there was nothing in the provinces like it. I wavered and I nearly fell; but suddenly a bell rang and the big man excused himself for a minute. As soon as he left the room, Whitten said quickly and softly and in the most friendly way: "Don't leave the *Guardian*: you'd be a fool . . ." The big man returned abruptly, but I had received the sign. I withstood the big man's blandishments and his impatience with provincial indecision. I mumbled something about letting them know in twenty-four hours; and I escaped to the Strand and saw a newsboy with a poster announcing the murder of Rosa stroke. . . ."

I walked back to Euston, caught the four o'clock train to Manchester, and at nine o'clock I went into the "M. G." office. It was my night off, and at half-past nine all seemed

so quiet and austere that I felt like a lost child that had found
a way home again. Nobody knew where I had been; I nursed
the secret until I wrote to Whitten next day declining the
offer with thanks and the kindest regards. I never saw Whitten
again. Would I have accepted the job if he had not spoken out
of his heart? It is certain that if I had joined the staff of *John
o' London 's* I never would have written on cricket. I think
my interest in music would not have suffered; but it is unlikely
that my duties would have led me towards intensive study of
and preparation for musical criticism.

I cannot remember half a dozen occasions in my life when
I have made a journey that had not some object in view connected with my work. I went to Salzburg and Vienna when
invitations and free tickets from these places were received
by the "M. G."; I went to Australia in 1936 and 1937 for
cricket. It was to earn a living that I returned to Australia
in 1940. Not for a quarter of a century after I had fallen ill
when I was Scott's secretary and "rested" for a week in North
Wales, did I take a journey anywhere for a holiday. And this,
holiday in Llanfairfechan, spent in early days of March,
remains in my memory for a walk by the sea alone one gloomy
evening; at any rate my solitude on the sands was only
enhanced by that other lonely figure that is always pottering
about on a deserted shore at twilight.

I climbed up a steep bank to a pathway, where bracken and
bush were tossing in the cold wind. A cloud suddenly blackened
the western heaven, and a storm of hail hit my face. Then,
in the bracken, I heard a bird singing like mad; and a ray of
sunlight revealed his gallant fluff of feathers. And, as though
spoken by a voice from out of the elements, the lines of Thomas
Hardy came into my mind:

> So little cause for carollings
>   Of such ecstatic sound
> Was written on terrestrial things
>   Afar or nigh around,
> That I could think there trembled through
>   His happy good-night air
> Some blessed Hope, whereof he knew
>   And I was unaware.

This was one of those mystical assurances of immortality which do not pass from consciousness and are beyond the reach of logic. It is not necessarily an assurance of a personal or even a human immortality. Such revelations of a spiritual connection between nature animate and nature supposedly inanimate, and the consummation of beauty achieved at such times, are not to be argued about in any known dialectic, either of believer or unbeliever.

So with all our journeys and decisions at the cross-roads; so at the end of all our living. "A path there was where no man trod." As far as the spark is in us at all, it must be tended and fanned not to illumine any way of our own planning but simply for the sake of the light itself. This is the one lesson I have learned in my life about which I am certain. The light is sometimes kindled in unlikely places and in unlikely hearts; and only the devil and his crowds can quench it.

.   .   .   .   .   .

The journey to Salzburg during the music festivals was good for spirit and sense alike; here, at last, was to be found the time, the place and the loved ones together. Drawbacks of course had to be admitted; the loud-voiced harridans amongst the foreign visitors, painted dames sporting the Tyrolean dirndl! Yet even these grotesques lent an appropriate touch of masquerade to a scene and atmosphere always very much related to rococo comedy of manners; they added delicious ironic point to Lehmann's "Siehst du! die alte Marschallin!" in *Rosenkavalier*, where she sings that some day she will grow old and walk bent and crooked on a stick, and people will mark her out from the gay present. Also there was the disturbance to one's aesthetic sensibility caused by the fact that nearly every Salzburg woman of the peasant-class and of middle-years was afflicted by goitre. But perhaps it was the same woman I was perpetually seeing in the streets; there is nothing like a goitre for nullifying individuality. There were, too, pests of German tourists who came to Salzburg for the "Aussichten," the views—this was as banal as to look consciously at the stage properties in a production of *Figaro*. In Salzburg there are no "views"; the setting, the

SALZBURG

picture, is the spirit of Salzburg made visible; the scenery
should be felt, not seen.

And often enough the "scenery" of Salzburg could be
savoured only by the mind's eye. The town was blotted out
and the rain it raineth every day. Clouds of mist everywhere;
they came down on us in great shrouds; they filled even the
cafés; clouds as men walking. When first I arrived at Salzburg
and went into my bedroom, high up in the front of the Stein
Hotel, there was nothing to see through the window, only
the river Salzach below, and the ghostly bridge across it,
leading to a void of mist. Next morning the hot sun woke
me up as it flooded my pillow, and when I looked through
the window I saw a castle on a rock, under a blue sky, enchanted
there in the night. I gazed at it in the silence of the dawn;
and I might have expected to see Sister Anne waving her
scarf from a turret.

Every August I fretted, impatient as a child, as the train
ambled along the electrical railway on the last lap to Salzburg,
after the day's journey beginning at break of day at Zürich,
with breakfast as we passed the lake and saw a Noah's ark
spilled tidily all about us. A breakfast taken so early that
time became a lunatic for a while, and noon and a craving
for lunch occurred at nine o'clock. Eight hours later I would
stand in the corridor of the compartment of the train, leaning
against the steel rail, and on the look-out for the first trace,
afar off, of turrets and domes which are Salzburg, standing
in the meadows on two rocks, cloven by the river, and as
unreal and as convincing as a mirage, a town suspended in
the sky, not of this age or of any terrestrial substantiality.

In Salzburg itself the illusion persists of a habitation not
normally dimensional; the sheer heights, the sudden declivities
straight down to a roadway; the river that winds through
the town's busiest centre; the packed roofs, castle on a mountain, café on another mountain; now the Gaisberg, now courtyard and palace and antique tram-lines and the aloof orna-
mental Mirabell-garten; and now the Capuzinerberg, with
Mozart's little summer house on it—all these contrarieties of
altitude and level, huddled together as though to go within a
proscenium, constantly delighted the fancy. And the medieval
cowled tonsured monks, some of fabulous age, passing us and

mixing with the contemporaneous throng; and the dark
green capes of the burghers, and the shaving brushes in their
hats, and the pretty costumes of the girls, and the shop-
windows being pulled open outward on to the pavement, and
the curved pipes and peaked caps and moustaches of the
incredible Dien mann, and the man who at all times was
standing in the middle of the flowing Salzach, high and dry
on a small island, fishing always; but nobody ever saw him
get a bite.

Schön! This word was in constant use. In the cafés, Salz-
burgers listened to broadcasts of performances from the opera.
Nobody made disturbing noises. When the music came to an
end, they said: "Schön." They couldn't afford to pay the
high prices demanded for tickets at the Festspielhaus. But
none the less, they said "Schön," and called for more coffee,
until their tables were crowded with glasses of water. Was it
hoped that these might clear my mouth of the rich flavour of
Kaffee mit Milch? But no; the Salzburg or Viennese waiter
brings a glass of water with every cup of coffee so that he
will be able at once to estimate how many cups of coffee you
have drunk when at long length you ask for your bill.

Schön. Do I write sentimentally of it all now? And why
not? It was all a theme of sentiment. And everywhere music,
or the echo of it. In the afternoons we would go to Morzg, a
few miles across the meadows. We sat under lilac trees at
tables which were covered with cloths in red-and-black check,
and members of the Wiener Philharmoniker were there,
witty, ironical and, of a sudden, as noisy as children. Mairecker,
the first violin (nobody could play with his verve the polonaise
from Strauss's *Le bourgeois Gentilhomme* suite) insists on my
having an omelette, despite that I have lunched on Forelle
and Kartoffeln. The omelette is brought to the table by a
Mädchen who carries the tray on high. Apparently the
omelette is made of snow and air and music. Mairecker
stands up, all attention like a soldier, salutes the omelette and
plays the first of the gorgeous melodies of the *Kaiserwaltzer*.
Sehr schön.

After lunch we go over the fields to Hellbrunn. There is
talk of Bruckner, and as an Englishman not yet in the secret
of this composer, I mention Mahler, with whom the name of

Bruckner is associated in England. Mairecker picked a wild flower from the grass. "This is Mahler!" he said. He then apostrophised the great Untersberg mountain. "And that," he said, "is Bruckner!"

At Hellbrunn there are gardens of an archbishop's palace, or rather, the palace was presented by an archbishop to his mistress. In these gardens, alluring and baroque, there is a waterfall and its power works a musical-box concealed at the bottom of the lake. From Hellbrunn we climbed up and down paths rank with growths, and now we entered the most secret place I have ever visited, dipping down and down, while the pines rose higher and higher, making a transparent roof. After we had crunched some way along a narrow path we came to a halt to listen. There was nothing to be heard; a cracking of a branch somewhere, nothing else. Sombre silence, the world a distant gleam. The light of day was but a visitant here, as it made the upper regions of the forest luminous for a while, and fell before us where we stood, gently dappling the dust and cones of many a summer.

We walked home across the fields as sunset glittered on the limestone hills, and on the greater heights the snows were rose red; in front of us the windows of Hohensalzburg seemed on fire. Schön, auch schön! After dusk there was music in the courtyard of the Residenz Platz. At different corners four groups of fiddlers sat in candlelight. They played the "Echo" nocturne of Mozart. Melody called to melody and sweetness answered sweetness. The crowd sat quite still, no chattering between the movements. Later, the orchestra came together and we heard the Serenade in D, the "Haffner." During one of the slow movements I saw a woman with her head bowed low on her hands, and I heard her breathing. Naïve? Well, and for what else did the great composers wear themselves out? Not to hear the sophisticated yawns of the Fashionable Intelligences who apparently think that it is provincial not to seem a little tired of everything. Mairecker's solo was the breath of the violin, soft on the air, poignant and wounding in its wondrous fragile line of song. The stars throbbed above; they seemed to echo the pulsations of the music of Mozart.

Days without time, from beginning and the cup of tea with lemon in the cool inner breakfast-room of the Stein

Hotel, flat square cubes of sugar and on every day except Sunday a crescent of crisp yet soft white bread and cold luscious butter. We were served by Rupert. And it was Rupert who would serve us if we came in to supper fourteen hours afterwards. In the corridors upstairs, on the way to one's bedroom, a servant would be sitting always, a Mädchen or old woman; every time we passed her she smiled and said "Guten Morgen" or "Guten Abend." Outside the Stein, where the life of the town passed over the bridge from dawn to midnight, the porters were endlessly busy in their green aprons, receiving cars and the hotel coach, carrying luggage in and out in large armfuls. Hans in particular, had a gluttony for cases and bags. He pounced upon them at sight, surrounded himself from head to foot in luggage. It wasn't safe to leave anywhere near him a case which one might happen immediately to need; he would see it isolated from the pile that was waiting for delivery to bedroom or car; he would dive at it and add it to his general plunder. He gave the impression of a man who had found the secret of eternal satisfaction—nothing like luggage, nothing like leather. You would see him on his way into the hotel laden with half a dozen suitcases, two under the armpits; and he would beam at you, the whole of his burden taking part in his gracious bow. When the hotel entrance was temporarily inactive Hans would stand outside on the steps looking for luggage; if he saw a taxi drawing up on the kerb, he would leap into joyful life; and when he saw the approach of the hotel conveyance—a very ample means of transport—his mouth watered. Year after year he remembered me. As soon as I emerged from the taxi he would raise his two hands and shout: "Ach, Mis-ter Kardoos!—so goot you for to see. Ja!" He gave the impression that all winter, and nearly the summer through, he had been pining for the sight of me once more. Then, after the welcome, he fell upon my luggage.

Rudolf did not share the gusto and glee of his fellows. He served us politely enough, and with friendliness; but I noticed now and again a touch of impatience in his face. One day after lunch I found him sitting on a seat under the trees on the path of the Salzach, and in a burst of confidence he told me he was an admirer of Hitler. His father had fought and died for Austria in 1916, and after the peace he and his mother had starved in Vienna. His sister had died of tuberculosis. He had wished to go to the University, but of course . . . There was no hope to be looked for from the old order; Hitler had done wonders for Germany, Herr Cardus. You could see, he argued, the well-being and health of the German youth who came on holidays to Salzburg. Hitler was a good man. We English didn't understand. Rupert, too, was a good man; he would ask us at supper, about the opera, about Richard Mayr, about Lehmann. Whenever his "night off" occurred he bought a ticket in the Stehplätze—the "standing-places." Where is Rudolf to-day? He tried once or twice to convert Hans, but the luggage got in the way just as he was coming to the height of the argument.

Arnold Bennett once said that nature at Salzburg rather ludicrously seemed to imitate art, opera in particular. On the contrary, panting art ran after nature in vain. If the Untersberg mountain was as a Bruckner symphony, towering over Salzburg, there were more than eight other snow and cloud-capped pinnacles, in stupendous sequence. *Rosenkavalier* of Strauss was a piece of confectionery in Salzburg, where only Mozart was *genius* loci in all its moods—moods that would match *Cosi fan tutte* (in the Mirabell-garten) and also the *Requiem*. When *Jedermann* was acted in Salzburg, the Domplatz was the natural-born scene, stage, air and habitation. Through the great door of the cathedral came the voice of the Lord calling for the testing of Jedermann. Trumpets sounded from the high towers. In the silences of the afternoon, as Everyman listened and heard his name echoed, now near, now far—"Jedermann! Jeder-mann!"—all sorts of common everyday sounds took on significance, the flapping of the wings of the pigeons, the chiming of the clock. The cortège of Jedermann entered the square in poignant perspective, slowly approaching, Sorrow and Repentance trailing behind. Then from behind our backs, as we sat there in front of old stone and dome, we heard the howls of the Devil; he ran out of our very midst to claim Jedermann, holding his tail in his right hand. And on the steps of the cathedral Faith and Good Deeds frustrated him. A street noise from a distance was mysteriously relevant and touching.

I have never seen acting of such pity, eloquence, power and sweetness. Moissi as Jedermann was by no means the master of all. There was an unforgettable representation of Death, gowned in black, a white pitiless but sad visage, not yet a skull but nearly so, a heartbreaking embodiment of half life, half extinction. Good Deeds, a figure of frail whiteness seemed too gentle for the stone steps upon which she drooped. And all around us visible beauty, medieval poetry and emotion mingled with the lovely spirit and presence of Salzburg as we could feel it now, this very minute, as it went by in sunshine and silence.

So with *Faust*, The great rocky background of the courtyard of the old riding-school contained the natural setting of the first part of the drama, needing only the eye of a Reinhardt to see it, the statue in the solid block! The height of the wall, stretched upwards into the night, was like the abyss dividing heaven from earth; at the top the three angels spoke the wonderful poetry of the opening of the prologue:

"Die Sonne tont, nach alter Weise . . ."

and a light coming from nowhere made them barely visible— visibly invisible. Far below we saw Faust bent in weariness over his books; while crouching on a higher ledge or plane, Mephistopheles harangued with the distant but somehow dreadfully near voice of the Lord. It was a masterstroke to show us the "compact" scene in heaven, and at the same time to give us a glimpse of Faust on the earth far below, oblivious that holy and satanic forces were already being set into motion about him and his soul. Reinhardt, collaborating with nature in Salzburg, could suggest vast spaces and, indeed, a whole universe of strange dimensions, all out of a rock. A light was thrown on the wall, and we discovered Margarete's chamber, quiet and withdrawn ("not every girl keeps things so neat"— to translate the untranslatable gibe of Mephisto). An extension of the same light unfolded the whole of the city—gardens terraces, bridges, playgrounds, towers and churches. Faust and Wagner walked arm-in-arm watching the simple enjoyment of the people. Out of the hollow gloomy gate of winter the motley throng came forth, each to hoard the sunshine, to rejoice in the day of Easter. . . .

> "Jeder sonnt sich heute so gern;
> Sie feiern die Auferstehung des Herrn . . ."

The scene and the light were mystical and magical, conjured from old stone and Salzburg soil!

At noon in the little square where we went for coffee (more coffee!) there was a Glockenspiel, and it would play "La ci darem" from *Don Giovanni*, tinkling above on the warm autumnal air, while the gay thoughtless life went by—not to be stayed, you would have sworn, by any care or weight from the outside world. This was the moment and the place when and where the Faust that is in all of us would surely have spoken the fateful words:

> "Verweile doch, du bist so schön!"

This was the time and the place; it was annunciatory. The journey's end.

In 1938 after the festival's close I returned direct to London. A Viennese girl saw me off. She brought me a present of a little bottle of Tokay, in a pretty wicker case. She came into my compartment and I opened the bottle and we drank together. "Good-bye," she said; "perhaps there'll not be Salzburg much more for any of us." As the train moved out of the station, she ran along the platform, waving her scarf. I saw her at the end of the platform, still waving. Then the train rounded the bend and my carriage seemed intolerably empty. A few minutes later I looked out of the window and saw the mountains dwarfing the beloved place and the castle on the rock. That was my last sight and impression of Salzburg; but I imagine the river still flows under the bridge that we crossed every evening, on the way to the Festspielhaus, and lounged on in the afternoon, watching the life go by.

. . . .

It has been a life of wider scope and variety than I could reasonably have prayed for in my years of hope and idealism; and being a young atheist I usually observed sense of proportion in my prayers. I realised in time the two ambitions

of my boyhood; I became a *Manchester Guardian* writer and
I travelled as far from my Manchester slum as Australia. I
heard music in Vienna and I saw cricket played in Sydney.
These were not so much ambitions as the dreams of a waif
and stray. I have described my emergence from a slough of
mean streets and meaner vistas; but I do not imagine that I
have explained how it all happened. The chances were a
thousand to one against any considerable development of
whatever gifts were inherited by me; there was little, on the
face of it, to mark me off from millions who went under
miserably and so contributed to what was known in those
days as the Problem of the Condition of England.

I did not, as I have shown, possess initiative, or the wish to
Get On. There was no parent, priest or schoolmaster to instil
in me an appropriate sense of responsibility as a citizen and
a wage-earner. I *dreamed* my way through; my studies, even,
were a dream. I was unteachable at school, because I was not
interested. I dissipated early mornings and late nights with
my own chosen books. I would not compromise, when I grew
older and understood something of worldly values; or perhaps
it would be truer to say that I would not sacrifice my main
pleasures. I was indifferent about my physical welfare. That
the end was not total downfall and defeat I cannot understand
to this day; and I can take no credit for it, as I must insist on
repeating, except on one point; I have never been attracted
from my heart's desire by material temptations. I have never
gone out of my way to seek any man's favour; I have often
gone the other way to avoid a certain kind of advancement.
I like, rather than dislike, unpopularity.

Thus, somehow, lacking home or influence, with gifts
that were very late to show themselves, and burdened by a
timid disposition and ill-health, I contrived in the end to get
out of my bones some seventy per cent of the assets granted
me by the inscrutable gods. No man can hope to do more; I
suspect that Shakespeare himself was conscious of at least ten
per cent of waste and frustration.

It has been a different struggle from most of its kind. The
rise of a Dickens from the underworld can be accounted for in
terms of imaginative genius calling for no specialist education.
In the England of my youth it was almost impossible for a

poor boy ever to hear a note of good music, let alone find the means for a comprehensive study of music. No musical education in the world—I am prepared to swear it with my last breath—has been earned harder than mine, or in a school more severely tested and proven by experience. Not abstract theory, but living contact out of sheer need and love.

I have stored my mind and heart with good things; if I live another fifty years there will not be enough time to explore and savour to the full this harvest. Such harvests need to be jealously preserved, and we should offer constant thanksgiving for them. I don't believe in the contemporary idea of taking the arts to the people; let them seek and work for them.

For the Kingdom of Heaven is there; it is in the arts that I have found the only religion that is real and, once found, omnipresent. For years I was as dogmatic an atheist as could be. It was when I understood for the first time the later quartets of Beethoven that I began to doubt my rationalism. "One cannot speak justly of the short idyllic movements of these later quartets," wrote Samuel Langford, "without regarding them as elysian in their nature, and removed by their ideality from every contamination of the world." "Removed by their ideality from every contamination of the world"—in this phrase there is illumination for us in the darkening corridors of existence. Without creative urge and imagination man would be less than the animals. There is for me no accounting in terms of evolution or survival-value for the sense of beauty, for laughter and tears that come and go without material prompting, for the ache after the perfect form and the ineluctable vision. If I know that my Redeemer liveth it is not on the church's testimony, but because of what Handel affirms. As Jowett put it to Margot: "My dear child, you must believe in God in spite of what the clergy may tell you."

SYDNEY,
   1942-1946.

THE END

INDEX

3768835R00167

Printed in Great Britain
by Amazon.co.uk, Ltd.,
Marston Gate.